Praise for *The International Self*

"Sucharov's attempt at introducing a new way to analyze the conflict is a courageous and definitely innovative one ... [it] is particularly pertinent in light of the recent American rhetoric of 'no choice' with regard to its war against Iraq."
— *International Journal of Middle East Studies*

"...Sucharov successfully provides a balanced account ... In the final analysis, this book does much more than provide important new insights into Israeli-Palestinian peace-making. It introduces innovative tools to analyze policy decisions in conflict situations, and should generate comparative studies in other regions of the world."
— *International Journal*

"This is an innovative case study of why the stronger party in an enduring international rivalry would negotiate for peace, perhaps more about social psychology and interaction than about psychoanalysis ... It is surprisingly readable, yet technically sound; more process oriented than the often-quoted Freudian pseudo analyses of governmental leaders."
— *CHOICE*

The International Self

SUNY series in Israeli Studies
Russell Stone, editor

The International Self

*Psychoanalysis and the Search for
Israeli-Palestinian Peace*

Mira M. Sucharov

State University of New York Press

Published by
State University of New York Press, Albany

For information, contact State University of New York Press, Albany, NY
www.sunypress.edu

Production by Kelli Williams
Marketing by Michael Campochiaro

Library of Congress Cataloging in Publication Data

Sucharov, Mira.
   The international self : psychoanalysis and the search for Israeli-Palestinian
peace / Mira M. Sucharov.
       p. cm. — (SUNY series in Israeli studies)
   Includes bibliographical references and index.
   ISBN 0–7914–6505–5 (hardcover : alk. paper)—ISBN 0–7914–6506–3
   (ppk. cover : alk. paper)
   1. Arab-Israeli conflict—Psychological aspects. 2. Political psychology.
   3. Psychoanalysis—Social aspects—Israel. 4. Israel—Ethnic relations—
   Psychological aspects. 5. Arab-Israeli conflict—1993—Peace.
   I. Title. II. Series.

DS119.7.S8875 2005
956.05—dc22

                                                                    2004020821

10 9 8 7 6 5 4 3 2 1

For Steve and for Rory

Contents

Acknowledgments

This book owes much to the nine months I spent conducting field research in Israel in 1999–2000. For the institutional and financial support that enabled me to get there, I would like to thank the Social Sciences and Humanities Research Council of Canada; the Chaim Herzog Center for Middle East Studies and Diplomacy at Ben-Gurion University; Canadian Friends of the Hebrew University and the Harry S. Truman Institute, and specifically Edy Kaufman and Emanuel Adler. Heartfelt thanks also goes to the many Israeli political, military and cultural figures who agreed to be interviewed.

Peter Feaver and Hein Goemans and the members of the Triangle Institute for Security Studies offered an excellent testing ground for my ideas mid-way through the project. Richard Betts, Stephen Biddle and Stephen Rosen, as the organizers of the summer Workshop on the Analysis of Military Operations and Strategy, gave me the opportunity to consider the relationship between military doctrines and security ethics more deeply.

Gratitude also goes to Charles Kupchan, Victor Cha, the late Joseph Lepgold, Mark Tessler and Alexander Wendt. It is indeed very sad that Joe—a devoted political scientist and loyal colleague—is not here to see the final product. Other colleagues were unfailing in their moral and intellectual support; in particular Alex Avni, Rick Avramenko, Ronnie Barth, Bridget Grimes, Bassam Haddad, Jenn Hazen, Brad Holst, Balbina Hwang, Yasu Izumikawa, Becky Johnson, Eric Langenbacher and Tammy Wittes. Jason Davidson deserves special mention for reading multiple draft chapters and for faithful service as a talented academic and overall friend. And Rivian and Brian Weinerman and Andrew Oros provided useful feedback along the way.

At Carleton University, my colleagues have furnished an extremely supportive working environment. Jonathan Malloy and David Mendeloff generously commented on earlier drafts. A University Teaching Achievement Award has also been important in enabling me to devote more of my thinking to the Middle East as I work towards expanding the Arab-Israeli relations curriculum at the university.

Thanks also goes to the editorial and production team at SUNY press, particularly Michael Rinella and Kelli Williams. And as editor of the SUNY press series in Israeli studies, Russell Stone of American University was instrumental in ensuring the project reached a wider readership.

A number of other individuals and institutions helped to shape my ideas in this book, whether or not they or I realized it at the time. Rex Brynen of McGill University introduced me to the complex pleasures of political science inquiry into the Middle East. Camp Massad of Manitoba and the Winnipeg Board of Jewish Education provided excellent and painless Hebrew instruction that eventually facilitated my grasp of the nuances of Israeli politics and culture. And the Jewish National Fund's annual Israel contest engraved in my ten-year-old brain the dates of Israel's wars and other sundry facts that proved most helpful for later graduate work.

Finally, the thinking that led to this book would not have been possible without the constant love and support of my family: my mother, Faye Margolis; my father, Max Sucharov; my stepmother, Rebecca Toolan; my stepfather, Ron Campbell, my grandparents Marian Margolis and Clifford Margolis; and my husband Stephen Gluck and daughter Rory Sucharov-Gluck. My paternal grandmother, Rose Sucharov, would have enjoyed reading these acknowledgments. Each of these powerful life forces taught me expression, in every sense of the word. Both my father and grandmother Marian read portions of the manuscript and offered keen critiques. My dad was an especially significant inspiration in shaping my thinking on the value of psychoanalytic insights and the analytic potential of constructivism. Intense love and gratitude go to Steve and Rory. Steve, for being first in his class from the beginning; for providing the *rugelach*, the Pac Man high score, the best route to the Jaffa Gate, and for knowing I could do it; and Rory (*Re'ut*), for joyfully accompanying me in her Jolly Jumper through final revisions as the book went to press, and for keeping me mindful of the global stakes involved in stemming violent conflict for this generation and the next.

Chapter One

Introduction

What leads long-standing adversaries to seek peace? Despite the violent setbacks that have overtaken the Israeli-Palestinian peace process since the second Palestinian Intifada erupted in September 2000, the 1993 Oslo agreement reached between Israel and the Palestine Liberation Organization (PLO) is a striking example of a concerted attempt—however fragile—by entrenched adversaries to shift from conflict to compromise. The phenomenon of longtime enemies deciding to lay down their arms and pursue a path of peace—a decision that almost invariably involves costly concessions of some sort—would be puzzling enough, yet this case is all the more surprising given the stark power asymmetry that characterized the Israeli-Palestinian relationship by the early 1990s. We are left to wonder why Israel, by far the more materially powerful actor, agreed to enter a peace process with the PLO that would likely entail significant material and symbolic costs. The Palestinians' limited military and economic strength—made worse by the end of the Cold War and the 1991 Gulf War—did not pose a threat to Israel's territorial integrity, and the gravest threat to Israeli security, namely Egypt, had already been neutralized over a decade earlier through the 1978 Camp David agreement and the 1979 Israeli-Egyptian peace treaty. Yet, in early 1993, Israel agreed to shift course and negotiate with the PLO—in the process reversing its position of outlawing contacts with the organization and of not recognizing the Palestinians as a distinct nation—to embark on the secret Oslo negotiating track from which the September 1993 Declaration of Principles emerged. And even the current stalemate reveals policy discourse at variance with the pre-Oslo period, as evidenced by Israel's hard-line prime minister, Ariel Sharon, labeling Israel's policies in the territories an "occupation" and openly contemplating the establishment of a Palestinian state.

While much has been written about cases in which the weaker side sues for peace, or when a "mutually hurting stalemate" brings both sides

1

to the table, this book addresses a more puzzling and understudied phenomenon: the stronger party agreeing to seek peace with a weaker adversary. There are many widely understood reasons why the study of conflict resolution is important to international relations. It allows international relations theory to contribute to the burgeoning field of peace studies, and enables the latter to illuminate broader ontological questions within the study of international relations. The issue also speaks to the question of radical foreign policy change, a topic that has received increasing attention in the last decade, yet whose research program has largely proceeded outside the ambit of conflict resolution theory and analysis. Perhaps most important, it allows conflict-resolution stakeholders to craft policies appropriate to the scores of enduring conflicts currently blemishing the international order.

Yet uncovering the conditions under which the *stronger* adversary agrees to seek peace is both more puzzling and more urgent: while most weak parties to conflict do not have to be pushed to the table, in most cases the stronger actor is more willing to prolong the status quo. This is particularly the case in anti-occupation uprisings, where any feasible settlement will more than likely entail withdrawal. Unlike in traditional warfare, where the stronger state may be motivated to terminate the fighting by prospective war spoils, for an occupier, withdrawal usually represents a net material loss.[1] This book questions that assumption by expanding the definition of utility to include psychic costs as well.

Accordingly, in this book I present a sociopsychoanalytic model to explain foreign policy formulation and policy change. Such a perspective is unique in contemporary international relations theory yet builds upon the central assumptions uncovered by the constructivist research program—which has typically been concerned with issues at the level of the state system—and by the insights of political psychology—a subfield that has largely fallen under the purview of foreign-policy studies. With its focus on a deep investigation of the individual within an interpersonal context, psychoanalysis is perfectly poised to operate at the nexus between the twin domains that have come to be known as foreign policy and international politics.[2]

Like many other political-psychological theorists, I begin from the premise that states, being collections of individuals, share some elements of human psychology. One of these is a self-image—the way a polity conceives of its specific place in the world. This self-image, or role-identity, usually leads to corresponding foreign policy actions, or role behavior. Yet if a state deviates from its self-prescribed role by adopting a sustained policy course that clashes with its role-identity, I argue that elites and masses will experience a cognitive dissonance arising from the contradiction between the state's actions and its identity. The dissonance is made apparent to decision-makers by international and/or domestic actors holding up a "mirror" that serves to dredge up unconscious counternarratives that represent what the state fears becoming. Once this dissonance has taken hold, we can expect elites to take radical action to realign their country's policies with its role-identity. Thus, a self-perceived "defensive" state that acts "aggressively" over time can be expected to extend an olive branch to its most intimate adversary, in order to restore its more pacific self-image.

A state's role-identity is transmitted and entrenched within society through popular and discursive artifacts such as folk songs, liturgy, plays, films, novels, school curricula, and advertisements, as well as institutional channels including conscription policies, war memorials, national logos, the national anthem, and the flag. This identity in turn, arises from the early regional and global experiences of the state, as well as whatever pre-state historical events the corresponding nation experienced and documented. In the case of young states, both the early state experiences and the pre-state experiences of the corresponding nation will be more readily remembered, such as the twentieth-century anticolonial "birthing" moment experienced by many states in the Third World. However, older states will usually have "foundational moments," including events occurring during the lifetime of the polity, such as the French Revolution for France, or the Norman Conquests for England. The sum total of these experiences is translated into historical memory that is retained and nurtured at the collective level.

As we will see, Israel's early state experiences emanated from three sources: the experiencing of rejection by the surrounding Arab states; ambivalence at the hands of its patron—the British mandatory power in Palestine; and an international community that seemed to be against the fledgling country—notwithstanding the 1947 UN Partition Plan that proposed the division of Palestine into one state for the Jews and another for the Arabs. Israelis' pre-state historical memories are sandwiched between such dichotomous events as the heroic David and Goliath myth and the tragedy of the Holocaust, and include significant episodes that embody the courageous fight of the few against the many that occurred on the actual territory of what is now Israel—including the fall of Masada (73 A.D.), the Bar Kokhba revolt (132–135 A.D.), and the Battle of Tel Hai (1920). These ancient and modern events, coupled with the early experiences of the state in its regional surroundings, led the State of Israel to develop what I call a "defensive-warrior" role-identity, alongside which the Israel Defense Forces (IDF) has nurtured a "security ethic" that sanctions only wars of "no alternative" (*ayn breira*) that employ "purity of arms" (*tohar haneshek*). Conversely, I argue that Israel's *unconscious* counternarrative approximates the idea that 'we are not only defensive, but sometimes we can be aggressive,' and it is this latent aggressiveness that Israel, being a self-perceived defensive state founded from the ashes of Hitler's genocide, fears in itself.

In examining Israel's decision to pursue Oslo, it is clear that Israelis considered the first five Arab-Israeli wars to be defensive operations—even when launched preventively (the 1956 Sinai Campaign) or preemptively (the Six Day War of 1967). And with the exception of the 1973 Yom Kippur War, in which Israelis faulted their intelligence establishment for failing to predict the Arab attack, Israelis accordingly celebrated these wars through artistic and national channels. However, I argue that two events in the 1980s—the 1982 Israeli-PLO war in Lebanon and the first Intifada (the 1987–1993 Palestinian uprising in the West Bank and Gaza)—cast a defensive-warrior Israel into the role of an aggressor, the realization of which forced Israelis' unconscious fears to battle with their conscious role-identity. Only by seeking compromise with the Palestinians were Israelis able to address these unconscious counternarratives and realign their state's policies with its role-identity, a dynamic that arguably sheds light on Israel's harsh response to the latest Palestinian Intifada.

It is true that at the time of this writing (late 2004), the Israeli-Palestinian peace process is in grave jeopardy following almost four years of clashes between the IDF and Palestinians in East Jerusalem and the West Bank and Gaza Strip, including scores of Palestinian suicide bombings within Israeli cities and Israeli reprisals in the territories. If and when the parties return to the negotiating table, it is unlikely that they will return to the organizing framework laid out in Oslo, though the contents of the recent "road map" proposed by the United States and sponsored by the so-called quartet (the United States, Russia, the European Union, and the United Nations) largely echo the spirit of the Oslo agreement. From the perspective of Israel's government, the Palestinians rejected the most generous Israeli peace offer to date (when, at Camp David II in July 2000, Israel publicly offered to share control over Jerusalem) by opening a protracted round of violence two months later, following a controversial visit to the Temple Mount by Israel's then-opposition leader Ariel Sharon. Israel-watchers had fixated on the Oslo decision as the heralding of a new era in Israel—some have called it "Israel's second republic," while others have decried the agreement as either invidious from the beginning or hopeful, yet misguided. As with many peace processes the world over, it is likely that this period of violence will eventually be viewed as a tragic bump on the road to peace.

However alarming the events in the region during these last four years, it cannot be said that Israel has decided to outright abandon its policy of peacemaking with the Palestinians. The Israeli government's decision to shift relations with the Palestinians in the early 1990s from a conflict to a negotiating stance remains significant to the study of conflict resolution, and within the history of Arab-Israeli relations. Finally, and not unimportantly, understanding what led to Oslo can help us understand the causes of its failure, and determine what sort of agreement might replace it.

THE EMPIRICAL PUZZLE

Before evaluating the utility of psychoanalytic theory for addressing the question of what leads international adversaries to seek peace, we must consider the many competing theories that can be used to explain the Israeli case, particularly since the Arab-Israeli conflict represents a subject not lacking in scholarly attention. The most obvious explanations for Israel's pursuit of peace with the PLO are materialist-oriented (or realist) ones, yet these do not stand up to logical and empirical scrutiny. Constructivism has been criticized for being the mopping-up approach of international relations theory—namely, that its theories end up explaining only puzzles that realism cannot solve.[3] Yet in our case, a number of other, nonmaterial approaches, such as learning theory, strategic culture, domestic politics, or cognitive-dissonance theory (absent a psychoanalytic mechanism) are also inadequate for explaining Israel's decision to seek peace with the PLO. First, positing that states act to maximize their material self-interest, a realist could formulate four potential explanations for Israel's pursuit of Oslo: what I call the "gather-ye-rosebuds" argument, the "lunch-money-handover" argument, the "weekend-dad" argument, and the "glass-slipper" argument. I will address each of these in turn, before examining the remaining, nonmaterialist, alternative explanations.

The Gather-Ye-Rosebuds Argument

Just as seventeenth-century English poet Robert Herrick implored the virgins to "gather ye rosebuds while ye may," one realist explanation for conflict resolution in this case would be that Israel was seizing the opportunity to make peace while the PLO was weak—before the Palestinians' depleted coffers from the end of the Cold War (whereby the PLO lost its Soviet support) and the Gulf War (where the PLO lost its Gulf patronage after siding with Iraq) could be replenished. According to this logic,

Israel *would be expected* to make peace with the PLO while the latter was vulnerable—in order to strike a better deal than it could expect were it to wait until the Palestinians had regained strength.[4]

From this perspective, there is no puzzle; rather, a puzzle would have been in why Israel *did not* make peace, had it refrained from doing so in the early 1990s, rather than why it did. There are at least two responses to this sort of argument. First, whether we assume that a state will more readily pursue peace with a weakened adversary, or whether that state is *less likely* to grant the concessions necessary to make peace if the enemy is weak, remains an open question in international relations. To a traditional realist who asserts that Israel would be *more likely* to make peace with the PLO in the aftermath of the Gulf War and the end of the Cold War, another might counter that Israel had *much less to fear* from an atrophied PLO and therefore could tolerate an adversarial status quo. Indeed, the last major event to precede the Oslo negotiations, the first Intifada, while morally burdensome on the Israeli polity, was arguably not enough of either a security threat or an economic drain to justify the major change in the status quo that Israel was prepared to accept in the lead-up to the peace process. And with the Soviet Union having disbanded and the Cold War having ended, neither could the PLO expect its arsenals of outdated Kalashnikov rifles to be replenished. Finally, it is true that the Intifada gave rise to new and more militant Palestinian groups, namely, Hamas and Islamic Jihad, who have historically garnered domestic support through their supply of social services to impoverished Palestinians in the occupied territories. While critics might argue that Israel would have been wisest to make peace with Arafat before his Islamicist rivals gained strength, neither did these groups pose a traditional military threat to Israel. The nature of their threat—terrorism—was little different from the guerilla tactics that had historically been employed by the PLO. The IDF had long ago dubbed terrorism a "current security" problem, as distinct from a "basic security" problem (large-scale, cross-border threats), the former a modest irritant that could adequately be dealt with on a day-to-day basis, and one that would not necessarily justify giving up broad swaths of land in the West Bank and Gaza, thereby paving the way for the likely formation of a Palestinian state alongside Israel. This is particularly so given that the Islamicist suicide bombings within pre-1967 Israel that have become so prevalent since the mid-1990s virtually did not occur prior to Oslo.

A second case against this strand of realist argument can be made from bargaining theory. This perspective would demonstrate that Israel was *less likely* to make peace with the Palestinians based purely on geopolitical calculations. That is, while the events of the early 1990s—the Gulf War and the end of the Cold War—could have led the Palestinians to lower their demands in any potential negotiation setting, making the PLO a more attractive bargaining partner for Israel, Israel's demands would have been concomitantly *raised* by those same events. The loss of Soviet and Saudi support for the Palestinians would have meant that the Israelis perceived themselves to be stronger than they had been prior to 1990–1991. The change in these two bargaining positions (the Palestinians having lowered their demands; the Israelis having raised theirs) does not necessarily mean that the Palestinians lowered their demands *more than* the Israelis raised theirs.[5] Since an overlapping bargaining space is logically necessary to enable an agreement, we would have to look for factors *other than* those suggested by the geopolitical scenario extant in the early 1990s.

As I will show in later chapters, Israel began to view the Lebanon War and the Intifada as intolerable from an ethical perspective. Over 160 soldiers had refused to serve in the Lebanon War on conscientious grounds, and slightly more than that—186—refused to serve in the occupied territories during the Intifada, as they increasingly experienced their mission as not being in line with the defensive-warrior role of the IDF. It was these events—not the end of the Cold War and the Gulf War— that lowered Israeli demands and enabled Israeli elites to contemplate making peace with the PLO.

The Lunch-Money-Handover Argument

Just as the high-school freshman must routinely give his lunch money to the senior-class bully in order to avoid being crammed into a locker, a "lunch-money-handover" argument could reason that Israel pursued peace with the PLO to placate its own two chief (potential) nuclear threats: Iran and Iraq. While Israel had been secretively nuclear since the late 1960s, only recently has it tacitly acknowledged having the bomb. Yet with the advent to the region of nonconventional weapons (laid bare during the Western probe of Iraq's arsenal during the Gulf War), a realist could argue either of two things. First, Israel could have come to realize that territorial depth was less important to facing down a potential threat from Iraq or Iran. Iraqi scud missiles (armed only with conventional tips, fortunately for the Israelis) had already penetrated Israel's fortified borders during the Gulf War. Second, Israeli elites could have viewed peacemaking with the Palestinians as appeasing Iran and Iraq, thus mitigating a nuclear threat from those states. These possible explanations are hardly groundless, and indeed the Iraq-Iran nuclear threat was a not uncommon interpretation for why Prime Minister Yitzhak Rabin made peace with the PLO.[6] However, even in the nuclear age, wars are still fought and won on the ground, and leaders have not succeeded in dispelling their population of this belief. Moreover, the deployment of nuclear weapons, given their devastation and the widespread presence of second-strike capabilities among most nuclear states, is seen almost universally as a weapon of last resort. Even nuclear states must possess and continue to hone conventional military power. Israel, despite its own nuclear deterrent, has accordingly invested enormous resources in maintaining its conventional superiority in the region, including keeping territorial breadth and depth, making it less likely to hastily withdraw from the West Bank and Gaza. Furthermore, territory still holds high symbolic importance for nations the world over, no less so for Israelis and Palestinians. Even though territory may have been *less* salient given the nuclear threat from the nonborder states in the region, it is still costly in both strategic and emotional terms for Israel to cede these areas. Elites are well aware of the symbolic attachment given to land in Biblical Israel by many Israelis and would be hesitant to alienate their political constituents. For all these reasons, it cannot be argued that the nuclear threat makes land insignificant—particularly within the context of the Israeli-Palestinian conflict.

In addition, Israel saw itself possessing a deterrent sufficient to withstand a missile attack. In response to a reporter's question in May 1992 regarding the "guarantee that we [Israelis] will not be unprotected if another fusillade of missiles [referring to Iraq's use of scud missiles during the Gulf War] is dropped on our heads," then-Prime Minister Yitzhak Shamir stated, "Our power of deterrence has undoubtedly not lessened; it is there." And that although "[t]here is no guarantee...that there will be no snags...Israel has means and a political infrastructure with which it can confront any kind of attack."[7]

Finally, it is not certain that Iran's Ayatollah Khamenei or Iraq's Saddam Hussein would have changed their belligerent policies toward Israel based on an Israeli-Palestinian peace agreement. These regimes had historically depended on rhetorical grandstanding for securing domestic legitimacy, and both leaders saw themselves as self-declared champions of their Muslim brethren in their struggle with Israel, particularly once Egypt removed itself from the immediate fray of the Arab-Israeli conflict following its 1978–1979 peace treaty with Israel.[8] Given Israel's view of these states as being outside the bounds of legitimate diplomacy—particularly after Saddam Hussein's attempt to link the Iraqi withdrawal from Kuwait in 1990 with an Israeli withdrawal from the West Bank and Gaza—neither would Israel's leaders necessarily have been inclined to make concessions along their immediate border in the slim hope of assuaging threats farther afield.

The Weekend-Dad Argument

A third type of realist argument would assert that without the Cold War drawing the United States to the Middle East to counter its Soviet rival, Israel could not be assured of continued American support should Jerusalem ruffle Washington's feathers.[9] Since the 1991 loan-guarantees crisis, where President Bush threatened to withhold American support as a guarantor for $10 billion in loans unless Israel froze settlement-building in the West Bank and Gaza, the United States had strongly been in favor of Israel's making a serious effort to reconcile with the Palestinians under a "land for peace" formula. Under this logic, Israel would be enticed to make peace with the PLO in order to retain its "special relationship" with the United States. However, the continued American-Israeli connection has never been seriously cast into doubt. It is still in America's interest to retain a foothold in the oil-rich region of the Middle East, and Israel remains the best entree for the United States into the area. Moreover, Israel could have simply stopped building settlements in order to restore friendly relations with the United States; thus it remains puzzling why Israel chose to negotiate directly with the PLO and suddenly reverse its decades-old policy toward the Palestinians, in the process committing to at least limited withdrawal from the territories.

Finally, the ties that have been forged between the two countries surpass Cold War considerations, and include a Judeo-Christian component that sees the Jews' repatriation in the Land of Israel as part of a biblical teleology. Alongside the pro-Israel lobby in Washington have operated increasingly prominent Christian-right groups who want their country to retain close relations with the Jewish state. Since the end of the Cold War and until 1999, American public opinion exhibited little change toward Israel, and U.S. elites even perceived the two countries as sharing an increased number of "vital interests."[10] Then-President George Bush summed up the intrinsic bond between the United States and Israel when he stated, amid the loan-guarantees tension of 1992, that "the U.S. commitment to Israel is a fundamental one."[11]

The Glass-Slipper Argument

By fitting into the glass slipper presented by the prince, and producing a matching one from her pocket, Cinderella is permitted to marry him, and the two live happily ever after. Similarly, a realist could claim that Israel pursued Oslo as a way of bringing Israel's remaining Arab neighbors to the table.[12] However, Israel's 1979 peace treaty with Egypt had already made Israeli-Palestinian reconciliation less important as a condition for peace with other Arab states. Moreover, with the exception of Syria, which could not be expected to wage war on a single front, the remaining front-line states—Jordan and Lebanon—were not a threat. De facto peace had already existed with Jordan, with a formal peace treaty to follow in 1994. As past-defense minister, foreign minister, and prime minister, Shimon Peres recalled, "From time to time, [Jordanian King] Hussein... would meet with Israeli leaders... to resolve common problems," and frequently "the participants would discuss, informally, whether the time had yet come... to negotiate a formal... peace between them."[13] Lebanon was all but immobilized from fifteen years of civil war coupled with Syrian occupation. In any event, Israel no longer deemed war with Syria at all probable. In May 1992, a "senior source in the General Staff" declared that *there is no danger that [a war between Israel and Syria] will break out.*"[14] The absence of a peace treaty (at the time of this writing) between Syria and Israel since the Oslo agreement was signed over a decade ago suggests that neither Hafez al-Asad nor his son Bashar, who succeeded his deceased father in 1999, were not simply waiting for the Palestinian question to be dealt with before making peace with Israel, unlike Jordan's King Hussein, who was eager to translate the de facto peaceful relationship into a formal peace treaty almost as soon as the ink was dry on the Declaration of Principles.

Non-realist Explanations

While materialist explanations indeed seem to fall short in explaining Israel's decision to pursue peace with the PLO, we still need to consider a host of nonrealist explanations. Learning theory, an offshoot of cognitive psychology, is a natural starting point for examining why political actors suddenly shift policy course. The theory posits that individuals possess cognitive templates that shape how they see the world, and that people draw analogies from significant events that inform the subsequent choices they make. Information that severely contradicts a person's belief system—particularly if it arrives in large chunks—will force that individual to adapt her cognitive template in response to such belief-challenging events.[15] In the context of Oslo, a learning theory explanation would suggest that Israel sought peace due to belief-challenging evidence presented by Palestinian actions. However, by the early 1990s, Israel had not necessarily learned new things about the adversary, nor did the polity change its collective worldview. Instead, Israel's policy actions clashed with its enduring identity. Psychoanalysis better accounts for such a durable view of identity.

Second, given constructivism's breadth as a theoretical approach, we can isolate one of its many applications—strategic culture—to assess its explanatory utility in the Oslo case. In its emphasis on the way a military conceives of its use of force, strategic culture comes closest to the explanation I advance in this book.[16] However, strategic culture focuses on the military's view of the effectiveness of certain types of force over others, and neglects to account for the perspective held by the overall polity (of which the military is but one component), as well as the *normative* aspect of military action and national identity. Regarding Oslo, a strategic-culture explanation might rightly uncover Israeli servicemen's frustration at having to act as "policemen" rather than soldiers, but would ignore the emotional and ethical clash—experienced across society—between actions and identity.[17]

Third, given the widespread presence of policy critiques emanating from Israeli society during this period, observers might point to domestic politics as best explaining Israel's shift toward peace with the PLO. It is certainly true that domestic politics plays a part in this story, yet it remains an unsatisfying explanation: in this case, the answer that a domestic-politics theory provides begs further questions. While the 1992 elections ushered in Rabin's Labor party on a platform of peace, we are left to ask *what led Israelis to vote for a leadership that would bring about a radical policy reversal on the Palestinian question?* By going farther back in the causal chain, this book seeks to answer that question.

Finally, we must consider the utility of a straight cognitive-dissonance model.[18] Yet the mere existence of dissonance between the two ideas—awareness of the state's behavior and beliefs about the state's role-identity—does not explain the *source* of discomfort experienced by the polity. Like others working in the cognitive-dissonance tradition who have noted the underspecified nature of the motivation caused by the dissonance that Leon Festinger first identified as being akin to a "drive state" like "hunger," I argue that we need a better causal mechanism to account for this motivation.[19] Some have since introduced the ideas of hypocrisy and the "self-concept"—challenges to one's sense of self—to explain the motivation for dissonance-reduction, and still others have suggested or affirmed a role for psychoanalysis in yielding a fuller understanding of the phenomenon of cognitive dissonance.[20] Accordingly, my model posits that unconscious counternarratives—representing what the actor fears becoming—serve as this catalyst for change, something that contradicts neither Festinger's original formulation nor

Elliot Aronson's useful amendment, but which situates both within a better-specified analytical framework.

Yet neither would a simple dissonance model explain why the dissonance is not simply brushed aside by altering the state's identity, and, instead, why the state experiences a need to radically shift its policies. The simple answer is that for identity to be a useful heuristic, it must be enduring to a degree.[21] While identity is subject to evolution, and certainly there is disagreement among observers as to the degree to which identity is continually remade, there is arguably a kernel of sameness that outlives such processes. Since the *existence* of identity is not what is contested in international relations theory but rather its role in determining outcomes, any identity-based explanation must maintain the integrity of the concept—which is essentially reduced to durability.

METHODOLOGICAL ISSUES

Psychoanalysis, with its view of identity as enduring and with its assumption that powerful unconscious fears can plague an actor who has strayed from the action path suggested by her identity, better explains the case of why Israel sought peace with the PLO. Accordingly, in this book I attempt to show how psychoanalysis can yield insight into the study of international relations and can solve empirical puzzles that many prevailing approaches—both material and social—cannot. The use of psychoanalysis has precious little precedent across international relations theory, and the particular argument presented here is a novel one. Yet it is by no means easy to uncover the content of collective consciousness—no less a collective *unconscious*. The risks associated with applying a psychoanalytic framework to the social sciences in general and international relations in particular are addressed in chapter two. Suffice it to say here that insofar as most social processes are relatively invisible—certainly compared to most physical, chemical, or biological phenomena (and, even then, physicist Werner Heisenberg and his successors found that the instruments of investigation can themselves affect what we observe in the material world), we need to consider hitherto neglected variables in the most scientific way possible, even if this means foregoing proof for plausibility, something to which most social scientists long ago resigned themselves.

In a psychoanalytic framework, the use of a single case study has obvious merits—namely, the opportunity for the researcher to immerse herself in the social and cultural context surrounding the foreign-policy decision process. Thus, to address the question of how identity is created and maintained, I have employed an ethnographic approach. Much has been written about the importance of identity in determining political outcomes, but, without a close observation of the society under study, it is difficult to discover the contours of that identity and to understand its role in shaping foreign policy. Three years of fieldwork during the 1990s, including interviews with almost all of the major Oslo participants on the Israeli side, plus a number of other military, cultural, and political figures, have provided the immediate background for understanding the Israeli decision to seek peace with the PLO. In addition, an examination of cultural symbols, including folk songs, plays, films, school curricula, and other social and political symbols help to determine the substantive content of the state's identity. Conscientious-objection trends across the various Arab-Israeli wars plus documented activities of the peace movement and other opposition groups illuminate the collective reaction to the foreign-policy events examined here.

Beyond demonstrating that the use of a single case is appropriate for theory development, we still need to consider whether or not Israel serves as a suitable example of the phenomenon under study. I would argue that Israel is indeed a good case for the following reasons.[22] First, Israel has intrinsic importance at various levels: popular, strategic, and academic. From a popular perspective, the Judeo-Christian tradition underpinning Western culture means that Israel/Palestine has held particular resonance within the popular imagination—from Mark Twain's famous voyage to the region in 1867 through Israel's dramatic declaration of statehood in the aftermath of the Holocaust. Indeed, the number of news items devoted to Israel in any given week worldwide belies its small size. Moreover, within the Muslim world, Israeli policy captures the interest of those concerned with their coreligionists along Israel's borders. Strategically, Israel enjoys the mixed blessing of residing in the vicinity of the oil-rich states of the Middle East—having made it a site of Cold War rivalry between the two superpowers. For this reason as well as the previous one, Israel has enjoyed the "special relationship" with the United States discussed earlier in the chapter. Academically, Israel is located in the developing world, but by almost all socioeconomic indicators is akin to a fully industrialized state. Its relative youth and ethnically heterogeneous population (Israeli society has been formed from a mix of Eastern European Jews and Jews from the Middle East and North Africa, and more recently, Ethiopia), as well as the high importance accorded security issues within a context of a deep-running religious-secular divide provide a fertile setting for what has emerged as the burgeoning field of "Israel studies"—although the question of whether Israel presents a *sui generis* case is by no means settled.[23]

Second, Israel provides an abundance of data—both through secondary sources, and through the primary sources of public opinion data, published memoirs, and easy access to political elites, being the relatively small and informal society that it is. For determining Israeli identity—the subject of chapter three—much ethnographic data is available in Israel, including the folk songs that are taught in schools and sung annually at multiple points in the calendar, commemorative sites—both temporal (festivals, remembrance days) and spatial (war and other memorials), politically self-conscious plays and films, and collectively oriented graphic works, such as posters issued to celebrate Israel's independence day. The discussion of the nature and outlook of the IDF, as examined in chapter four, draws on the wealth of studies that the Israeli military has inspired among military historians, given the battlefield prowess of the small army. Finally, the Lebanon War and the Intifada—the two events crucial to this story—have resulted in many academic and other works—both inside and outside of Israel—chronicling the operations and their social and political consequences.

Third, there is large within-case variation on the dependent variable: Israeli-Palestinian relations. The Israeli-Palestinian relationship has changed drastically from the time of the state's founding to the signing of the Oslo agreement and beyond. These four-and-a-half decades were punctuated by such events as the spate of anti-Israel and anti-Jewish terrorism of the 1970s, the 1986 Israeli law banning contact between Israeli citizens and the PLO (except under the auspices of academic conferences), and PLO leader Yasser Arafat's 1988 speech at the United Nations in Geneva where he declared his acceptance of a "two-state solution" (a Palestinian state alongside Israel, rather than the rejection of Israel's existence outright) in the Middle East. There is also much variation on the independent variable—that is, Israelis' attitudes toward their country's actions. Despite the controversial international reaction to some Israeli operations (particularly the 1956 Sinai Campaign and partially the 1967 Six Day War), Israelis perceived all of their country's pre-1980s wars as falling well within the limits of Israel's role-identity. Conversely, and as we will see, the Lebanon War and the Intifada led Israelis to experience their country as an aggressor.

Fourth, the theoretical framework developed here lends itself to testing across a variety of types of conflict cases—including traditional protracted violent conflict (such as between the Catholics and Protestants in Northern Ireland, or between Greeks and Turks in Cyprus), anticolonial war (such as the United States in Vietnam, and France in Algeria); and even intrastate constitutional conflict (such as the conflict over Quebec) that may or may not be violent. Finally, as discussed earlier, the most obvious alternative explanations—including realist and nonrealist arguments—make divergent predictions.

PLAN OF THE BOOK

The book is divided into eight chapters. In chapter two, I elaborate on the theoretical framework outlined briefly in this chapter, through reference to sociology and contemporary psychoanalytic theory. There, I present a typology of six role-identities that may occur over time across the international system and across state and nonstate actors, predict what an actor might do after deviating from that identity, and address the question of why states might ever deviate from their role in the first place. In chapter three, drawing on popular channels of narrative dissemination, along with a discussion of five significant events that form the backbone of Israelis' memorialized history, I sketch a picture of the Israeli Self and its attendant defensive-warrior role-identity. Chapter four examines the history and doctrine of the IDF, detailing what I call its "security ethic" in the realm of defense policy; that is, the normative underpinnings of the use of force as viewed by the military. The assumption here is that like the overall role-identity of the state, the military's security ethic has the potential to shape and constrain security policy. Chapters five and six explore the Lebanon War and the Intifada, demonstrating that these two operations served to challenge Israel's role-identity as a defensive warrior and helped to precipitate an Israeli policy shift toward the Palestinians, from belligerency to compromise. Chapter seven examines the path of Israeli policy leading to the Oslo process. In chapter eight, I conclude by situating the book within the broader discipline of international relations, and by discussing what the argument says about the current crisis in the Middle East and the prospects for peace between Israel and the Palestinian Authority.

Chapter Two

Psychoanalysis and International Relations

The psychological turn that international relations took with the rise of behavioralism in the 1960s has begun to expand beyond focusing on cognition—how individuals think—to a wider appreciation of the role of emotional determinants of action, one of many factors that were long dismissed as unscientific. Part of the reason for this hesitant courtship is no doubt the long strides that international relations theory has taken toward refining its investigative lenses, such that less easily observable phenomena can be more confidently incorporated into the solid theoretical infrastructure that the discipline has now adopted. A central example of this evolution is the analytical watershed inaugurated by neorealism, which fashioned a conceptual playing field where little had existed before. Neorealism, a theoretical school that views international relations as taking place within an anarchical state system with no overarching authority, in turn spawned the constructivist turn in international relations—the approach that stresses the importance of social identity in determining international outcomes—and subsequent counterarguments that built on yet other social and psychological precepts—all of which agree that there is such a thing as an international system—though they understand the effects of anarchy differently.[1] Introducing psychoanalysis to international relations can therefore be seen as the next logical step for a relatively young discipline that seeks to understand why political actors behave the way they do.

While all psychoanalysts draw on Freud's unique contribution, subsequent approaches have altered many of his assumptions. This trend has kept pace with the embracing of new epistemological and ontological perspectives by other scientific and social scientific fields, such as the quantum revolution in physics—a paradigm shift that has since influenced other disciplines.[2] The form of psychoanalytic theory that I use here is the contemporary relational strand, one that analysts have alternately termed "relational-model theorizing," a "dyadic systems perspective," and "intersubjectivity theory."[3] This approach shares an ontology basic to constructivism in international relations: the psychology (identity) of the person (state) is not hard-wired into the unit, but develops in part from the actions of other actors in the social environment (the family; the therapeutic setting; the international system), and in part through the shared assumptions that permeate that system. As an approach centered on the individual mind, contemporary psychoanalysis takes into account the broader social context within which actors act.

Psychoanalysis also provides a coherent theory of behavior incorporating three elements that have mostly been invisible in international relations theory, but that provide a fuller understanding of how states and nonstate actors interact: emotion, the unconscious, and the possibility for actors' own cognitive and emotional insight to be a source of behavior change. In drawing on these principles, perhaps the most significant contribution that psychoanalysis can make to international relations is in improving on prevailing theories of identity, which in turn illuminate questions about international action. Within international relations, constructivism has been criticized for neglecting the question of how identity is, in fact, created. Cognitive psychology—which international relations has begun to draw on liberally—in part helps to fill this gap.[4] Yet with its assumption that the emotional legacy of early interpersonal relationships is essential in shaping personality and subsequent behavior, psychoanalysis offers a more comprehensive model of identity creation than those put forth by cognitive theorists. Recognizing these explanatory benefits, constructivists have recently called for exploring the potential that psychoanalysis holds for understanding international politics.[5] Thus, unlike the prevailing psychoanalytic approaches in international relations—namely, psychohistories of individual leaders, and the focus-group potential of micro-level conflict resolution, the psychoanalytic approach I use here is meant to coexist happily alongside other streams of systemic theory in international relations.[6]

HOW PSYCHOANALYSIS CAN HELP

It has long been argued that even within the confines of rational-choice approaches, the nature of a decision-maker's preferences cannot be assumed a priori, and indeed their distinctiveness derives from factors ranging from emotion to personality to the selective use of historical analogies.[7] Emotion, in short, can be considered the *sine qua non* of social life, a realization that has recently begun to permeate international relations theory.[8] Moreover, the concept of the unconscious that anchors psychoanalysis can illuminate the question of why an individual experiences a sense of dissonance when her actions do not conform to her identity; the *mechanism* by which the dissonance between action and identity can become unbearable; and therefore *why* humans experience the need to match the two.[9]

The unconscious is that aspect of the self that remains the most untapped yet potentially the most satisfying determinant of action, coming, as it does, early in the causal chain. At its most basic, the unconscious is simply the repository for those characteristics that an actor fears adopting; in other words, "action fantasies" that the actor despises but can *plausibly entertain*. This fundamental tension between the feared and the imaginable is what normally keeps these fantasies in check, and is what makes the unconscious so potentially powerful as an explanatory tool. And while the unconscious is an admittedly contested concept, scholars from various fields have issued tentative calls for its exploration,[10] and convincing deductive and empirical research certainly justify its consideration.[11]

One theoretical perspective that has been criticized for ignoring the unconscious is sociology's symbolic interactionism, an approach that underpins constructivism in international relations.[12] Part of the reason for the tension between sociology, including symbolic interactionism, and psychoanalysis arguably lies in an antiquated understanding of psychology: the false belief that to employ psychology as an explanatory approach, one must ignore the impact that one's social environment has on one's personality, self-image, and behavior. However, contemporary psychoanalysis presents a view of the self that is more relational than what Freudian drive theory had suggested. A psychoanalytic approach does not have to assume that unconscious or otherwise emotional factors arise from the actor independent of the shared understandings that define the social environment. Admitting an explanatory role for the unconscious therefore does not imply a rejection of intersubjectivity, mutual-constitution, or any of the other organizing principles of sociology and constructivism. Rather, it simply means that ideas held in the unconscious serve as one filter through which actors interpret social interaction.

The unconscious, therefore, may be understood either as *one element of agency* that the actor brings to interpreting his social script, or as itself the product of social forces that interpret and constrain action. The first perspective assumes that agency does not have to be conscious to be meaningful; agency at its most basic can simply imply action, and intentionality can therefore encompass an unconscious component. The second view means that the unconscious does not have to be understood as a pre-wired component of the unit that in turn shapes behavior; rather it can be viewed as an emergent and mediating phenomenon. We can therefore understand cognition as being inherently situated within social processes.[13] This is consistent with a relational view of social life, and yet it is an important theoretical addition to the prevailing wisdom in international relations about how social understandings ultimately shape behavior.

A final contribution that psychoanalysis can make to our understanding of international relations—and conflict resolution in particular—is its assumption that entrenched behavior patterns can be altered through cognitive and emotional insight. In addition to challenging the static conception of "human nature" that underpinned classical realism (arguably the first theory of international relations) and that provided a rather pessimistic view of human affairs, this assumption is a valuable addition to any theory of international relations in which the prevailing theories of action—material power in the case of states, polarity in the case of state systems—are difficult, if not impossible to manipulate. As a result, many of the most prominent international relations theories have lacked meaningful policy implications. Conversely, psychoanalytic theory suggests tools for ameliorating some of the most pressing global problems, including protracted conflict and war. While some psychoanalytically based conflict-resolution approaches use the focus-group format to simulate the healing function of the therapy setting,[14] this book demonstrates that the gaining of conscious insight into one's role deviation—a prerequisite for policy change—can come about through real-life international interaction that requires neither a skilled conflict practitioner nor the willingness of elites to participate in such an exercise. Rather, under certain conditions, role conflict can prompt domestic and international elements to hold a "mirror" to the face of elites, resulting in a collective cognitive dissonance that can lead to policy change. This mirror can take a number of forms—acts of protest by domestic groups, media coverage, and actions by allies, adversaries or international structures. These sources will be discussed further.

THE INTERNATIONAL SELF

Rather than referring to a notion of collective selfhood that is shared by multiple states—as some constructivist theorists of "collective identity" would maintain—the title of this book, "the international self," is meant to suggest not only that each state possesses a distinctive identity, but that this identity develops out of the state's relationship with other international actors.[15] This concept also implies that decisions emanating from the polity are derived from a process *not simply the sum of the state's "parts."* Yet while we have already shown that psychoanalysis can accommodate a role for environmental processes in shaping behavior, we still need to be aware of the risks of anthropomorphizing the state, a practice that gets to the heart of the debate between two analytical positions that cut across the social sciences: methodological individualism and holism. While methodological individualism views social life as the product of actions taken by individuals, holism understands the group to be a meaningful unit in and of itself.[16] Yet, to an extent, the debate between the two perspectives is already fixed. While the holists have in their favor a precedent of semantic habit—we tend to anthropomorphize the state in everyday speech more often than not (e.g., "*Washington* decided to wage war against al-Qaeda")—methodological individualism is allied with the rich literature of rational choice, and more prosaically the commonsense discomfort that arises when we ascribe human characteristics to things, including groups. Groups do not have "minds" any more than do other social facts, and group behavior is, after all, the product of individuals acting on the group's behalf. Finally, given the presence of disparate individuals and subgroups constituting any society, it can be misleading to attribute a single group "consciousness" to a political entity. In a foreign-policy context, accordingly, adherents of this view would focus on elite attitudes, bureaucratic politics, and/or interest group activities to tease out the causal relationship between intentions and outcomes.

Yet a strong case can be made for the *emergent* properties of states and their policy processes: something happens between the point at which citizens articulate preferences and those preferences are translated into policies. Insofar as elite decisions do not always reflect the opinion of the majority, there remains some degree of independent agency that may very well accrue to the state as a whole. Under this reasoning, it would be plausible to assert the existence of an overarching group self, as Alexander Wendt does when he claims that "states are people too."[17] In addition to the views of significant strands of psychoanalytic thought (which would not necessarily be expected to assume that units other than the individual can be psychoanalyzed), the idea of a group self enjoys far-reaching support across the social sciences—international relations included. This includes neorealism's assumption that the state is a unitary actor, the collective self-hood implied by social identity theory,[18] the concept of "political culture,"[19] early psychoanalytic assumptions about the group,[20] as well as studies on obedience, group-think, and the "crowd" phenomenon.[21] There is a reason why scholars are drawn to the group as a unit of analysis—witness anthropologists' concern with tribes and civilizations, sociologists' focus on street gangs and societies, and political scientists' emphasis on states and transnational actors. Group behavior and individual behavior are not necessarily identical. Nor can an individual be expected to behave the same way in the context of a group as he or she would alone. Moreover, constructivism goes so far as to assume the possibility of shared norms across states, a claim that has enjoyed much empirical support during the first active decade of constructivist research.[22] It is much more defensible to argue the existence of a collective identity *within* a state, the boundaries of which contain degrees of centralized media, language, and other discursive channels for cultural dissemination, and which prescribe the roles that the group's members are expected to perform within the context of that group. And if different subgroups within the state disseminate disparate narratives, we can assume that the most dominant group within society (as defined by some combination of ethnicity, class, or gender) has custody over a single, consequential 'dominant' narrative. Finally, even if we choose to ascribe a state's national ethos to its elites, we need to remember that state leaders are the product of the society in which they were reared. This view would effectively mitigate the tension between elite- and mass-level phenomena in international relations, since both elites and masses are socialized by the overarching structure of the collective.

Next, we must ask how we go about identifying a collective self. A group manifests its identity through collective consciousness, an idea that suggests an opposite (the collective unconscious) and that differs from the more common concepts of beliefs and attitudes. Beliefs and attitudes can be adopted or discarded depending on social pressures or the exposure to new facts. Even religious beliefs—those that are the least likely to be refuted by worldly evidence—can be swapped through religious conversion, adapted at the suggestion of religious elites, or rejected outright. Conversely, consciousness refers to one's entire arsenal of beliefs and attitudes that, like the self, is more than the sum of its parts. While new to international relations theory, the idea of a collective *unconscious* has been invoked by others in the humanities and social sciences, but typically without systematic exploration.[23] The major exception, not surprisingly, has been in psychoanalytic theory, namely, Jung's treatment.[24] However, Jung's presentation of the collective unconscious is problematic in its claim that there are universal, primordial "archetypes" that accrue across civilization. Jung's position is useful for what it suggests about humanity writ large, but says little about the effects of social categories—namely, states and societies—on consciousness and action. Instead, the assumption underlying this book is that states develop particular self-images that, due to the particular historical experiences that nations undergo, as well as the nation-building tools at the disposal of state regimes, are more particularistic and culturally informed than the universal archetypes that Jung sets forth. This view also addresses the criticism that psychology is either too individually oriented to serve as a meaningful determinant of group behavior, or else that the dominant psychoanalytic narratives (such as Jung's archetypes or Freud's notion of the oedipal complex) do not account for differences across cultures. This strand of psychoanalysis therefore serves to bridge individual-level psychological dynamics with collective processes—a stance that is certainly appropriate to international relations, where actions are taken by individuals on behalf of political entities that shape the subjectivity of individual leaders.

Yet compared to asserting that *nations* have identities (a nation being simply a group of people with a common past and common destiny), assuming a *state* identity is a more difficult leap, but one that is plausible nonetheless. This is a point that merits elaboration as constructivists have largely taken state identity to be an unproblematic unit of analysis, following neorealists, who, while neglecting identity, similarly focus on states as meaningful actors. One problem lies with the misleading use of terminology in the discipline. While we often interchange "nation-state," with "state," the two are not synonymous—as the phenomenon of intrastate, ethnic conflicts illustrates. Another lies with the lack of attention that international relations theory has given to the question of the evolution of the state from a territorial entity to one defined along nationalist lines.[25] Yet, especially since regimes wield the power to disseminate information, it is certainly possible to imagine that regimes fashion at least the kernel of a "state identity" in a top-down format—intentionally or otherwise. And in those cases in which regime-instilled identity is contested by the masses, the result may be either the maintenance of elites' version of state identity (achieved through coercion)[26] or else a product of a dialectical interaction between the two narratives.

ROLES AND ROLE-IDENTITIES

Now that we have established the ontological possibility of a group self in the form of a state identity, we need to consider the most relevant aspect of a state self in the context of foreign policy making: that is, a state's role and its role-identity. Currently making a comeback within international relations theory after decades of benign neglect, the study of roles still remains stymied by a lack of clarity as well as disagreement over basic ontological assumptions. Role theory draws on the tradition of social psychology that explores the interaction between individual subjectivity and social constraints, and as such is uniquely suited to studying the foreign-policy process, which entails individuals acting within the boundaries of the state, as well as the state acting within the confines of the international states system. Role theory's central contribution to international relations has been to predict a state's foreign-policy orientation from the determination of its "national role conception," a concept containing two complementary aspects: the "role prescription" *conferred on* the role-occupant by others, and the role-occupant's own self-image. Role theory therefore predicts a state's foreign policy on the basis of its self-perceived function in the international system, coupled with the behavior expected from it by others.

Being a social construct, roles are a natural complement to constructivism, streamlining constructivism's predictive capacity. Roles allow for the identification of particular "packages" of identity. In so doing, they encourage generalizable and concrete claims about the origins of identity and the behaviors associated with particular identities. Roles can therefore explain and predict the general pattern of behavior associated with a particular role-occupant (e.g., the degree to which a state can be expected to adopt cooperative or competitive strategies). Roles also capture the intersubjective nature of social life, and as such can predict the outcomes associated with specific dyadic interactions, particularly insofar as partners in a dyad develop repetitive patterns of interaction. Finally, when states *deviate* from their role, the latter can explain the important but understudied phenomenon of radical foreign-policy change that is under investigation here.

While roles refer to the actual positions that individuals occupy within a structure of interaction, *role-identity* refers to the internalized manifestation of the role.[27] This means that while identity refers to the overarching concept of who an actor *is*, role-identity is but one type of identity—one that refers to action.[28] In this way, role-identity is a particularly salient type of identity for investigating foreign policy and especially foreign-policy change. Moreover, role is a structural phenomenon, while role-identity is a unit-level concept that nevertheless accounts for intersubjective knowledge: one's role is the part that one acts out in relation to others; one's role-identity represents the way in which that role has been internalized by the actor.

The distinction between "role" and "role-identity" is an important one, and is helpful on a number of counts. First, the term role-identity provides semantic clarification: role-identity conveys the idea of a state's self-image, a concept relevant in accounting for role-deviation and illuminating the consequences of such deviation. Second, role-identity implies self-consciousness, while role implies a function not necessarily known to the actor and thus could be considered overly mechanistic. Finally, role-identity, while a unit-level approach to understanding and explaining behavior, nevertheless manages to account for the relational field surrounding interstate interaction: role-identities are derived from the parts one plays *in relation to others*.

So how *do* states develop role-identities? Looking at two related processes help us determine a state's role-identity—that aspect of the "international self" that is most relevant to policy and policy change. Paralleling the function of early interpersonal experiences in shaping the personality of an individual, we can consider the early interstate as well as pre-state experiences of the state as forming the backbone of its role-identity.[29] Whether pre-state experiences are as crucial as early state events will depend on the age of a state. States founded in the twentieth century are more likely to sustain narratives encapsulating pre-state memories. Israel, for instance, is an easy case in that the country is relatively young, and the circumstances surrounding its founding have remained an integral part of the national narrative. So too do postcolonial states in the Third World share memories of national liberation born out of a collective struggle—violent or otherwise—against Western imperialism. However, many older states nurture equally powerful historical memories that influence subsequent generations of regimes and citizens, such as the principles of individualism and liberalism enshrined in the American constitution. For states whose existence spans multiple centuries and who may even lack a precise birth date, watershed events when the state's identity was significantly transformed—such as the French Revolution—can be thought of as akin to early experiences. Finally, as has been argued in the case of the United States, some societies predate actual state-formation, with the former being held together by a system of shared ideas.[30]

Early relational experiences include such things as whether the state was born through secession or war; whether other actors recognized the incipient state's sovereignty; and the degree to which the state's economy was initially self-sufficient. These early experiences bestow upon the state a role—a patterned set of actions that is targeted toward a designated Other or Others—that shapes the state's behavior, and leads to complementary behavior by other states. Over time this pattern of behavior is replicated, with the state's role becoming further entrenched. The enacting of corresponding roles subsequently leads to degrees of internalization that culminates in the idea of a role-identity previously discussed. The relational field between states therefore determines roles and role-identities.[31]

The second constitutive aspect of a state's role-identity is the way the polity remembers these experiences—the *narratives* that a society weaves about its place in the international order. Narratives are actively nurtured and transmitted across generations, taking the form of stories that groups construct about their past, present, and future, as states and their members see themselves as "protagonists" within their respective histories.[32] Listening to the state's dominant narratives helps us identify the state's role-identity and is therefore instrumental in predicting policy and policy change. Seen functionally, narratives are forces intended to bind nationals together socially and culturally; they are the glue of socio-cultural "imagination." Imagination has been discussed in political science primarily in the context of forging nationalist bonds throughout societies that are too large to allow for face-to-face interaction among their members.[33] A sinister view of the imagining process would posit a political-corporate-media complex shaping the nature of public attitudes toward domestic and foreign policies for the good of the few and at the expense of the many.[34] Yet this "binding" function does not have to be enacted by manipulative elites, though of course elites—particularly those governing during the formative years of a state—possess powerful institutional channels of dissemination through such things as school curricula and the media, and such state symbols as the national anthem and the flag. However, as I will discuss later, a strong case can be made that elites are no less the product of cultural influences within the polity as are masses. This is particularly true of the second and subsequent generations of political elites, who have themselves been socialized by the same institutional symbols as their compatriots. This does not mean that the masses are passive recipients of state culture; rather, ordinary citizens are able to recast national narratives through their own interpretive lenses, an act that in turn shapes elite ideas, and so on.

Moreover, unlike biological, geological, or some psychological (e.g., personality) types—that exist as an observable aid in classification, a role-identity does not exist apart from the actor's own awareness of it. Moreover, while many states include citizens who possess different narratives about their state's history and destiny, for our purposes we can understand the relevant role-identity as that which is represented by the *dominant voice* in society. This voice may emerge from a particular political, ethnic, racial, religious, or gender group (or some such combination), but usually informs the creation and transmission of state symbols. This point will be elaborated in chapter three, in the context of the Israeli Self.

Just as individuals and groups possess consciousness and an unconscious, I argue that every society maintains not only a dominant (conscious) narrative, but an unconscious *counternarrative* as well, which the former has in part arisen to conceal. As the counternarrative represents the role that society most fears adopting, it resides in the unconscious, where it will not interfere with the day-to-day transmission and fulfillment of the dominant narratives and the dominant roles. For instance, a "defensive" state's counternarrative would encapsulate the view that 'we are not only defensive, but sometimes we can be aggressive.'[35] Narratives and counternarratives can coexist in two ways— either with the counternarrative being simply an unactualized fear, or with the counternarrative corresponding to an actual role being enacted alongside the dominant role-identity. Thus, while an actor may *consciously* be aware of a counterrole that she abhors (e.g., the "good student" who avoids cheating on exams), the unconscious reminds us that the "cheater" is latent in the "self-portfolio" of the good student. In the event that this student cheats, radical change can only come about once the self has been reconciled with its unconscious opposite. Actors will not become aware of the divergence from their dominant identity without the aid of a "mirror," however. Only with the help of outside forces drawing attention to the clash between the two narratives will elites experience a cognitive dissonance necessitating a realignment between actions and role-identity.

One of the most salient transmission belts for the creation of state narratives is collective memory. Memory—active or latent recall of things occurring in the past—has begun to be understood as not solely a private activity, but as representing a group phenomenon as well.[36] On the collective level, memory can be either experience-near-active, one-step removed, or distantly removed. Active memory would be represented by Holocaust survivors in Israel and the Diaspora, for instance; one-step removed would be the surrogate memories that their immediate offspring carry with them,[37] and distantly removed would be exemplified by the Rabbinic injunction that Jews experience the annual telling of the Exodus from Egypt as if "they were there." While a case could be made for discounting the importance of actual experiences in favor of the way those experiences are remembered, both of these are crucial for ascertaining role-identity. Just as traumatic events in a person's life may be repressed in memory but still shape that person's identity, the international observer needs to account for actual experiences, yet view these as embedded within a narrative context. Similarly, some historical events undergo a process of memory revision; in these cases the observer must be sensitive to the effect that the new discourse has on the society's perception of these events, whether or not these stories accord with fact. The clinical parallel in psychoanalysis is that while the analysand's relationship with her parents is considered crucial to uncovering the contours of her psychology, the analyst as a rule does not attempt to meet the parents firsthand: rather, the patient's recounting of these experiences is considered to be the most important channel of investigation—and hence transformation.

Since we are talking about collections of individuals, memory needs to be actively transmitted to the society's members in order for it to influence the citizens' sense of collective identity. One of the ways this can be done is through ritual. Being repetitive while symbolically imbued, ritual gains meaning only through the symbols attributed to it by the group, and is a collective process that serves to link actors to a series of past events for which they may not have been physically present. Moreover, private rituals that are collectively prescribed, such as prayer, serve to bind the individual to the collective, particularly when there is a formalized liturgy. Most collective rituals occur according to the calendar, and therefore can encompass regular ceremonies that come to act as markers for the individual's personal time cycle.[38]

Sometimes particular collective memories that have been sustained over time are ruptured, with citizens contemplating new facts about their country's past. Revisionist history is an example of an attempt to bring forth these sorts of new facts. When history is reinterpreted, the society can either shun the dissenting voices, or else gradually reevaluate the original narratives. When this reevaluation occurs, society is more apt to uncover the hitherto unconscious counternarratives, a discovery that can lead to the realization that the state's behavior might be contradicting the state's role-identity. In other words, revisionist historians and other domestic dissenters can serve as the "mirror" referred to later.

Given these proposed dynamics, two sets of questions remain. First, in order to produce a cognitive dissonance revealing unconscious counternarratives and precipitating a shift in policy, what *kinds* of national values must be challenged, and to what degree? On this issue, we can look to the substance of role-identities. As we will see, these identities rest on the fulcrums of capabilities and ethics. Yet it is the ethical component—the degree to which a government pursues policies that contravene the most basic moral stance of the military and the polity—that will elicit a policy change. As to *how much* these values must be challenged, it seems clear that if either of the basic principles of *jus ad bellum* or *jus in bello* are violated as a central defining feature of the given operation—that is, just cause and discrimination between combatants and civilians, *and* if the operation forces the state and its military into a role that is anathema to its most basic role-identity, then the threshold of public tolerance for the action will have been reached.

Second and importantly, *under what conditions* will the polity react to the dissonance by pressing for a wholesale policy shift, rather than simply by "bunkering down" and attributing the conflict to the enemy, thereby maintaining the policy status quo, or even intensifying the level of conflict-laden behavior? I argue that the *first series* of role-identity-challenging actions taken by the state will precipitate a policy shift. Conversely, role-identity-challenging actions taken in the aftermath of an attempt at compromise—particularly if viewed as such by the polity—will go unnoticed, and will more likely result in such a bunkering down stance, a dynamic that has been in play among Israelis during this second Intifada that has shaken the region since September 2000.

A TYPOLOGY OF ROLE-IDENTITIES

While the character of role-identities varies across states, the concept of role-identity is nevertheless generalizable. This section outlines a typology (shown in Table 1) of ideal-type role-identities that is meant to encapsulate most, if not all, nation-based international actors across time. Operationally, a state's role-identity can be gleaned by examining discursive artifacts of popular culture—including plays, folk and pop songs, films, jokes, advertisements, newspaper editorials, school curricula, academic treatments of history, and popular attitudes toward the military—as well as institutional symbols such as national anthems, war memorials, state logos, constitutions, parliamentary proceedings, and levels and types of defense spending. It is true that for a state, such as Israel, whose overall identity is largely defined by issues of war and peace, discursive artifacts will most readily reveal a state's role-identity. However, all states possess foundational myths and emergent narratives that help to define how that polity experiences itself in the international system. More often than not, these narratives contain messages about the polity's strategic and ethical attitudes toward war and peace.

The typology is fashioned along three dimensions: capabilities, ethics, and activeness, together representing the material and normative dimensions of a state's power.[39] Capabilities are arguably the baseline from which to explain outcomes, yet we also need to account for whether the state chooses to deploy these capabilities—a dimension that

resembles the concept of "resolve" but which I call "activeness" in order
to broaden the connotation beyond the idea of deterrence. Finally, capabilities and activeness are both affected by whatever ethical constraints
are in place within the state that define when and how force ought to be
used. An approach centered on these three indicators therefore recognizes the importance of relative power in shaping state identity, an
assumption that addresses critiques that both realists and poststructural-
ists have levied against constructivism.

Each axis yields two dichotomous possibilities. The capabilities axis
suggests either "weak" or "strong" states, referring to the state's material
power relative to its most significant adversary. The ethics axis refers to
whether or not a state imposes ethical limits on its own use of force
("limited" vs. "unlimited")—including limits directed at out-groups. For
instance, even though Nazi doctrine arguably espoused an "ethical" view
toward what it perceived as "advanced races," we would classify Nazi
Germany as "unlimited" since that ethic did not extend universally.
Finally, the activeness dimension refers to whether a state takes "active"
military and/or diplomatic measures to secure its own existence, or
whether it is "passive" in pursuit of its own territorial, economic, or ideological goals. Activeness includes such things as preemptive or preventive warfare, swaggering, or promoting diplomatic relations. A passive
state would find itself on the receiving end of both peacemaking and
warmaking overtures.

These three axes reveal eight possible attribute combinations: weak-
limited-passive, strong-unlimited-active, weak-limited-active, weak-
unlimited-active, weak-unlimited-passive, strong-limited-passive, strong-
limited-active, and strong-unlimited-passive. Two of these combinations—weak-unlimited-passive and strong-unlimited-passive—are illog-
ical in practice; a state cannot be passive in pursuit of its security while at
the same time exhibit no ethical limits on its use of force. Eliminating
these two, we are left with six *plausible* role-identity types, which I have
labeled more concisely for descriptive clarity: *passive victim, passive
defender, defensive victim, defensive warrior, aggressive victim,* and
aggressive warrior. I will now elucidate each type, beginning with the
three victim states.

Passive victim states are both unable and unwilling to defend
themselves, and they accordingly possess an ethic of limited force. This
type is rare among states—most of whom have the requisite capabilities and willingness to employ them—but is more common among
stateless nations, particularly those harboring myths about divine
intervention such that the will to pursue collective defense—were these
capabilities to exist—is subsumed under a metaphysical teleology that

ascribes little agency to political actors. An example is the Jewish people during the Exilic period who were characterized by passivity in the face of persecution, a stance that culminated in the Holocaust. A *defensive victim* state is the more common role-identity type among small states or stateless nations. Such a state takes active and ethically bounded measures to defend itself (hence the "defensive" label), yet does not necessarily possess capabilities superior to its enemies (hence the term "victim"). An example is the contemporary Baltic states, who are comparatively weak but take active measures to secure themselves through their attempts to join NATO, and who espouse liberal democratic values.

Finally, like defensive victims, *aggressive victim* states possess inferior capabilities to those of their significant adversaries, but use force—wherever possible—to advance their interests. As these states do not value the protection of out-group life and hence impose no significant ethical limits on the use of force, I have identified them as aggressive. Aggressive victims, given their limited military capabilities, are more likely to use terrorism to achieve their goals. An example is the PLO prior to its renunciation of terrorism as a legitimate means of resistance under the terms of the 1993 Oslo agreement, and its adoption of diplomatic measures—at least until the latest Intifada broke out in 2000, whereby the PLO has appeared to have adopted more violent means of protest, the military offshoot of Arafat's Fatah wing (the al-Aqsa martyrs brigade) being linked to a number of suicide bombings.

Next, I have identified two types of warrior states—defensive and aggressive. A state surrounded by enemies and enjoying power parity or superiority will develop military capabilities in line with a self-image of a *defensive warrior*. The "warrior" identity refers to the state's self-perceived need to take active measures to secure its existence. Thus, a defensive warrior, while possibly strong enough to inflict the damage of an aggressive warrior, limits its use of force by an ethical view of "just cause" and "discrimination" in which military might is to be used in the service of defense, with care taken not to harm civilians. The more physically vulnerable the state, as measured by the offense-defense balance between it and its adversaries (i.e., territorial and demographic size, technology, and natural barriers), the more defensive (ethically) it will view its own actions in war, yet, given this vulnerability, such a state will favor preemptive or preventive war strategies.[40] The defensive-warrior role-identity is more common among medium-to-large states who possess the requisite defensive capabilities and see themselves as beleaguered. An example is Israel, which has a long tradition of utilizing offensive military doctrines in the service of defense—a strategy employed most markedly in the preventive war that was the 1956 Sinai Campaign and the 1967 Six Day War, a preemptive operation.

Finally, an *aggressive warrior* can also be thought of as a "revisionist" state. This is a state that both possesses defensive and offensive capabilities, yet, unlike defensive warriors, aggressive warriors use force in an attempt to change the status quo—as defined in territorial or other (i.e., economic or ideological) terms. Similarly, an aggressive warrior places few—if any—ethically imposed limits on its use of force (hence the label "aggressive"), and may even value expansion—at the cost of harming others—over its own security.[41] An example is Nazi Germany or contemporary Iraq; Saddam Hussein's 1990 invasion of Kuwait exemplified an attempt to revise the status quo in the face of strong evidence that Iraq would be soundly defeated by a U.S.-led coalition. A final role-identity type is what I call a *passive defender* state. This is a state, such as Canada, that possesses the basic material capabilities to defend itself, but takes relatively few explicit measures to hone its military capacity—perhaps due to the particular social understandings that characterize the region in which the state resides, or perhaps due to its ability to enjoy a "security umbrella" provided by a stronger, neighboring state, as Canada arguably does vis-à-vis the United States.

From this typology, we can expect that *the greater the distance between the current aggressive actions and the level of aggressiveness implied by the role-identity, the greater the likelihood of compromise-seeking.* Therefore, a *passive victim*—in the event that it aggresses using its meager capabilities—will be most likely to seek compromise following that aggressive behavior, because the distance between behavior and role-identity is greatest. Conversely, an *aggressive warrior* is least likely to pursue compromise under similar conditions since the distance between behavior and role-identity is smallest.

ROLE-IDENTITIES AND COGNITIVE DISSONANCE

Like most individuals, states possess a complex arsenal of motivations that are not all palatable to the polity's sense of self—not least of which is due to the discrepant voices vying for influence in any society. Yet the dominant self—that overarching group ethos that does not necessarily reflect each single (sub)voice—implicitly prescribes a set of normatively acceptable behaviors. Should a state adopt a policy course that contradicts the state's role-identity, we can expect some sort of cognitive dissonance to arise, leading to a radical realignment between actions and identity. Just as a man who once struck his wife might offer the apologetic plea that "I don't know what got into me!," it is up to the analyst to help the subject come to terms with the aggression that has, evidently, been very much inside of him all along. The policy shift therefore results from the force of the "role-identity" prodding the "self" back into behavioral consistency.

Table I: A Typology of Role-Identities					
Role-Identity	*Capabilities*	*Ethical Limits on the Use of Force*	*Stance*	*Example*	*Likelihood of Seeking Compromise**
PASSIVE VICTIM	Weak	Limited	Passive	The Jews in Exile (c. 70 A.D. - 1948)	HIGHEST
PASSIVE DEFENDER	Strong	Limited	Passive	Canada	HIGHER
DEFENSIVE VICTIM	Weak	Limited	Active	Baltic States	HIGHER
DEFENSIVE WARRIOR	Strong	Limited	Active	The State of Israel	HIGH
AGGRESIVE VICTIM	Weak	Unlimited	Active	The PLO (pre-Oslo)	LOW
AGGRESSIVE WARRIOR	Strong	Unlimited	Active	Nazi Germany, Saddam Hussein's Iraq	LOWEST

*after acting aggressively.

Note: The greater the distance between aggressive actions and role-identity, the higher the likelihood of seeking compromise.

However, acting in contradiction to one's role-identity does not necessarily result in a behavior shift. The dissonance between role-identity and behavior must be both unbearable and experienced at an emotional level in order for such a shift to result. If the dissonance remained at a cognitive level, it is likely that the subject would employ one of a number of cognitive biases in order to rationalize the discrepancy.[42] The dredging up of the unconscious counternarrative assures that the dissonance is experienced deeply enough to result in the taking of radical action to realign actions with identity.[43]

This hypothesis of "cognitive-emotional realization" is grounded in the clinical findings of psychoanalytic theory that suggest that, under certain conditions, actors may become consciously aware of previously

unconscious processes.[44] The classic understanding of cognitive dissonance—as articulated by Leon Festinger—is that inconsistency between
behavior and belief results in "psychological discomfort" that leads to
"activity oriented toward dissonance reduction just as hunger leads to
activity oriented toward hunger reduction."[45] In line with psychoanalysis, the actual cognitive-emotional realization brings to light what had
previously been stored in the unconscious areas of the state's subjective
world. In actuality, the assumption here is that the role-challenging
behavior (paired with domestic challenges) causes elites to "reflect" on
the state's role-identity. Moreover, my use of "cognitive-emotional realization" imbues the concept with a distinctively emotional component as
well. Whereas pure "cognitive dissonance" refers to the challenging of an
individual's worldview (i.e., the revelation of new "facts"),[46] I am introducing the more ontologically powerful notion of challenges to the
self.[47] When this behavior undermines the very legitimacy buttressing
the state's *raison d'etat*, the dissonance is particularly acute.

Catalysts for Realization

Once decision-makers come to realize that the state's foreign-policy
actions have contradicted the state's role-identity, a policy shift may
result. The important question that remains is: what contributes to this
realization? Numerous sources may act as the "mirror" necessary for the
state to reflect on its behavior. For clarity, I have divided them into three
categories: domestic elements (including the military, the peace movement, revisionist historians, artists and the domestic media), other states
(including allies and adversaries, as well as those state's news media), and
international structures (including international organizations, norms,
and regimes).

Domestic Elements: The Military

If the military acts in a way that the populace sees as contradicting the
state's self-image (even if the military is merely carrying out governmental policies), society can experience a corresponding cognitive dissonance. In a democracy, the military takes its directives from the
government; however, military culture is instrumental in shaping the
broader strategic culture encompassing foreign-policy decisions—and
role-identity—more generally. Most of the time, the relationship
between the civilian and military spheres resembles a symbiosis: com-
mands are given by civilians and implemented by the military, which in
turn will advise and reshape subsequent policies. In some cases, ex-mili-

tary personnel will pursue a career in government on being discharged. However, it is possible for the military to experience a sense of dissonance between a particular policy and its overall defense doctrine, or ethic. Soldiers might articulate discomfort in carrying out a particular mission, or the number of conscientious objectors may rise. In a country in which conscientious objection is previously unheard of, the founding of such a movement will therefore signal an even higher degree of dissonance between behavior and institutional role-identity. In examining foreign-policy shifts, the role of the military is crucial in representing the degree of concordance between national role-identity and foreign policy. In states where the military has particular salience for establishing national identity—those states with mandatory and universal conscription, for instance—that institution will be particularly salient.

Domestic Elements: Civilians

The second group that can serve as a "mirror" aiding in the state's realization that its behavior is contradicting its role-identity is the nonuniformed segment of society: particularly the peace movement, revisionist historians, and artists. Although peace movements can contain membership crossover with the military, much of the movement's momentum emanates from the civilian sphere. Peace movements often take their initial impetus from a particular foreign policy event to which there is much domestic dissatisfaction. Furthermore, peace movements do not necessarily advocate pacifism; rather, they can simply critique what their members see as overly aggressive state policies. Revisionist historians are typically a much less numerous force, and are less accessible to the public than are peace movements that actively garner new members. The effect that revisionist historians have on the public at large as well as elites depends on the level of interest within society in exploring its own history, as well as the media exposure they receive. In societies particularly conscious of their own historical experiences, historians can play an important role in defining and reshaping collective narratives.[48] When such scholars are shunned (as in the case of Holocaust deniers in Canada), the result is a marginalization of their work and a consonant lack of policy impact. However, in those cases in which the historians are perceived as loyal to the state and conduct legitimate scholarship—including holding respected academic positions—they can serve as an impetus for a reexamination of the state's history. Such a reexamination, in turn, can serve to reshape the narratives that guide state policy. However, it is the premise of this book that narratives are more durable than they are malleable and, therefore, such challenges will more likely be channeled toward present policies that will subsequently be better aligned with the state's role-identity. A good example here is the plight of the Aboriginal peoples in Canada. Rather than Canada's coming to see itself as an historical oppressor in response to native-rights research and advocacy, Ottawa redirected any potential "guilt" into a celebration of current Canadian magnanimity with the 1999 creation of Nunavut, the Aboriginal-run territory in the country's north.

Of potentially more impact than revisionist historians but with less institutional legitimacy are artists. Different types of artists will have an impact on different segments of the population; protest rock singers will appeal to the younger stratum, while visual artists will have an even more narrow following due to the exposure limitations of the medium. However, as controversial art exhibits are mounted, inevitably media attention will serve to compound their effects. And in cases where artists face censorship, these restrictions may unintentionally amplify the dissenting message.

Finally, domestic media can act as a check on policy by creating and transforming the contours of national discourse. Especially salient are instances when a state suddenly gains access to international media stations hitherto unavailable to the mass public. The degree to which the media is independent from the state obviously affects whether it can act as a catalyst for realization. Moreover, media fora with a known political slant will also be viewed as such, and may carry less resonance among those opposed to it. However, the dissemination of ideas—no matter the political stripe—can shape the way members of society think about an issue. This claim rests on the assumption of the power of language and visual images in shaping attitudes, and is reflected in the efforts of some states to implement "hate laws" to stem racist or other inflammatory rhetoric.

Other States: Allies and Adversaries

Other states' actions can influence the foreign policy of an ally to a degree, but success often depends on the level of autonomy that the target state both desires and is able to achieve. Small states might be more determined to assert an independent foreign policy in the face of outside interference, yet at the same time are constrained by the economic or military aid they may receive from these allies. Similar to the dynamic linked to the media and to international norms, allies may serve as a normative check on action through informal censure. The role of adversaries in acting as the catalyst for realization is somewhat more obscure. As previously discussed, the pattern of interactions that develops between states (allies or adversaries) can be described as the enactment of roles. When one member of the dyad breaks this pattern, the other may be forced to reflect on the role it has hitherto been enacting as well as any actions it has taken that deviate from the original role position. For example, a "defensive warrior" state that sees the other as an "aggressive warrior" and that is suddenly presented with an olive branch may have the opportunity to examine its interactions. If the former state has been acting aggressively, the peaceful overtures from its adversary will act as the "mirror" to reveal this deviant behavior to the state, thus setting in motion a process of cognitive dissonance.

International Structures

The role of international norms and ideas in shaping foreign policy is the channel most often pointed to by constructivists.[49] This dynamic is also suggested by anthropologists such as Margaret Mead as well as symbolic interactionists as discussed earlier; that is, the idea that the self operates within a shared process of meanings that are constantly being interpreted and acted on. Given the assumption of roles being a patterned activity, international norms must shift suddenly for them to be able to rupture the role pattern. Thus, an international community that brands small, state-seeking activists as "terrorists" will contribute to the victim state seeing itself as a "defensive warrior" surrounded by hostile enemies. Conversely, once the international community recognizes these state-seekers as legitimate (i.e., shifting their policy discourse from labeling them "terrorists" to calling them "guerillas" or "freedom fighters"), the original role-occupant might reflect upon its role and any deviant behavior that it has subsequently enacted.

WHY ROLE-DEVIATION RATHER THAN ROLE-CHANGE?

It might seem curious that, given the supposed explanatory strength of the concept of role, a state would ever deviate from its role in the first place. Two perspectives shed light on this issue. One answer suggests that individuals and groups can—and often do—function with multiple roles motivating parallel sets of actions—one set representing the conscious role-identity, the other corresponding to an unconscious counternarrative. The teenagers depicted in the Oscar-winning 1999 film *Traffic* represent such a coexistence of conflicting roles: the protagonist's daughter is a straight-A student whose resume boasts multiple extracurricular achievements at the same time that she is becoming a heroin addict. Opportunities may simply present themselves to the actor, leading her to either abandon her primary role (but not her role-identity, which is the internalized manifestation of the primary role and quite durable), or to supplement her role with a concurrent but conflicting action. Enacting multiple roles is not uncommon, and does not challenge the basic assumptions of this book, as long as one role has been internalized consciously to yield a role-identity, while the other remains in the unconscious.

However, in order to help explain role deviation, we can turn to another psychoanalytic proposition: the experience of narcissistic rage that can result from a lack of recognition. The issue of recognition is central to maintaining a healthy sense of self, and is at a premium in many ethnic and interstate conflicts. In ethnic conflicts, recognition spans the idea of articulating the other group's right to exist, through to supporting the existence of symbols of self-determination. Some groups contest others' right to exist down to the level of the individual, which, in the extreme, can lead to a policy of genocide, or to coexist within the borders of the first polity (leading to mass expulsion or ethnic cleansing), or as a state (which can spur attempts at politicide—the attempt to eradicate the state as a political unit). While the denial of statehood does not necessarily entail perpetrating violence, the way this denial is internalized by the target-group can lead to varying degrees of narcissistic rage.

The theory states that narcissism is an integral part of selfhood, and is normally held in check through healthy self-affirming interaction coupled with "reality-checks." For example, I feel strong when I lift weights but I need to know that I am unable to lift a car. If my early caregivers consistently convey to me either that I am a "weakling" or that I am "superwoman," my intrinsic narcissism will be out of kilter. When an individual feels negated, narcissism builds up, resulting in the expression of "narcissistic rage." This rage can be expressed through violent means, and can be used to explain ethnic conflict or political terrorism.[50] While in international relations this explanation is most often applied to acts of terrorism, a similar logic could apply to organized military offensives. On an individual level, the political terrorist can be understood to have internalized this lack of recognition from the international community and hence strikes out as a representative of the group. On the macro-level, a state that internalizes a lack of recognition from its surroundings may lash out through organized violence.

Yet a second potential problem remains: why does the dissonant behavior result in a policy shift, rather than a shift of role-identity? The simple answer is that for identity (and therefore role-identity) to be a useful heuristic device, it must be durable to a degree.[51] Thus, while identity is subject to evolution—especially in response to significant life-changing events—there must be a degree of "sameness" to merit the term. The self is constantly evolving in response to interactions with others; however, there is a kernel of sameness that outlives such processes. Another way to understand this tension is to conceive of the self as initially almost wholly relational, while becoming more durable through time. This view would support our emphasis on the actor's early relational experiences as being formative (an idea that is revealed semantically in the way we typically use the phrase "formative experiences"). It then follows that subsequent experiences, while partly able to shape the self, are incrementally weaker at doing so. From either a "nature" or "nurture" perspective then (a fault line that in any event many now see as antiquated), we can assume that once the actor reaches a degree of maturity (state-formation coupled with nation-building in political terms), the self is already formed. In terms of our framework, expecting every dissonant behavior to result in a role-shift would be tantamount to asserting that there is no such thing as identity. Since the *existence* of identity is not what is contested in international relations theory but rather its relative weight in determining state behavior, any explanation that rests on its existence must maintain the integrity of the concept—and that notion of integrity is most basically reduced to durability.

CONCLUSION

Applying psychoanalytic precepts to the ultimate political unit—the state—is not free of methodological challenges, but can ultimately yield explanatory payoffs through an appreciation of the psychic effects wrought by power and memory. In this chapter, I have explained how we can consider the state to have a "self," and I have outlined a sociopsychoanalytic framework for predicting conflict resolution and radical foreign-policy change. I have posited that when a state acts in contradiction to its role-identity, a cognitive dissonance will result—spurred by the holding up of a "mirror" to the face of elites by domestic and international elements—in which unconscious counternarratives are brought to the fore. In the case of a self-perceived "defensive" state acting aggressively over time, this process will result in a foreign-policy shift toward compromise with the significant adversary. The likelihood that a state will pursue compromise after acting aggressively depends on its "role-identity type." For this purpose, I have outlined six types that represent international actors across time. The next chapter will turn to the Israeli case, where we will explore the substantive content of Israel's "defensive-warrior" self—a role-identity that would eventually clash with Israel's actions in the Lebanon War and the Intifada, setting the stage for the Oslo process of the early 1990s.

Chapter Three

The Israeli Self

For the Lebanon War and the Intifada to have elicited a cognitive dissonance between Israel's policy actions and its role-identity, that identity must have been apparent to Israeli elites, coherent enough to reveal any dissonance, and collectively understood. Yet the nature of collective identity and the process of identity creation have been understudied in international relations, perhaps because of the particularity of the endeavor. That is, theories of identity-creation (which, in any event, are few) can suggest *what* we might look at (early statehood experiences, historical narratives, commemorative rituals, etc.), yet the task of teasing out the meaning of these symbols to uncover the content of a state's identity requires the researcher to become immersed in the cultural nuances of the case—a strategy that suggests an anthropologist's stance. While in the preceding chapter I outlined a typology of six role-identities that capture the variance across states and nonstate actors over time, determining a particular role-identity type is best approached inductively, with an understanding of how symbols are propagated and internalized by the members of the collective.

Therefore, in this chapter I train an ethnographic lens on Israel, drawing on historical and contemporary motifs that together represent the role-identity I am terming a "defensive warrior." In Israel's case, this defensive-warrior state is primarily concerned with protecting its right to national realization *(hagshama)* through the vehicle of state sovereignty. It is a "warrior," in that central to the Zionist enterprise is an attempt to regenerate the Jewish people through an activist stance; and it is "defensive" in that the state touts an ethic of fighting only wars of "no alternative" *(ayn breira)*. Historically, Israelis understood this defensive-warrior role-identity as defining their country's relations with the Arab states and with the Palestinians—with the latter relationship adopting a rather different tenor given that the latent Israeli-Palestinian war was primarily an antiterrorism one. Once the lack of consensus during the

1982 war in Lebanon exposed that venture as a war of "choice," the dissonance between Israel's policy actions and its role-identity began to emerge. That process was accelerated during the Intifada when the Palestinians traded their rifles for stones, Molotov cocktails, riots, and general strikes. Both by the harshness of its response and the fact that Israel was quelling another nation's call for independence, Israel experienced a cognitive dissonance necessitating a radical foreign-policy shift, one that resulted in Israel's decision to pursue the Oslo track.

WHOSE VOICE?

However parsimonious, it can be misleading to extract a single voice from any polity, no less one as diverse as Israel. Israeli society revolves around crisscrossing fault lines of Ashkenazim (Jews from Eastern Europe) versus Sephardim (those from Spain, the broader Middle East, and North Africa); religious versus secular Jews; Palestinian Arabs—both Muslim and Christian—versus Jews; and, of course, the gender divide. However, I make the case here that these disparate groups, while not unimportant in Israeli society, nevertheless have not been equally influential in creating and sustaining what I call the Israeli Self. This dominant narrative, embodied in the Labor Zionism of David Ben-Gurion, primarily a secular Ashkenazi movement, was ultimately institutionalized within the almost three decades of Labor Party rule in Israel, until the "upheaval" of the 1977 elections in which Likud gained power for the first time in the country's history.

The Likud, led at the time by Menachem Begin, took its ideological inspiration from Ze'ev Jabotinsky's Revisionist Zionist movement, an ideological grouping that has historically stood on the sidelines of Israeli national discourse. The leaders of the Yishuv (the pre-state, Jewish community in Palestine) consistently referred to the Revisionists' paramilitary organizations—Lechi and Etsel—as "secessionist movements,"[1] and upon assuming office, Prime Minister Ben-Gurion proclaimed that he was willing to form a coalition with any party *other than* the Communists and Herut (the precursor to the Likud and the successor party to the Revisionist movement). At the level of security policy, the Revisionists differed from Labor mainly in their goals vis-à-vis the British and the local Arabs. Lechi and Etsel favored an activist approach, believing that Jewish interests could be advanced only by forcing the local Palestinians and the surrounding Arab states to come eye-to-eye with the "iron wall" of Jewish force, a strategy that did not eschew terrorist tactics. By contrast, Labor under Ben-Gurion and embodied in the

Haganah (the precursor to the IDF) favored a policy of restraint, a fault line that will be explored in greater depth in chapter four.[2]

There are two other reasons for the entrenchment of a singular, dominant voice in the Israeli case. First, the institutionalization of a military censor vis-à-vis the Israeli press has meant that alternate voices have not had the same audience as they might in other democracies. Given that the censor operates according to the broad criterion of "national security," certainly the Arab position, were it to be raised in the mainstream press, would likely be muted. Similarly, it is likely that positions that undermine the unity of the nation might be viewed as constituting a security risk in themselves—resulting in a limited smattering of alternate voices being aired publicly. A second reason to assume the existence of a dominant voice relates to the strong ethic of collectivism that permeates Israeli culture.[3] As we will see, although some battles commemorated as heroic entailed settlement-losses to the Arabs, the Yishuv as a whole ultimately secured Palestine for the Jews, thus underscoring the importance of a collective effort in forging national independence. The ethic of Israeli collectivism has been translated into a lofty goal of ensuring that "all Jews are responsible for one another,"and that Israel serve to "ingather the exiles" into a melting pot of Jewish unity, a dictum that one scholar-politician has referred to as Israel's "myth of integration."[4] Collectivism also underpinned the Israeli founders' push toward establishing a socialist state, embodied in the kibbutzim that served to defend the country's borders.

ISRAELI COLLECTIVE NARRATIVES

For the Jews, the founding of the State of Israel embodied a grand narrative of 2,000 years of exile characterized by centuries of persecution, and culminating in a rebirth of Jewish sovereignty guarded by military might. As Israel's national anthem, Hatikvah ("the hope") declares, "The hope is two thousand years old; to be a free nation in our land." Zionism, from its origins in the nineteenth century, was set upon two prongs: the rebirth, or "normalization," of Diaspora Jewry from a landless, withered entity into one rooted in the soil of the land of Israel, the latter to be cultivated by intense pioneering; the other, a form of "Jewish self-defense," as one Israeli observer has termed it.[5]

Yet given the centuries of anti-Semitisim that had cast the Jews into perennial victimhood, we are left to wonder why Israel's role-identity became characterized by a defensive rather than an aggressive ethic. By contrast, German self-perceived victimization surrounding the post-World

War I Versailles settlement is often used to explain the rise of the Third Reich's aggressive policies. An answer to this puzzle lies in the "normalization" theme of Zionism, which is arguably the unifying kernel of the disparate currents of Zionist thought. This normalization took the form of Jewish nationalism that arose in part from the many instances of persecution experienced in the face of anti-Semitism: what are generally referred to as the "push factors" of the Zionist movement. Yet important "pull factors" confronting nineteenth-century European Jews drew them toward an experiment in self-determination in which they would be masters of their own fate—physically, spiritually, and intellectually. So focused were the Zionists in abandoning their self-perceived spiritual and national parasitic existence within their host countries, that the achievement of national sovereignty—to be a "nation like all others" in Zionist parlance—would not have to be accompanied by an expansionist or missionary zeal in order to thrive. The decades-old Israeli quest to have the Arab states recognize Israel's legitimacy is evidence of this basic need to live within secure and self-contained borders, rather than to fundamentally alter the status quo.[6]

Thus, in addition to events such as the Russian pogroms of the 1880s, and the Dreyfus Affair in France,[7] collective identity played an important role in precipitating a Hebrew national renaissance in Palestine. The changes that the Enlightenment brought to Europe forced the Jews to create their own form of secular nationalism. No longer were Jews cloistered, books in hand, in the *heder* and *yeshiva*; they were now being treated as citizens of the larger polity; one that transmitted and maintained collective memories different from those in the Jewish imagination. Although the Enlightenment led to greater equality among Europe's disparate ethnic groups, in order to maintain a narrative consistent with the Jewish experience the Jewish people would have to reenact their own experiment in national self-determination.[8] Part and parcel of this attempt to sustain a Jewish historical narrative was the perceived need to redirect the course of the Jewish national character. Accordingly, some Zionists began to call for the rebirth of a "new Jew"—a transformation that would take place even at the corporal level. The product of this collective revolution would be a Jew less tied to scholarly pursuits at the expense of physical prowess; a Jewry that could shape its fate against the ravages of the desert and the threats of Arab intruders on the Jewish experiment in self-determination—a Jewry of Muscle, in the words of Zionist philosopher Max Nordau. In so doing, these Zionists recalled the historical experience of Jewish sovereignty in the ancient land of Israel, in the process rejecting the 2,000 years of Diaspora life that had intervened between ancient history and what would be the modern reenactment of Jewish sovereignty. Leaders of the Yishuv encouraged its members to break with the Jewish past of passivity and victimization, and, instead, create a new Hebrew state based on defensive strength and the ability to maneuver within the international system like any other member. In some cases, collective memory was recast in order to serve the ends of national redefinition; in others, the Exilic past was derided (*shlilat hagola*) and its collective membership scorned.[9] For a nation that had sustained narratives encapsulating the need to defend itself against enemies that persistently sought its destruction, the pull to the historical locus of Jewish sovereignty by politically savvy Zionist leaders who provided hoe and gun was strong indeed. Unfortunately for the modern Zionists, the inhospitable environment awaiting them in Palestine (at the hands of Great Britain, the Palestinians and the Arab states) would provide a rude awakening as to the nature of "normalization" in the regional system of the Middle East.

These explanations point to a broader trend taking shape among broad swaths of nineteenth-century Jewry: an acute appreciation of the role of history and memory in defining the Jewish condition. Central to the Zionist enterprise was a philosophical canon embodying religious and secular variants, as well as a prominent socialist strand that would come to be known as Labor Zionism. While writers like A. D. Gordon and Nachman Syrkin outlined the philosophical contours of Zionism, leaders like Ben-Gurion and Golda Meir (both of whom would serve as Israeli prime minister) enacted their vision. Out of the layers of historical memory coupled with the need to nation-build in the Middle East, there emerged three sets of narrative tropes around which Israeli collective consciousness ultimately solidified: *ayn breirah* (no alternative) and *tohar haneshek* (purity of arms); "a light unto the nations" versus "a nation like all others;" and the ethic of agriculture as a means of regeneration and defense. The remainder of the section will discuss each in turn.

Ayn Breirah (No Alternative) and Tohar Haneshek (Purity of Arms)

That Israelis experienced themselves as being born out of centuries of Diaspora persecution into the arms of Arab intransigence meant that the State of Israel quickly cultivated a role centered on existential self-defense and the need for requisite military capabilities. Yet crucial to this situation were the notions of fighting only wars of "no alternative" (*ayn breirah*) under the maxim of "purity of arms" (*tohar haneshek*)— two tropes that parallel the Just War philosophical categories of *jus ad bellum* (just cause) and *jus in bello* (just conduct). Wars of no alternative mean those in which Israel is defending itself against the threat of annihilation, where war is seen as a last resort. According to the IDF mission statement, purity of arms refers to the idea that "[t]he IDF servicemen and women will use their weapons and force only for the purpose of their mission, only to the necessary extent and will maintain their humanity even during combat. IDF soldiers will not use their weapons and force to harm human beings who are not combatants or prisoners of war."[10]

The concept of "no alternative" quickly became the label Israelis gave to every war fought by the Jewish state from its 1948 War of Independence until the 1982 Lebanon War broke the national consensus. Explains an Israeli to an American Jewish tourist in the 1953 Israeli film *Hill 24 Doesn't Answer*, Israel's "secret" for being able to defeat the more numerous Arab states: "No choice. *This* is our secret."[11] Israeli Foreign Minister Abba Eban, reflecting on the Six Day War a year later, would declare, "Nobody who lived those days in Israel will ever forget the air of heavy foreboding that hovered over our land...For Israel there would be only one defeat. If the war had ended as those who launched it planned, there would be no discussion now of territories, populations, negotiations....There would be a ghastly sequel, leaving nothing to be discussed."[12] While *ayn breirah* is a slogan that has penetrated everyday Israeli discourse, so conscious are Israelis of behaving within the limits of the law during war itself, that a phrase has emerged that encapsulates both the "option" and "obligation" that IDF soldiers have to choose to disobey "blatantly illegal orders" (*pkudot bilti hukiot be'alil*).[13] As indicated in the IDF's mission statement, "[IDF servicemen] will take care to issue only legal orders, and disavow manifestly illegal orders."[14]

Tied in with the *ayn breira* ethos is the idea of "peace" as an absolute value. The Hebrew word, *shalom*, permeates every realm of Israeli life: from given names to surnames, the greetings "hello" and "goodbye," business names, street names, song titles, and is generally the first word any new Hebrew speaker learns. A popular folk song states, "We've brought peace unto you!" (*Heveinu shalom aleichem*). And a 1966 curriculum guide for elementary school mandates a teaching unit called "the value of peace."[15] In Jewish thought, peace is understood to be the "ultimate purpose of the whole Torah: 'All that is written in the Torah was written for the sake of peace.' (Judges 18)."[16]

Underlying the ubiquity of the word "peace" in Israeli culture is the assumption—propagated by successive Israeli governments—that Israel has always had an arm outstretched with olive branch, only to be rebuffed by intransigent Arab states.[17] Even amid criticism of the Arabs for using "terrorist methods," and while claiming that "[t]here is virtually no chance of an agreement with them," Ben-Gurion wrote in 1939 that "we should make every possible attempt to negotiate with them, and if there is any chance of it—to come to terms. We owe this to ourselves, we owe this to the Government [the British Mandatory power], we owe this to our future relations with the Arabs."[18] By 1971, after four Arab-Israeli wars, Ben-Gurion's belief that peace depended on the Arabs had deepened. "For us no possibility exists of a final solution to the conflict between us so long as the Arabs do not want this.... We do not have the possibility of terminating the conflict, but they do."[19] The idea of Israelis being forced into a conflictual stance by their enemies—who are only enemies by dint of their denial of Israel's right to exist—in part helps to explain the eventual acting out of Israel's unconscious counternarratives in the form of the events of the 1980s, a theme that will be explored further.

Political cartoons, printed in the popular dailies in the wake of the Six Day War, help to convey the Israelis' view of their own readiness for peace in the face of Arab bellicosity and international resistance. One such illustration depicts a sunhat-clad Israeli holding aloft a placard calling for "direct negotiations." Behind him stands a motley crew of medical personnel labeled ("the powers" which,) wearing surgical and gas masks, appear to be disinfecting the hapless, would-be peacemaker. Another cartoon from this period, entitled "the circle," displays an Arab running around a circular path flanked by a brick wall on one side and an exit marked "peace" on the other. The figure's blood-stained head bandage and the spatters on the wall suggest that the Arabs refuse to simply avail themselves of peace with Israel.[20]

Along these lines, Israelis have viewed the achievement of Arab-Israeli peace as synonymous with the receipt of sovereign recognition from the Arab states, a feat that plagued Israel from its inception until the arrival of Egyptian President Anwar Sadat in Jerusalem in November 1977, followed by the 1978 Israeli-Egyptian peace agreement at Camp David. As Foreign Minister Moshe Shertok (later Sharett) stated in 1948, "Peace [is] conceivable only in terms of the Jewish State as a neighbour of the Arab States, and not in terms of a Jewish community endowed with some form of 'autonomy' and existing as a tolerated minority within an Arab state."[21] Another political cartoon conveys the Israeli perception that it has had to fight for its existence since the days of the Yishuv, only to have the conflict magnified with the state's founding. Here, an Israeli man, accompanied by a pair of menacing guards, stands in a courtroom before two dour judges. The caption reads, "I plead guilty to the main charge: I exist!"[22]

From Israel's perspective, the Jewish state's attempt to achieve recognition from its neighbors has been the mainstay of the Arab-Israeli conflict, and has contributed to Israel's defensive-warrior role-identity, one that takes its inspiration from the self-perceived experience of the Jews existing as "the few against the many." This attempt has also led to political sloganeering on both sides of the Israeli spectrum. In the early 1990s, as the Labor-led coalition demanded public support for the "land for peace" formula explicit in the Oslo agreement, the right wing countered with a call for "peace for peace."

In opposition to the conscious narrative trope of "no alternative" is the unconscious counternarrative of a state taking action outside the bounds of necessity. This counternarrative thus suggests that a state might fight aggressive wars for the sake of domination, rather than for existential or defensive purposes. During the Lebanon War and the Intifada, Israelis tasted that counternarrative as the IDF laid siege to Beirut, indirectly oversaw the massacre of hundreds of Palestinians in the refugee camps of Sabra and Shatilla, and later clashed with Palestinian protestors throughout the occupied territories. Neither of these operations were essential to self-defense in the "no alternative" sense of the term; as we will see, the Lebanon War was even termed a "war of choice" by Prime Minister Menachem Begin. One phrase that circulated within Zionist circles as the Arab-Israeli conflict wore on was Golda Meir's: "I can forgive my enemies [the Arabs] for killing our children, but I can never forgive them for making our children kill theirs," a sentiment that suggests the despised-but-plausibly-entertained aspect crucial to an unconscious counternarrative.

Given that Israeli military doctrine has largely centered on the assumption that "the *central aim of Arab countries is to destroy the state of Israel whenever they feel able to do so*,"[23] the perception that most states of the world have denied Israel's right to exist has no doubt endowed the country with an acute existential fear. It is plausible that the intensity of this fear (perhaps tinged with unconscious self-loathing), while masked by boisterous efforts at self-preservation and even self-congratulation, nevertheless left Israelis primed to experience a sharp psychic conflict when their state acted aggressively in the Lebanon War and the Intifada. Given the high value Israelis have historically placed on the receipt of sovereign recognition from the Arab states, the IDF's suppression of Palestinian demands for national independence during the first Intifada would engender a cognitive dissonance. Indeed, until the eve of the Oslo agreement, Israel had not reciprocated its demand for recognition vis-à-vis the Palestinians, whom it had always viewed as part of the broader pan-Arab nation. Where national statehood was conceived of, the expectation was placed on Jordan to house the Palestinian refugees and end the conflict along Israel's eastern front. This scenario makes Israel's decision to seek peace with the PLO even more puzzling, given that a peace agreement would entail not only territorial and symbol-rich concessions, but would include an implicit acknowledgment of the Palestinian narrative of dispossession resulting from Zionist settlement and the establishment of the State of Israel.

"A People That Dwells Alone" versus "A Nation Like All Others"

Two other phrases have come to represent two partly opposing and partly overlapping perspectives of Israel's role in the international system: a "people that dwells alone" and a "nation like all others." The former is a Biblical phrase that refers to a self-conception of "chosenness," with a related view of Israel as a self-contained, morally pure ghetto within a sea of malevolence. These two aspects—moral superiority and geographic isolation—have led to competing views of what kind of foreign policies Israel should adopt. Chief among the proponents of the "people that dwells alone" position were the Jabotinsky's Revisionist Zionists, and continuing with the Likud's Menachem Begin and Yitzhak Shamir. Conversely, to be a "nation like all others," while potentially used to justify a realpolitik stance, in the Israeli context came to be associated with the mandate for peace associated with Yitzhak Rabin and the Labor Party, and was the view that ultimately prevailed. According to this perspective, Israel is neither sublimely unique in its "chosenness," nor is so isolated by enemies that it is unable to take the risks associated with peace.

While eventually forming an ideological fault line in the 1992 elections,[24] the two views have meaningfully overlapped in particular ways in the Israeli imagination. The idea of Israel's being a nation that dwells alone had historically been articulated by a segment of society, yet the dominant narrative of the polity as a whole—that of the Labor Zionist stream—would consciously espouse the "nation-like-all-others" idea, while retaining the "people-that-dwells-alone" view in its collective unconscious. The latter perspective would justify acting aggressively, since a people that dwells alone has no friends or protectors and is therefore responsible to no one. Conversely, a view that understands the state to be a nation like all others will more easily accommodate a role not only for enmity but also for friendship—in constructivist terms, such a view will leave room for a Kantian anarchy.[25] Along with pockets of interstate friendship come trust and the confidence to make concessions for peace.

However, trust does not come easily to Israel; central to the Jewish and Israeli experience has been a sense of embattlement, a notion that has justified the imperative of constructing a formidable defensive fighting force and maintaining the military as a central part of day-to-day consciousness at the individual and collective level. Says the eleven-year-old protagonist of an elementary-school text entitled *Our Country's Ports*, "In our time, it possible to reach Israel only by sea or by air, since our country is surrounded by Arab states, and it is impossible to reach Israel by land."[26] While until the 1979 Israeli-Egyptian peace treaty and the 1994 agreement with Jordan access to Israel *was* limited to sea and air, the passage implies that it is the very existence of "Arab states" that has led to Israel's isolation, rather than the absence of peace agreements with those same states per se. This sense of embattlement had lessened somewhat by the early 1990s, once a Labor government was elected to replace the Likud in 1992. Thus, while a sense of embattlement certainly was among the essential narrative tropes of the Israeli collective, and strengthened the defensive warrior identity, the events of the 1980s, particularly the Lebanon War and the Intifada, led Israelis to conclude that their policy actions were in discordance not only with who they saw themselves to be, but with *who they aspired to be*. By 1992, Israelis had opted to embrace a vision of a nation that would behave like all others— the vision espoused by Herzl—rather than one that would seek refuge behind the veil of chosenness and moral isolation.

Moreover, while the modern Israeli voice is overwhelmingly secular, there is no doubt that Israeli historical memory carries with it vestiges of fulfilling God's mission as the Chosen People in the ancient land of Israel. While a segment of ultraorthodox Jews, some of whom are among Israel's citizens (although they do not identify as Zionists), reject the establishment of a Jewish state until such time as the Messiah arrives, for most Jews it is enough to hear the word "the chosen people" to identify with a historical-devout mission, however unconsciously.[27] Biblical tropes abound in modern Israel, military rank titles are taken from the Bible,[28] the West Bank is referred to in contemporary Israeli discourse as the biblical regions of "Judea" and "Samaria," and Rabin's speech at the September 1993 Oslo signing ceremony quoted Ecclesiastes.[29] Early Israeli leaders viewed their country as a morally pure force within a region dominated by backward peoples. Stated David Ben-Gurion to President Truman in May 1948, "continued sympathy and support for [a] final solution of [sic] [the] Palestine question...will end [the] age-long Jewish tragedy and enable [the] State of Israel to become [a] stabilizing and progressive force in [the] Near East, and to contribute its humble share to [the] welfare and peace of [the] human race."[30] This view of the Other as being *un*stable and *un*progressive helped Israelis to sustain a narrative of themselves that represented the mirror-image. When the Lebanon War broke the national consensus, an air of "instability" permeated Israeli national discourse; when Israel's Intifada policies led to domestic and international accusations that the state was behaving barbarically toward the occupied Palestinian population, Israelis feared themselves becoming "unprogressive"—those same attributes that they had historically reviled in their enemies. The idea that the enemy is the repository for one's unconscious counternarratives helps to keep those counternarratives concealed from consciousness. And if or when those counterroles are enacted, the dissonance will be that much more acute.

Agriculture as Regeneration and Defense

Central to the Zionist ethos, particularly the Labor Zionist strand, is the importance of cultivating and settling the land. And with settlements came border outposts to defend against attacks. Yet the pioneering ethos, centered as it was around human physical prowess and the harnessing of nature, imbued the goal of building fortress-like settlements with a benignity that is not usually associated with security affairs. As the early Zionists would have seen it, it would be difficult to lay moral blame on a people who, with their own hands, were attempting to drain ditches and plant trees, all while living in primitive conditions and battling malaria and dehydration. Thus did the Zionist attempt to cultivate the land and build agricultural settlements serve a dual purpose in the national narrative. First, and particularly in the early period of the state, the pioneering enterprise underpinned a military doctrine of defensiveness, with the settlements serving as the backbone of Israel's front-line security. In line with this, Israelis could consider themselves to be a defensive force vis-à-vis the surrounding Arab states who sought to "drive them into the sea"—another common trope within Israeli discursive history. Second, as previously suggested, agriculture served to regenerate the Jewish body to adopt a warrior role in the face of aggression, and to meet the challenges of intense physical labor under trying conditions. As Yitzhak Rabin recalls his adolescent dream of attending the Kadouri Agricultural School: "[A]s a city boy I had never...developed a private passion for agriculture. But the return to the soil—and especially the establishment of collectives—was something of a national passion in those days."[31] Every tree that the early Zionists planted and every road they built drove home the idea that the New Hebrews were liberating the land from a state of natural neglect, while participating in a process of collective regeneration—from the Diaspora Jew to the landed Hebrew. With every till of the soil, the Zionists experienced themselves as taking an activist stance toward

securing their own spiritual and physical transformation while defending themselves against those who sought to preclude them from joining
the family of sovereign states. This process, in turn, helped to bestow a
"defensive-warrior" role-identity on Israelis. Moreover, by creating
arable land out of swamps and deserts, Israelis had more self-perceived
reason for displacing the Arab residents of Palestine. So, too, was Zionist
settlement seen as the "first" settlement, despite their unconscious
awareness of the Arab presence in Palestine. This belief was best encapsulated by the phrase "a land without people for a people without land,"
in the words of early Zionist publicist Israel Zangwill. As Golda Meir
described it, "Zion [was] the land from which the Jews had been exiled
2,000 years before but which had remained the spiritual center of Jewry
throughout the centuries and which...up to the end of World War I,
was a desolate and neglected province of the Ottoman Empire called
Palestine."[32] Similarly, an elementary-school textbook titled *Roads in
Our Country* states, "Many years ago, with the beginning of settlement
in the Land of Israel, most of the roads in Israel were paths. Let us read
the story of Rachel Yanait Ben-Zvi about her adventures on the paths of
Israel, at the time of *the beginning of settlement*." Rachel, who would
later become the wife of Israel's second president (Yitzhak Ben-Zvi),
was a prominent voice from the Yishuv period. In that text, she discusses
walking through the countryside, while not being totally unaware of the
Palestinian presence: her stroll included "passing by an Arab village."[33]

The pioneer ethic was instilled in generations of young Israelis.
Primary-school songs recommended by the Ministry of Education in the
state's early years included lyrics such as "We are fellow pioneers, strong
and brave...with a bulldozer, we will uproot rock and boulder.
Pioneers!"[34] The Zionists viewed reclaiming the land as spiritually justifying their mission. As Golda Meir writes, the Labor Zionists "believed
that only self-labor could truly liberate the Jews from the ghetto...and
make it possible for them to reclaim the land and earn a moral right to it,
in addition to the historic right."[35] Tied in with this ethic has been the
importance of the IDF's Nahal brigade, established in 1949 in part to
replace the youth-movement spirit of the Palmach. Nahal *garinim* (small
groups of young men and women; literally "seeds") established commu-
nal agricultural settlements along Israel's borders to defend against infil-
trations, in the process helping to entrench a fertile, Jewish presence on
the soil.[36]

The cognate narrative was that not only did the Zionists see themselves as the first to develop the land of Israel, but that swath of land was
collectively seen as their first home. Said the Israeli writer S. Y. Agnon in
his 1966 Nobel Prize acceptance speech, "I was born in one of the cities

of the Diaspora. But I always deemed myself as one who was really born in Jerusalem."[37] The New Hebrews saw the land as waiting to bestow riches on them: they dubbed it the "land of milk and honey," in the words of a popular folk song. By the early part of the twentieth century, this narrative was forced to compete with the view of America among Eastern European Jews as representing the *goldene medina* (Yiddish for the "golden land"). It was clear that not all Jewish residents of the towns and shtetls of Europe were Zionists, and many Jews who aspired to leave the persecution of Eastern Europe behind chose to immigrate to the United States. As a result, many adolescents who became smitten with Zionism clashed with their parents over the perceived rightful place of Zion in Jewish consciousness. Both Golda Meir and David Ben-Gurion note that their parents, who remained in the Diaspora while their children immigrated to Palestine, did not share the same level of commitment to Zionism.[38] Perhaps because of this tension, Zionists viewed the relationship to the land of Israel as a reciprocal one. Israeli schoolchildren sing, "Our homeland; For eighty generations we waited for you; you kept the faith. We have returned to you from the corners of the earth; you are a strength for us and we are a wall for you."[39] Declares one Israeli folk song, "Land, my land, generous to my dying day, A great wind has heated your ruins....I have wedded thee in blood that reddened and was silenced on the hills of Shech Abrek. *I chose the land.*"[40] To instill this love of the land among succeeding generations, Israeli children are instructed in the details of *moledet* (homeland), an amorphous school subject devoted to all aspects of *yediat ha'aretz* (knowing the land). Hikes throughout the country form an essential part of formal education, as does a familiarity with the region's flora and fauna.

To achieve these settlement goals, the Yishuv inculcated the values of *avoda ivrit* (Hebrew work) and *avoda atzmit* (self-sufficiency), meaning that all manual labor on Jewish settlements would be performed by Jews. In this way were the Zionists able to resist the charge of imperialism. Instead, they saw themselves as liberating the land from a feudal system of underpaid Arab toilers and their greedy patrons,[41] hence underscoring an identity that is defensive—and even liberationist— rather than rapacious. *Avoda ivrit* also signified a new collective identity: a "Hebrew," as distinct from a "Jewish" one. Whereas "Hebrew" was the name associated with Zionist settlement in Palestine, "Jew" symbolized the passivity of exile, where Jewish life was more religious and intellectual than national and physically productive in its pursuits. The passivity of the Diaspora was represented by the idea of "waiting" for Jewish suffering to reverse itself. In contrast, Zionist philosophy stressed the Jews reshaping their own fate. As Ben-Gurion wrote to his three children in 1938, "in the Diaspora our history is made by others. In Palestine—by ourselves. And whatever others scheme and foreigners do, if we are able *to create history* even in the worst possible conditions, they will not be able to overcome us."[42] Similarly, Golda Meir recalls that from an early age she realized "the fear, the frustration, the consciousness of being different [in the Diaspora] and the profound instinctive belief that if one wanted to survive, one had to take effective action about it personally."[43] Cultivating the land was a tangible embodiment of the attempt to control the Jewish destiny.

To this end, Zionism turned to the development of the body through the "Jewry of muscle" archetype. As Max Nordau wrote in 1903, in eery ignorance of the worst physical decimation yet to be wrought on the Jews, "now, all coercion has become a memory of the past, and at least we are allowed space enough for our bodies to live again. Let us take up our oldest traditions; let us once more become deep-chested, sturdy, sharp-eyed men."[44] The connection between the tanned, muscular sabra and the land of ancient Israel was inextricable. Thus did David Ben-Gurion, Israel's first prime minister, favor an outfit of desert khakis over that of the dark trousers and white shirts popular among his contemporaries. Perhaps for this reason, the occasional success of Jewish athletes has always fired the Jewish imagination, such as the image that baseball greats Hank Greenberg in the 1930s and Sandy Koufax in the 1960s instilled in the minds of Americans of those generations.[45] A 1913 Zionist film entitled *The Life of the Jews in Palestine*, designed to encourage Russian Jewish *aliya* (emigration to Israel), depicts in great detail a Jewish sporting event held in Rehovot. Since 1932, this interest has manifested itself in the World Maccabiah Games, now held every four years in Israel for young Jewish athletes around the globe.

This property-defense duality was also expressed in many of the advertisements, political posters, and folk songs of the early state period. As the caretaker of Jewish land and its cultivation, the Jewish National Fund (JNF), founded in 1901 by the World Zionist Organization, spearheaded fundraising efforts in the Diaspora. By the 1930s, one million "blue boxes" designed to collect nickels and dimes for the JNF were in circulation in homes and institutions across the Diaspora, a trend that would continue throughout the decades.

Initially an undisputed Zionist value, after the Six Day War Jewish settlement became tinged with controversy as successive Israeli governments—beginning with Labor—encouraged the spread of Jewish outposts in the newly occupied territories of the Golan Heights, the Sinai, the West Bank, and Gaza Strip. By the 1980s, the settlement push had been adopted by the right wing; one slogan of the Likud party was to "create facts on the ground," a phrase that became maligned by leftist Zionists who viewed the establishment of these settlement "facts" as obstructing a peace deal with the Palestinians. While the Israeli-Palestinian conflict has centered around competing land claims, insofar as longstanding settlements could be pointed to, the Israeli claim to the lands of Palestine would be apparently strengthened, went the right-wing-nationalist reasoning. As a counterpoint to this, Palestinian historical memory has been infused with claims to individual houses in various towns and villages, with many Jaffa-or Haifa-born Palestinians retaining keys to their abandoned dwellings. Central to these competing narratives was an attempt by Israel to decide what kind of polity it wanted to be. Israelis have almost never questioned the basic right of Jews to a state in the Land of Israel, believing that "at the end of the day, we are justified; justice is on our side," in the words of one senior IDF officer.[46] However, what would remain an outstanding question confronting Israeli policymakers after twenty-five years of occupying another people would be the extent to which settlement should be pursued; for what purposes and within which borders. The land-defense duality also suggests a powerful—yet repressed—counternarrative, one describing the role of the Zionists in dispossessing the Palestinians. The same settlement activity that served to rejuvenate the Hebrew nation also resulted in many Palestinians becoming refugees from that same land. While the counternarrative of aggression mentioned above has generally served to check the government's actions—as the widespread protests during the course of the Lebanon War attest, the counternarrative of dispossession is so deeply rooted that it arguably has never surfaced on any widespread level. True, a number of Israeli revisionist historians have sought to call attention to the role of Zionism in precipitating the Palestinian refugee problem, yet the vast majority of Israeli policy critics do not call into question the very premise of their state—something that would have to be done if one were to fully acknowledge the Palestinian narrative. No doubt the Zionist account of the birth of Israel contains an element of projection onto the Palestinians. That is, while the Jews hesitantly embraced it, the Arab residents of Palestine (and the surrounding Arab states) rejected the November 1947 UN proposal to partition Palestine into two states—one Jewish, and one Arab. This decision on the part of the Palestinians enabled generations of Israelis to maintain a view of the Arabs as rejectionist and aggressive, at the same time that the Arabs would have viewed those fateful days of 1947–1948 as acts defending their national existence. This is all to suggest that the actions of others in part help to maintain roles and to structure role-identities, but there is a powerful element of subjective interpretation that molds incoming actions into particular forms of identity.

While these themes provide a general framework for understanding Israeli collective consciousness, an important second step in determining Israel's role-identity is to trace the pivotal events in Israel's early years that have helped shape the national self. We can consider two periods as being critical for this end: the events spanning Jewish history from the biblical period through the end of the Yishuv; and the early, post-1948 experiences of the state itself.

ISRAEL'S PRE-STATE HISTORY

Israel's pre-state history, stretching from antiquity through 2,000 years of exile, forms the foundation for modern Israeli collective memory and Israel's defensive-warrior role-identity. Prior to the tumultuous years surrounding Israel's emergence as a state, the Jews had experienced centuries of wars, expulsion, and persecution, joined with study and prayer; all of these against a distant memory of self-rule in ancient Israel. Modern Zionism sought to replace the weakest moments of Jewish history with a renewal of Jewish power. Ideally, this experiment was to be played out in the land of Israel, although in 1903 the Zionist leadership flirted with the possibility of Uganda as a site for resurrecting Jewish sovereignty—at least as a way station until Palestine was more hospitable to mass settlement. Threatening to divide the movement along political lines, these deliberations became known as the Uganda Crisis.[47] And in at least one essay, Herzl suggested the possibility of Argentina as a locus for the Jewish national home.[48] Rather than present a comprehensive account of Jewish history, in this section I will outline five events in the pre-state period that have come to occupy a central role in Jewish historical memory and that were therefore pivotal in shaping the role-identity of modern Israel: the David and Goliath myth, the fall of Masada (73 C.E.), the Bar-Kochba Revolt (132–135 C.E.), the battle of Tel Hai (1920), and the Holocaust. Three of these (Bar-Kochba, Tel Hai, and the Holocaust) are commemorated annually in the Israeli calendar (through Lag Ba'Omer, Tel Hai Day, and Holocaust Remembrance Day) and have physical memorials (the lion monument in the settlement of Tel Hai, the excavated fortress of Masada, and the Yad Vashem Holocaust memorial); and one (the Holocaust) has much documented evidence, as well as survivors still alive to recount their experiences. The David and Goliath story has none of these physical or calendrical manifestations, but is arguably so entrenched in Jewish and Western consciousness as to require none. Moreover, given that a solid grounding in Old Testament biblical studies is a requirement for high-school matriculation in Israel, almost all Israeli adults will presumably be familiar with that myth.[49]

David and Goliath

> *And David put his hand in his bag, and took thence a stone, and slang it, and smote the Philistine (Goliath) in his forehead, that the stone sunk into his forehead; and he fell upon his face to the earth.*
>
> —*(I Samuel 17:49)*

The story of David and Goliath doubtless holds such resonance for its depiction of the triumph of the weak and righteous over the strong and brutal. As a single, fledgling Jewish state in the predominantly Arab Middle East, from its birth Israel fostered the myth of heroic struggle against those bent on its destruction. Just as God's will helped David defeat the Philistines (who, along with the Canaanites, were the ancient precursor to the Palestinians), so too would the Jews prevail in their mission. In so doing, they would achieve collective immortality—a feat that has been central to the Jewish narrative from the time that, according to the Bible, God prophesied that Abraham's progeny would be as numerous as the grains of sand on the earth, and through the periods where Jews have had to fight for their collective survival. Says a Hebrew folk song, "Saul smote his thousands and David his tens of thousands; His name endures forever."[50] With few exceptions (such as the Bar Kochba revolt and the Warsaw Ghetto Uprising), while Jews had diligently studied the Bible for centuries, it was not until their arrival in Palestine that they were actually able to reenact the David and Goliath myth. While their Arab enemies were more numerous, the Zionists succeeded in establishing a sovereign presence in the Middle East—both by force of arms vis-à-vis the Arabs, and by dint of diplomacy vis-à-vis the British.

Years later, as the Intifada began to expose the dissonance between Israel's defensive-warrior role-identity and Israeli policy toward the Palestinians, the David and Goliath myth would reappear in a subverted form. At a 1989 anniversary celebration of the founding of a kibbutz in the Negev, the following song written by children of the kibbutz was awarded first prize: "Dudi you wanted to be like David / Red headed and nice eyes, And always with a smile / In an alley in Nablus you forgot everything and turned into Goliath."[51] While the Palestinians were not a significant actor in the Zionist imaginary during the first few decades of the state's existence, once the IDF confronted unarmed Palestinians, and as Israel struggled to suppress Palestinian nationalism, significant segments of the Israeli polity began to see itself as a Goliath vis-à-vis the Palestinians' David. Given the intimacy of the battles between Israeli troops and Palestinian youth, the Israelis no longer viewed themselves as being embattled by menacing Arab states. In sum, the David and Goliath myth can be understood as forming a central part of Israel's role-identity, while also containing the seeds of that identity's most painful challenge. In the context of the narrative tensions discussed here, the David and Goliath story contains both a conscious narrative of the possibility for good to triumph over evil, and an unconscious counternarrative of acting as a Goliath against the Other's David.

Masada

In 73 C.E., a group of 960 Jewish zealots holed themselves up at Masada, which, along with Herodium and Macherus, was one of three remaining fortresses in Judea. As the Jews faced the oncoming Romans, the group's leader, Elazar Ben Yair, convinced the 900 residents to commit suicide rather than submit to the enemy. Accordingly, the group decided that the men would slaughter the women and children before falling on their own swords. Curiously, the Masada legend was rarely mentioned in Jewish historical texts until nineteenth-century Jewish scholars revisited Josephus's account, leading to the first Hebrew translation of the work in 1862. It was not until 1927, though, with the publication of Yitzhak Lamdan's poem "Masada," that the event was brought into the forefront of the collective consciousness of the Yishuv. The revived interest spurred many youth-group pilgrimages to the summit, with several of these hikes leading to deaths along the way due to exhaustion and dehydration. Nevertheless, it was not until the mid-1960s that the Israeli government sponsored extensive excavations of the hilltop fortress and opened it as a tourist attraction, with the ancient Snake Path restored, and a cable car built to facilitate access to the summit. Soon after, the excavated synagogue became a popular site for Bar Mitzvah ceremonies, the IDF's armored corps held their induction ceremonies atop the summit until the early 1990s, and the hill became a must-see on tourist itineraries.[52] Eventually, the 1980s American made-for-TV-movie of the Masada story would serve to reinforce the Zionist imaginary, just as the film version of Leon Uris's *Exodus*, two decades earlier, had invited an American film star into the national consciousness of Israelis, with Paul Newman's image even being used to promote Israeli Goldstar beer.[53]

Within Israeli collective memory, the physical site of Masada represented the most striking aspects of Jewish persecution and daring. Like the Bar Kochba revolt sixty years hence, Masada represented the last stand against hostile enemies. However, as a fragment of historical memory, Masada's suicidal ending has been wrought with controversy within the Israeli grand narrative. Suicide is not only expressly forbidden by Jewish law, but the act in a military context represents partial defeat. (A total defeat would arguably have been torture or death at the hands of the Romans.) While the Masada zealots indeed refused to go passively into the hands of their enemies, they did not, in fact, brave the risk of battle. Such a narrative falls uncomfortably within the limits of the perception of Holocaust victims as going "like sheep to the slaughter" on the one hand, and the modern Israeli warrior who actively confronts the enemy, on the other. Notwithstanding its lack of a purely activist stance, the event has remained powerful for its physical symbolism as a fortress of purity in a desert-sea of enmity. The IDF officers who were instrumental in using the site as an educational motif in their recruits' military socialization stressed two themes that appear to justify the use of an historical event containing a suicide motif: that IDF recruits should be prepared to sacrifice their life in defense of the state, and that given that the Masada event occurred during the Jews' Exilic years, such an event will not happen as long as the State of Israel exists.[54]

Once the events of the 1980s exposed the "few-against-the-many" part of the Israeli narrative as being counterproductive for the aims of peacemaking within the Middle East, the appropriateness of the Masada myth, among others, began to be questioned.[55] And just as Yitzhak Rabin declared in 1992 that Israel can no longer view itself as a nation that dwells alone, some Israelis began to distance themselves from the story of Masada. Nevertheless, in its fortress aspect, Masada clearly represents a defensive stance against a hostile enemy. Accordingly, whether Israel views itself as wholly embattled or as relatively strong in the face of weaker enemies, the Masada myth instilled a justification for Israel to wage war when necessary—in order to avoid annihilation. Israel's preventive attack leading to the 1956 war is a case in point. While the Arab states and some historians may have viewed Israeli behavior as "aggressive" in that instance, Israelis viewed their country's actions as necessary for the country's survival, and thus as falling well within the confines of the state's defensive-warrior role-identity.

The Bar Kochba Revolt

As a last stand against the Roman Empire, in 132 C.E. Bar Kochba (Aramaic for "son of a star") led the Jews in a revolt in Judea. While garnering initial success, the Romans ultimately defeated Bar Kochba's forces at the mountain town of Betar in 135 C.E., following the killing of 500,000 Jews.[56]

The narrative of the Bar Kochba revolt that was fostered throughout the Exilic period focused on his ultimate defeat to the Romans, and commemorated the event through the most somber of days in the Jewish calendar: the fast day Tisha B'av (the ninth day of the Jewish month of Av); this date eventually served as the commemorative repository for all the tragedies having befallen the Jews throughout history. Similarly, Jewish tradition throughout the Rabbinic period viewed Bar Kochba as a messianic charlatan, dubbing him "Bar Koziba" ("son of a liar"). But as Yael Zerubavel points out, modern Israeli collective memory reconstructed his image as a hero worthy of his original name. Despite the tale's bitter ending, modern Israeli tradition has focused on the courageousness of the protagonist and the temporary gains he made during his three-year revolt. Israel has since imbued the otherwise mystical holiday of Lag Ba'Omer with Bar Kochba symbolism. Israeli schoolchildren play at archery during the day and light bonfires at night. Generations of young Israelis were reared on stories of Bar Kochba engaging an initially hostile lion in friendship, and were encouraged to fulfill the valiant mission in Israel that his story suggests. As goes a children's song in the Ministry of Education's file of songs recommended for kindergarten, "There was a man in Israel, Bar Kochba was his name. He was young and tall, with shining eyes. He was strong, he called for freedom; all the nation loved him; he was a hero, a hero!"[57] Like Tel Hai and Masada, the Bar Kochba revolt ended tragically, but eventually led, two millennia later, to renewed Jewish sovereignty.

For modern Israel, the Bar Kochba revolt emphasized the moment of strength that characterized ancient Jewish life on the eve of Exile. That the revolt took place in Judea rather than in the ghettos of Europe links Israelis with their ancient sovereign roots, thus underscoring the historical attachment to the land. For Israel's role-identity, nurturing the Bar Kochba revolt as a highly symbolic event has served to entrench the state's self-image as a defensive warrior, one not afraid to fight for the right to exist in historic Israel. And unlike the Masada myth, which has seen a partial distancing by Israelis, the Lag Ba'Omer holiday remains a thriving day of celebration in the Hebrew calendar.

Tel Hai

In 1920, the Jewish settlement of Tel Hai in the northern Galilee was attacked by a band of Arab guerillas who succeeded in overrunning it, in the process killing the leader of its resistence, Joseph Trumpeldor, and several of his comrades. On his deathbed, Trumpeldor, who had lost his left arm in the Russo-Japanese War as an officer in the Czarist army, allegedly uttered the phrase "Never mind, it is good to die for our country." While the details of the legend have since been partially discredited, with more recent historians asserting that he merely cursed in his native Russian,[58] the phrase became celebrated in Israeli folklore. One children's song around the theme was taught to schoolchildren in the 1960s as part of the Ministry of Education's music program, commemorating the anniversary of Tel Hai: "On the night of the eleventh of Adar; 'It's good to die—we'll die in glee for our country, in the Galilee.' "[59]

In addition to the professed value of loyalty to the state, and like the David and Goliath story, the Tel Hai myth symbolizes the possible triumph of "the few against [the] many"[60] so integral to the Israeli national narrative. However, unlike the David and Goliath story, the outcome of the Tel Hai battle was less than sweet, with the chief defender ultimately dying in the face of enemy fire. Thus, crucial to the Israeli narrative is an inherent tension between strength and vulnerability. Coupled with this is the notion that the collective is manyfold stronger than the individual. While the attack resulted in several deaths, and the settlement itself was lost to the Arabs,[61] the Jews ultimately prevailed in Palestine.

In its current manifestations, Tel Hai boasts an imposing lion monument at the settlement, which has historically been the site of youth pilgrimages on the state's annual Tel Hai Day. Nevertheless, by the 1980s, some Israelis began to question the accepted symbolism of Tel Hai. In addition to the new history that cast doubt on Trumpeldor's final words, some artistic works sought to satirize or outright condemn the place of the myth in contemporary Israel. Pre-inductee protagonists during the War of Attrition in the popular 1987 Israeli film *Late Summer Blues* created a musical revue that satirized Trumpeldor's famed last words with, simply, "It's good to die." And a 1989 Israeli play titled "*Tov Labut Be'ad Artzeinu*" (It's good to club/bludgeon for your country; labut is a play on the word lamut—"to die"—and refers to the army-issued clubs used by IDF troops during the Intifada) was staged.[62] The founding myths that formed the core of the Israeli narrative thus became natural fodder for societal critiques against the government's policies in the 1980s. Rather than view these narratives themselves as undergoing drastic change within historical memory, we can understand them as concealing the unconscious counternarratives of aggression, counternarratives that reverse the few-versus-many divide, as Israel became progressively stronger than its most intimate enemy, the Palestinians. The relationship between these conscious and unconscious narratives therefore set the stage for Israelis to experience a collective cognitive dissonance once they perceived their state to be acting aggressively. As the Lebanon War and the Intifada unfolded, Israelis asked themselves whether they were enacting a role closer to Trumpeldor/Bar Kochba/David/the Masada Zealots, or to that of the Arab bandits/Goliath/the Romans. As we will see, it was the Israelis' realization that they were acting like the latter trinity that forced large segments of the population to push their government to reconcile the state's policy actions with its role-identity through the decision to negotiate with the PLO.

The Holocaust

The fourth pivotal event in constructing the Israeli narrative is one that did not occur on the site of present-day Israel, but in part led to the state's creation. Although the emergence of Zionism as an organized movement predated World War II by more than half a century (the first "wave" of *aliya* was in 1882), the story of pre-Israel, Exilic Jewish history culminated in the Holocaust and the attendant slaughter of six million European Jews. Although the role of the Holocaust in determining the establishment of the State of Israel in May 1948 remains a point of scholarly debate, the fact is that fresh in the collective memory of Israel's founders was the worst atrocity ever perpetrated on the Jews.

The Holocaust has been a highly ambivalent event in the formation of Israeli national identity, with the Yishuv period and the early years of the state characterized by a pronounced derision of Holocaust victims amid the accusation that they had gone "like sheep to the slaughter." A derogatory label for an overly compliant member of an army unit is "soap"—a macabre reference to the fate of many concentration camp victims.[63] The Zionist imaginary cast the archetype of the Holocaust victim/survivor in opposition to the vision of the New Jew, whose transformation into a citizen of Israel paralleled the desired shift from "Jew to Israeli," a process that was depicted in much of cinema in the late Yishuv/early state years.[64] Conversely, one of Israel's most prominent monuments is *Yad Vashem* ("a hand and a name") a memorial-museum dedicated to Holocaust victims. The monument is not only the site of Jewish pilgrimages, but also one of the stops for official state visitors to Israel.

A likely explanation for this ambivalence is the need by Israelis to justify their past victimhood in the context of present strength, given the hostile reception they were accorded by their new neighbors during the independence era. In addition to this spatial locus of commemoration (although one not directly linked to the actual site of occurrence, unlike Masada and Tel Hai), Israel has created an annual day of commemoration called *Yom Ha'shoa Ve'hagvura* (Holocaust Remembrance and Martyrs Day)—the precise Hebrew translation is "Holocaust and Valor Day"—in an encompassing reference to victims of the Nazis as well as to those Jews who stood firm in the face of the atrocity, especially the Warsaw Ghetto fighters. Given the collective Israeli attempt to fashion a defensive-warrior identity out of the Zionist narrative, Israelis are most comfortable commemorating moments of resistance during the Holocaust and World War II. This sentiment is embodied in the "Song of the Partisans" sung by generations of Israelis and, indeed, Diaspora Jews. "From the land of dates to the frosts, we are here amidst pain and anguish; and through our flowing blood, the strength of our spirit and bravery will yet emerge."

Israelis were forced to confront their attitudes toward the Holocaust during the 1960s when Israeli secret-service agents captured Adolf Eichmann in Argentina and brought him to Israel. His much-publicized trial riveted the nation, and his haunting defense of being merely a "cog in the wheel" of the Nazi regime would serve as a soul-searching point of reference for generations of Israeli soldiers. For scholarly Israelis, Hannah Arendt's treatise on the trial would similarly bring home the idea that extreme evil begins with seemingly ordinary humans.[65] Thus, the memory of the Holocaust brings to light a more nuanced set of conscious narratives versus unconscious counternarratives than does the starker tale of David and Goliath. While Israel's conscious narratives represent the idea that "we are defensive warriors who are in the process of reshaping our destiny," the unconscious counternarrative that the Holocaust represents is not only one of aggression against the weaker party, but is also one of not being strong enough to prevail against aggression. This suggests that in moments of utter weakness, Israelis might experience a reverse shift than the one examined in this book. For instance, in the aftermath of the Yom Kippur War, where the Egyptian and Syrian attack caught the Israeli intelligence establishment unawares, Israelis demanded a judicial commission to investigate the military's failure. Subsequently, the intelligence branch fell from grace in the collective Israeli imagination—yet in a direction different from both the Lebanon War and Intifada. All this is to say that a role-identity implies a fairly constrained set of actions, as the role-occupant must occupy a middle ground between strength and weakness, and between aggressiveness and passivity.

ISRAEL'S BIRTH AND THE EARLY STATE YEARS

Coming on the heels of a tumultuous history and corresponding historical memory of victimhood and divinely inspired moral battles between
good and evil, Israel's formative years were characterized by what we
may see as three, at times contradictory, forces: acute hostility from its
more numerous and seemingly more powerful regional neighbors (the
Arab states); hostility tinged with powerlessness from the Arab residents
of Palestine, many of whom became refugees during the 1948 War; and a
"mother-figure" who alternated between benevolence and antipathy, in
the form of Great Britain, which held the Palestine Mandate. Ultimately,
the great-power support that Israel came to enjoy—first from France,
then from the United States—supports the claim that the Israeli-Arab
antagonism was germane in shaping Israel's early selfhood, in that the
former patronage relationships cast the latter situation of enmity into
stark relief.[66] That Israelis enacted the first experiment in Jewish sovereignty in two millennia under the shadow of Arab intransigence led to a
curious mix of pride and disdain—a perception that the "six-against-
one" ratio of Arab to Jewish states was something to be overcome at all
odds, and that those six were spoiling the fun.[67] Israel's early leaders
believed that the Arab states were, in the words of one leader of the
Yishuv, attempting to do "everything through [the] Arab League to
crush [the] Jewish State out of existence."[68] These perceptions of the
Other as being bent on Israel's destruction led to a strengthening of
Israel's defensive-warrior role-identity. Israel needed to maintain its
warrior stance to stave off annihilation; and, since force was being used
in the service of self-preservation, the defensive aspect was consciously
(and unconsciously) ingrained in the Israeli collective psyche.

For Israelis, the pre-state historical legacy of Diaspora persecution
coupled with the ancient biblical tropes were instrumental in constructing the meaning of the events surrounding 1948. For instance, while
more numerous than the Israelis by a ratio of forty-to-one at the start of
the 1948 war, the Arabs' conscripted manpower outnumbered Israel's
only by a hair. In May of that year, Israel's manpower strength was
29,677 compared to the Arabs' 30,000. Yet by October, Israel clearly
prevailed numerically with 99,300 men while the Arabs had approximately 70,000.[69] The *perceived* relationship between Israel's fighting
forces and those of the Arab states on the eve of the June 1948 Arab-
Israeli truce, however, reveals an Israel that saw itself as having "marked
inferiority in planes, guns, tanks and heavy armour" and suffering from
"numerical inadequacy of our effective fighting strength."[70] As Rabin
recalled about the War of Independence years later, "At the most tragic

moments of the war, tormented by the thought that we were sending these men to face death—poorly armed and frighteningly outnumbered...I undertook a personal commitment...we...would never again be unprepared to meet aggression."[71] The dominant Israeli narrative understands the 1948 war as a victory of the "few over the many," and this, therefore, is the narrative conception that we must privilege in order to understand Israeli identity.[72]

While the Israelis perceived the Arab states to be much stronger than their own fledgling entity, they also viewed the local Palestinian population as embodying both dangerous strength and pathetic weakness. The Arab riots of 1936–1939, in which local Palestinians attacked Jews in the Yishuv, had led the Zionists to associate the Palestinians with the legacy of anti-Semitism that Diaspora Jews had faced at the hands of their host countries. However, the 1948 war saw the mass flight of Palestinians to the surrounding Arab countries; it would have been clear to the Israelis that the Palestinians did not constitute a formidable political or fighting force. Nor was it possible, given the Zionist narrative of returning to a "land without people for a people without land," to acknowledge the national uniqueness of the Palestinians. Only recently has Israel begun to confront the origins and fate of the approximately 700,000 Palestinian refugees who either fled out of encouragement from the surrounding Arab states who promised them a safe return to their homes following a projected defeat of Israel (the conventional Israeli account), or who were evicted by Israeli forces (the Arab/Palestinian account), or, more likely, some combination of these two factors.[73] This lack of recognition on the part of Israel helped maintain a defensive-warrior identity. Israelis saw themselves as defending their right to exist surrounded by hostile Arab states, rather than as colonialists whose national project was inherently linked with the dispossession of another people. The process of recognizing the Palestinians' national aspirations—something that was necessary for the Israeli-PLO talks to begin—was ultimately linked with the events of the 1980s, whereby Israel acted in discordance with its role-identity. It was during this period that Israeli "revisionist" historians (as they are called in Israel) published accounts of the events surrounding 1948 that lay more blame on Israel in bringing about the refugee problem than the dominant Israeli narrative had allowed.[74] Yet, on some unspoken level, the Israelis must have been aware of the tragic fate awaiting the refugees and knew that they themselves, in their sovereign position (however beleaguered), were more fortunate and surely more powerful than those thousands of Palestinian families, many of whom were forced into the squalor of refugee camps in the neighboring Arab states for decades to come.

Indeed, Israeli leaders at the time viewed the Palestinian exodus as sheer good fortune visited on Israel, without any of the perceptions of self-blame later experimented with by those Israelis harboring a critical view of the country's history. Wrote Shertok to World Jewish Congress leader Nahum Goldmann in June 1948, "The most spectacular event in the contemporary history of Palestine—more spectacular in a sense than the creation of the Jewish State—is the wholesale evacuation of its Arab population."[75] Elsewhere Shertok emphasized that "300,000 Arabs had left the Jewish areas of Palestine *of their own accord*."[76] A month later, in considering whether Israel would readmit those Arab residents who had fled Palestine, Shertok issued an unequivocal refusal, citing the "introduction [of a] fifth column" and that the question of return would only be determined by a reciprocal move on the part of the Arab states to discuss the fate of the Jewish residents and property in their countries. Nevertheless, he acknowledged that those Arabs remaining in Israel would be "unmolested and [would] receive due care from [the] State as regards services.[77]

Ultimately, however, one of the factors motivating Rabin to pursue a settlement with the Palestinians was a personal awareness of the suffering the Palestinians had undergone—some of it by Israeli fault, such as the extension of military rule over the Israeli Arab population until 1966, and the unequal funding accorded Arab villages compared to Jewish locales.[78] As Rabin declared to the Knesset in his opening parliamentary speech in June 1992, "It is proper to admit that for years we have erred in our treatment of Israel's Arab and Druze citizens. Today, almost forty-five years after the establishment of the state there are substantial gaps between the Jewish and Arab communities in a number of spheres."[79]

With regard to the British, the Israelis came to realize that even a like-minded, Western power that had promised to back a Jewish attempt at self-determination could not ultimately be counted on to follow through. The most glaring example of this inconsistency, was, of course, the 1917 Balfour Declaration, in which Lord Balfour promised to support the Jews in "establishing a Jewish national home"[80] being followed by the 1922 White Paper, which, though affirming the Jews' right to settle in Palestine, severely limited Jewish immigration to that which would not be "a burden upon the people of Palestine as a whole."[81] By 1939, British policies toward the Jewish community in Palestine had hardened; the White Paper of that year limited Jewish land purchase to 5 percent of the total area, restricted Jewish immigration to 15,000 per year for five years, and pledged to support the Palestinian "evolution toward independence."[82] And while the Balfour Declaration was ambiguous in its stated aims (the establishment of a Jewish "national home" rather than "state," and the accompanying warning that nothing should be done to "prejudice the civil and religious rights of existing non-Jewish communities in Palestine"), Jewish leaders interpreted the document as highly supportive of Zionism. As Moshe Shertok wrote to British Foreign Secretary Enest Bevin in May 1948, "[the] Balfour Declaration... will rank forever in [the] annals of history as [a] great act of reparation and creative statecraft."[83] Nevertheless, by the late 1930s, even Ben-Gurion recognized the inherent ambiguity in the language of the document. In a 1937 letter written to his son, he acknowledged, "But what is a 'National Home'? No one knew exactly what it meant and what its purpose was. Was it a Jewish State? If so—why did they say National Home' and not 'Jewish State'?"[84] This vague wording would be etched into the history of Israeli-Arab studies, and would be recalled as one of the clever uses of "constructive ambiguity" in Middle East diplomacy.[85]

Extreme reactions among Yishuv leaders to British policies occasionally took the form of terrorist acts, as when members of Etsel, along with the Hagana, bombed the British headquarters at the King David hotel in 1946, resulting in 95 dead—including Jews, Arabs, and British. Actions such as these on the part of Jewish forces demonstrated to Britain that its actions in Palestine stood in stark contrast to its self-image as an enlightened Mandatory power. As one Israeli scholar observes, "the British troops found the experience 'repugnant' and 'frustrating'; the struggle ended by taking away their self-respect, whereupon they turned tail and left. It was a lesson that...the Israelis themselves were destined to learn later."[86]

The actions taken by the British, and by the local Palestinians and surrounding Arab states toward Israel were almost wholly perceived by the early Zionists as a negation of their existence, leading Israelis to construe the Other as "aggressive" and the self as a defensive warrior. Israel's continued rejection of the PLO and the Arab League during the next four decades would help to solidify Israel's role-identity. The more entrenched this identity became, the greater would be the dissonance between Israelis' collective self-image and their state's actions in the Lebanon War and the Intifada.

CONCLUSION

This chapter has described the process by which Israel's defensive-warrior role-identity emerged within Israeli collective consciousness. The identity of being a "defensive warrior" entails pursuing military and strategic decisions within an ethic of fighting only wars of "no choice" and by following the "purity of arms" maxim. On a more subtle level, though, the idea of being a warrior is meant to encapsulate the activist stance taken by Israelis throughout their short history; a value that has been celebrated in Israeli commemorations of historical events, such as the importance ascribed to the battles of Tel Hai and Bar Kochba, and the refusal to die at the hands of the enemy embodied in the Masada story; and which was manifested in such pursuits as the regeneration of the land and the creation of a "Jewry of muscle." Intrinsic to this identity is a tension between the two halves of defensiveness and warrior-ness: to be a successful warrior one cannot be passive, and hence the ethic of "defensiveness" implies self-control out of a position of strength, including taking preventive actions when deemed necessary. This view is contrasted with a position of "waiting," an activity associated with Messianic yearnings in the Diaspora, and which was derided by modern Zionists who sought to create a state out of an activist ethic. Paired with a value of self-restraint, however, this ethic would ultimately have to contend with Israeli policies toward its nearest enemy. The next chapter will examine the ethical underpinnings of the IDF's doctrines, illustrating the degree to which they are infused with the narrative tropes discussed here.

Chapter Four

The Security Ethic of the IDF

As the military fashioned out of pre-state, clandestine forces, the IDF is the first centralized use of force by the Jews since the biblical period. This, along with the salience of national security concerns within the Jewish state, the policy of universal, dual-gender conscription, and the many wars that Israel has fought within its relatively short history, has given the IDF a central place within the Israeli imagination. Security issues form the basic fault line of left-to-right in Israeli politics, making the social and economic debates that are essential to the political landscape of most Western democracies recede to the background. In contrast to Europe, which boasts one war monument for every 10,000 fallen soldiers, Israel has one for every 17 fallen.[1] Historically, service in the IDF has been a pivotal rite of passage for young Israelis, providing the ticket to employment and basic government services, and has played a socializing role similar to the college experience for American youth. As such, the IDF's "security ethic"—that is, the military's normative attitude toward the use of force, including the consideration of under what circumstances force should be used, and the manner in which force may be justly employed within a given operation—is a crucial part of the Israeli popular consciousness, and is the institutional repository for the Israeli defensive-warrior role-identity that we examined in chapter three. Whereas Israel's overall role-identity derives from the citizens' view of themselves as arising from a beleaguered minority into a people that has taken charge of its own destiny—and which seizes on the narrative tropes of land and regeneration, the IDF's security ethic maintains that the military must maintain a sharp deterrent sword that may only be used in the service of self-defense.

With its pre-state forces formed during World War II, and its official inauguration in 1948, the IDF intended its fighting stance to be in sharp contrast to the victim years of Holocaust and Exile. And like the memory of the Diaspora, where the Jews operated as the few against the many, the IDF has been a small army in terms of recruitable population, yet a highly effective one that sees itself harboring all the potential energy bundled in David's slingshot against a lumbering and ill-equipped, but much larger, adversary: the Arab Goliath. The same self-less sentiment allegedly uttered by Joseph Trumpeldor on his deathbed at Tel Hai ("It is good to die for our country") was echoed by the government's call for universal conscription, where every Jewish male in the state—and indeed some women—might one day have to suffer the same fate as the one-armed warrior.[2] In this spirit of volunteerism, Israeli military commanders are known for their battle call of *"aharai!"* (After me!). Related to volunteerism is a policy of inclusion: the IDF has historically been receptive to gays and lesbians in service, an attitude that the organization formally enshrined in its 1993 policy of nondiscrimination based on sexual orientation.

The collective perception of Israel existing as a defensive state surrounded by hostile enemies meant that the IDF developed a deterrent fighting stance, but with the eschewing of aggressive campaigns whose sole purpose would be to revise the status quo. Israel saw itself as the only peace-loving member of the Middle East state system, wherein it had to wait patiently—and fight when necessary—until its neighbors were willing to accept its existence. With Israel having been reared by an ambivalent patron (Great Britain) and born into the arms of Arab hostility, the IDF had to develop a strong ethic of self-reliance, whereby great power patronage, while actively sought, could not entirely be relied on.

THE EMERGENCE OF THE IDF

Prior to Israel's independence, the Yishuv's security services were splintered into disparate arms, including the two anti-British, underground guerilla organizations Etsel (also known as the Irgun) and Lechi (also known, particularly by its detractors, as the Stern Gang—after its leader, Avraham Stern); as well as the more mainstream Palmach—the strike force of the Hagana. The Palmach was founded in 1941 to resist the advancing German forces, and as an infrastructure for a future Israeli army to defend itself against the Arab states. Palmach forces formed a key part of the state-building enterprise, engaging in such nontraditional activities as bringing boatloads of Holocaust refugees to Palestine. With independence, the underground movements were replaced by the IDF under the unifying leadership of Prime Minister David Ben-Gurion. And while Etsel and Lechi would hitherto be associated with the Revisionist Zionist movement led by Ze'ev Jabotinsky, and later embodied by Menachem Begin—who commanded Etsel from 1943 onward—and subsequently Yitzhak Shamir (who was active in Lechi), the dominant Zionist narrative would hearken back to the days of the Palmach to gain historical inspiration.[3]

Ben-Gurion's statist policies revolved around the twin fulcrums of socialism and Zionism. This so-called *mamlachtiut* (statism) has been described by one critic as stemming from Ben-Gurion's view of himself "as the founder of a kingdom, as an armed prophet, and not as a social reformer."[4] Ben-Gurion's subsequent appellation within popular Israeli discourse as "the old man" conveys this mix of veneration tinged with irreverence. Ben-Gurion's centralized policies in the political and economic spheres were equally manifested in the military arena, with the elimination of both Etsel and Lechi as independent organizations on the one hand, and the disbanding of the independent Palmach brigades (which were absorbed into the IDF), on the other.[5] Ben-Gurion's tight control over the military doubtless contributed toward the entrenchment of the IDF in collective consciousness as the sole security arm of the State of Israel, and one that was closely led by the state. While commentators have emphasized that Ben-Gurion's motives for disbanding the pre-state forces were intended to ensure a "unified and concentrated armed force" in order to prevail over the Arabs,[6] it seems evident that his consolidation had the effect of preventing the emergence of a garrison state. Moreover, the close civilian control meant that despite being a "nation in arms," Israeli society would not be permeated by a spirit of militarism that could threaten the democratic functioning of the civilian sphere. Whatever tensions in civil-military relations observers would henceforth identify could therefore not be attributable to a heterogeneous command structure within the IDF in its early days.

Within this process of centralization, the *Altalena* affair has assumed a prominent place in Israeli historical memory. On 20 June 1948, an Etsel ship named the *Altalena* approached the Tel Aviv coast carrying hundreds of volunteers and a significant quantity of armaments. Fearing an Etsel coup, Ben-Gurion ordered the ship to be bombed. In the event, sixteen people were killed, and the armaments lost.[7] For the formation of the Israeli national narrative, the episode represented the consolidation of the Labor Zionist voice and a consequent muting of Jabotinsky's Revisionist narrative, as well as a signal that the civilian command of the IDF would brook no opposition from renegade military groups. Past members of Etsel, many of whom ended up as members of the Herut and later Likud parties, pledged "never to forget" the episode. (The Holocaust is referred to similarly by Jews worldwide.) In an eery mixture of the realms of the public and private, Israeli collective memory was easily jogged by the Altalena affair as the scorched shipwreck was visible to sunbathers on Tel Aviv's beaches for a number of years hence, until the remains finally sank to the sea bottom.[8] And while the episode indeed was not forgotten, Ben-Gurion's version of the national narrative—that only a centralized IDF would lead the state through its annals of war and peace—remained dominant.

Given that Israel is a relatively young country, most of whose soldiers during its formative years were either themselves immigrants or sons and daughters of recent arrivals, the Israeli state during the 1940s and 1950s faced the task of actively creating a unified body of national consciousness where few or disparate common historical memories may have existed. The geographic, cultural, and historical divide between Sephardim and Ashkenazim, the two groups that each later came to represent roughly one-half of Israel's Jewish population, is a case in point. The Sephardim mostly immigrated to Israel during the 1950s when the basic infrastructure of the state had already been put in place by what was quickly becoming an Ashkenazi elite. And while Sephardi Jews had experienced varying degrees of discrimination (and sometimes tacit acceptance, with Jews and Christians being viewed under Islamic law as "people of the book") at the hands of the Arab states and their Islamic precursors, Sephardi Jews were untouched by the Holocaust. Neither were they at the center of the debates within Zionist thought that took root in Eastern Europe at the end of the nineteenth century. Thus, the new Israelis—a mix of Ashkenazim and Sephardim—possessed varying degrees of a sense of belonging within their previous host countries and with varying intensity expressed their hope of returning to Zion. (Much of this would have depended on the level of familiarity with the Jewish liturgy and the level of devoutness in various Jewish communities across the continents.)

Yet, as the government soon realized, all new arrivals to Israel had to become imbued with an immediate attachment to the physical and symbolic contours of their new land if the Israeli nation-building project was to succeed. The Israeli leadership was keenly aware of the unifying possibilities inherent in a mass conscript army, and capitalized on their captive audience of young recruits. Conscription thus served not only to provide the state with a loyal fighting force, but to forge a cohesive set of historical memories that would facilitate the state-building enterprise. Thus, the IDF—particularly in the early years of the state—took on the task of teaching its recruits the Hebrew language, along with a basic understanding of Jewish history and *yediat ha'aretz* ("knowledge of the land/country"). This has meant that while the military represents Israel's role-identity in the realm of security, the IDF's ethic and policies are also able to shape generations of Israeli citizens who in turn reflect back upon the IDF's mission and occasionally critique its policies. The reservists who fought in Lebanon were the sons of Israel's founding fathers, and had been raised with the ethic of fighting only wars of no alternative. As such, they were uniquely poised to critique the war as contradicting the IDF's security ethic—once it was made clear to them by Prime Minister Begin that the war indeed *was* a "war of choice."

Given that the elite of the IDF in its formative years consisted only of Ashkenazi officers—with Sephardim eventually trickling into the upper ranks following their mass immigration to Israel in the 1950s—at a rate similar to their integration into the civilian elite, the collective narratives contained within the IDF security ethic better corresponded to the Ashkenazi historical consciousness, at times embracing it; at other times subverting it. The yeshiva scholars who had feebly endured sporadic pogroms and anti-Semitic state policies in Europe had now shed their *tefillin* for mortars and rifles to become a formidable fighting force against the invading Arab armies. While the Sephardim in the Diaspora had by no means represented a warrior class, they did not emerge from the same yeshiva context and thus the contrast between their own transformation from a Diaspora people into a Jewry of Muscle within the proto-state would have been less apparent as was that of their Ashkenazi counterparts.

THE MISSION OF THE IDF

The self-perceived mission of the IDF is to underwrite Jewish sovereignty against a sea of hostility, the ebbs and flows of which vary according to cease-fire agreements and occasional peace treaties. More than simply a defensive body, in the words of one of its past chiefs of staff, the IDF is an "existential instrument."[9] IDF soldiers are instructed in the importance of safeguarding Israel's borders and, by extension, the country's existence. This task is made all the more prominent by the government having declared a "state of emergency" for the first eighteen years of Israel's history. The preface to a 1964 IDF-issued Passover *hagadah* (the story and prayer booklet accompanying the ritual meal) states, "The road to true redemption is still long, we have not advanced enough in the realization of the spiritual vision of the nation of Israel, the enemy still stands at the gate and schemes our destruction."[10] While it is true that Israel's neighbors, certainly before 1967, were committed to overcoming the state by force to the point of its extinction, this passage was written after Israel had emerged victorious in two major wars (1948 and 1956) and had assumed a relatively secure—if despised—place within the region. Yet this collectively-maintained narrative of self-protection would only be strengthened by the 1967 war (the lead-up to which involved a build-up of Egyptian forces along Israel's southern border and Nasser's closing of the Tiran Straits) and the 1973 war, in which Israel faced a surprise attack by Egypt and Syria.

Historically, Israelis have seen the IDF as providing an "insurance policy" against whatever peaceful overtures Israel makes toward its neighbors. In addition to the view of captured territory serving as a bargaining chip toward future negotiations, the latter phases of the Oslo negotiations saw the introduction of IDF personnel at critical stages.[11] In return, Israel views its soldiers as worthy of loyalty and protection. Until a recent spate of kidnapings and murders by Palestinians posing as Jews, Israelis routinely transported hitchhiking soldiers from home to base; a poster from the early state period depicts a rifle with a tag tied to it with the words, "Soldier! Protect me and rely on me."[12] As an institution, the IDF is aware of the reciprocal relationship between active duty and national loyalty. States a 1960s IDF pamphlet issued by the Educational Division, "the fighter who struggles for the sovereignty of Israel...acquires for himself a deep and durable connection with his homeland."[13]

Part of the way Israel has prepared itself to defeat the Arab states has been by stressing the need for a qualitative, rather than a quantitative, advantage over the enemy. As Major General Israel Tal wrote in 1977, "Israel's military supremacy would have to be based on her qualitative advantages—ethical, cultural, scientific and technological— on a difference in kind, not only in degree."[14] Reflected in this statement is the belief in Israeli moral superiority over the Arabs permeated by a David and Goliath narrative coupled with a Western-imbued Orientalism, a sentiment that has informed much of Israel's view of the Arab-Israeli conflict. Whereas Israeli national consciousness emerges from a Judeo-Christian ethic of moral righteousness, attributing to the Other qualities of barbarism and cultural inferiority can help to prop up the sense of we-ness so crucial to collective identity. The idea that the goodness of a *culture* or an *ethic* can be ordinally measured lacks sense, of course, but has been central to Israel's view of itself relative to the Arab states, a belief that has paralleled a similar one on the part of the Arab states toward Israel; yet the dominant Arab goal toward the Israeli state had historically been to annihilate it as a political entity.[15]

Israel has historically seen itself as the recipient, rather than the initiator, of war overtures. As Prime Minister Yitzhak Rabin declared at the August 1993 commencement exercises of the National Security College in Israel, "Our task, our objective is to bring peace. Your task is to be victorious in war and to defend peace, if, God forbid, war *is imposed on us.*"[16] Even the Six Day War of 1967, in which Israel launched a preemptive strike, was described by Rabin as being fought by "a nation that desired peace but was capable of fighting valiantly *when enemies forced it into war.*"[17] The belief that the Six Day War was a purely defensive operation has remained widespread among Israelis. That Nasser amassed troops along the Egyptian-Israeli border, and closed the Tiran Straits to Israeli shipping, doubtless contributed to Israel's sense that a preemptive strike was ethically akin to reacting to an actual military strike by Egypt—a view that in any event is, in large part, confirmed by just war theory. But, as discussed later, given Israel's lack of a hinterland (particularly prior to the 1967 war), Israel could not trade space for time and thus militarily would have had to preempt in order to stave off defeat. A so-called "objective" reading of the military-political situation leading up to a given war is not necessary for understanding a state's view of its own actions. Nevertheless, it is helpful to understand the external situation to the extent that mapping the particularities of a given strategy to Israel's view of its own actions can help us predict when a subsequent military operation will be met with collective skepticism, thus generating the cognitive dissonance that was manifest in the 1980s.

The IDF's view of itself as fending off would-be destroyers of the entire enterprise of modern Jewish sovereignty meant that the "defensive" aspect of the IDF's security ethic was deeply ingrained from the beginnings of the Zionist attempt at state-building. Even prior to independence, the Hagana adopted an operational stance of passive defense, such that ethical and tactical issues combined to form a major fault line in the late 1930s between the Hagana traditionalists and the formidable leadership of Yitzhak Sadeh. Ultimately, the clash was resolved by agreeing to maintain a defense-oriented *ethic* while engaging in offensive *tactical* operations against Arab guerilla bands.[18] This combination of defensive norms and offensive operations would later come to form the core of Israeli military doctrine as well as the IDF's security ethic.

While a mission rife with such existential pains could have led Israel's army to assume a Machiavellian stance, such that no action would be deemed out of the bounds of Israeli attempts at self-preservation, the IDF was quick to embrace as legitimate only those operations that actually did aim to stave off politicide. Thus, while the 1956 and

1967 wars were preventive and preemptive operations, respectively, they were both understood by Israel's political-military establishment to fit within Israel's security ethic. For instance, the Suez Crisis of 1956, in which Britain and France collaborated with Israel in attacking Egypt, was viewed by the West as unnecessarily offensive, yet Israel's accompanying Sinai Campaign was seen by Israelis as simply an attempt to keep the country's trade access open and its southern flank peaceful. In the process, Israel would be attempting to neutralize its most daunting threat in the form of Nasser's Egypt, including the guerilla raids that had been staged from the Egyptian-occupied Gaza Strip into Israel.[19] Indeed, emanating from the ranks of the Arab states since the aftermath of the 1948 war had been the ominous promise of executing a "second round" so as to finally defeat the Jewish State. So pessimistic did Israelis feel in the years leading up to the war, that a "Second Round" children's board game was marketed.

Despite the absence of a full-scale Arab-Israeli war between 1948 and 1956, the years prior to the Sinai Campaign were characterized by a series of *fedayeen* attacks from the Arab states into Israel, followed by IDF reprisal raids against military installations.[20] Similarly, Israelis remember the Six Day War as representing a lightning strike over Egyptian, Syrian, and Jordanian forces who were poised to attack Israel with the aim of eliminating the small state. So careful were the Israelis not to stray from their defensive ethic that, on the eve of the war, Prime Minister Levi Eshkol opposed a preemptive strike out of fear that Israel would be perceived as an aggressor.[21]

All this is to suggest that while Israelis do not shy away from employing military might, they believe in using it to ensure Israel's existence, rather than for predatory purposes. As the commemorative album of the Six Day War, issued by the IDF and the Ministry of Defense, proclaims, "The Israel Defence Forces, *ready for battle, but eager for peace,* must guard the cease-fire lines until they are replaced by secure and agreed frontiers."[22] By contrast, the war in Lebanon and the Intifada were both instances of military episodes that, to broad swaths of the Israeli population, contradicted their state's role-identity. It was this break with Israel's security ethic and hence its self-image in the realm of security policy that led Israel to seek peace with the PLO.

Force and Legitimacy

Essential to a state's security ethic is the military's normative attitude toward the use of force, including what types of force are deemed legitimate within the collective consciousness of the polity. In Israel's case, the need to safeguard the state's existence along with Israel's view of itself as wholly desirous of peace has led Israel and the IDF to harbor an ambivalent attitude toward the use of force. The IDF's logo, a sword entwined with an olive branch set against a Star of David, perhaps best expresses this tension, and the defensive-warrior role-identity. Rather than being portrayed as a murderous weapon, the sword suggests defending the biblical patrimony of the Land of Israel, with the Star of David reminiscent of Jewish claims to the land hearkening back 2,000 years. Israelis have long viewed their state as wielding the sword only in the interest of self-preservation, if not of peace. Intrinsic to the Israeli attitude toward the use of force is the debate that evolved within the pre-IDF forces between adopting a policy of "restraint" (*havlaga*) versus "reaction" (*tguva*).[23] In advocating that the Yishuv employ restraint when dealing with the local Arabs, Ben-Gurion condemned members of his population for smashing the doors to an Arab shop, asking "whether this will be the Land of Israel or the Land of Ishmael."[24] Here, it is evident that Israel's leaders attached great importance to the role that the would-be Jewish state would play vis-à-vis its neighbors and its own Arab-other population. The idea of restraint was popularized within early Zionist discourse by Zionist thinker Berl Katznelson, who presented his views—in the context of purity of arms—at the twenty-first Zionist Congress in 1939. As Katznelson declared, "*Havlaga* means: let our arms be pure. We are studying arms, bearing arms, we are facing up to those who attack us. But we do not want our weapons to be tainted with innocent blood."[25] It was in part this distinction between restraint and reaction that distinguished the dominant Labor-Zionist discourse from that of its Revisionist opponents. This distinction was one that evolved from a nearer identity of aims, as the bombing of the British Mandate headquarters at the King David Hotel by Etsel and the Hagana illustrates. However, Hagana leaders later claimed that Etsel had not provided sufficient warning time to enable the hotel to be evacuated. For this reason, as at least one interpretation allows, the Hagana subsequently ceased large-scale terrorist-type operations, and specifically ended its cooperation with Etsel.[26] Seen in the context of the eventual policy shift that would come about in the early 1990s, this example of the Hagana's reaction can be viewed as a more minor example of the type of dissonance that results when an actor's self-image is contradicted by its policies or the effects deriving from them.

Connected to the issue of the use of force is the state's attitude toward victory over the enemy. Typically in warfare, victory not only implies defeat of the adversary, but significant loss of life as well—usually for both sides. In the aftermath of the Six Day War, then-Chief of

Staff Yitzhak Rabin acknowledged the ambivalent feeling that had emerged from the battlefield. "It may be that the Jewish People never learned and never accustomed itself to feel the triumph of conquest and victory and therefore we receive it with mixed feelings."[27] While Jews in the modern period were forced to contend with their new status as collective wielders of sovereign power, so too did they need to accommodate a view of themselves as the governors of an army capable of inflicting severe pain. Where these victories were perceived to be in the service of self-defense, whatever existential tension existed was so manageable as to elicit a forgettable reaction in a single speech by the chief of staff. However, once Israel—in the 1980s—launched offensive operations that lacked national consensus, the psychic conflict became unbearable, and Israel was forced to contend with unconscious fears of becoming an aggressor.

With the IDF's view of itself as entrusted with the task of defending the state comes a disdain for enacting a police-role—one that Israeli soldiers had to play during the Intifada—as well as an antipathy toward terrorism as a legitimate means of statecraft. While by no means inherently excluding the ability to prevent and punish terrorist actions, the IDF's doctrine has largely centered around the conventional battlefield. Conversely, with terrorism a constant threat, the IDF has had to devote considerable resources to what it dubs a "current security" (as opposed to "basic security") problem, the latter referring to the traditional cross-border threats that have been the mainstay of the Arab-Israeli conflict. In contrast to this position, Israelis have sought to reduce terrorism to the morally lowest form of warfare. As Amos Elon points out, while years earlier the Zionists had carried out terrorist actions against the British in Palestine, once statehood was achieved Israel often used the terrorist label to villify its Arab adversaries.[28] Prime Minister Menachem Begin was known to refer to the PLO as "two-legged animals," and dubbed the group the "Palestinian Murder Organization."[29] And as right-wing Knesset Member Raphael Eitan would say during the Intifada, Israel should seal off the occupied territories to make the Palestinians akin to "cockroaches in a jar." In the 1964 Israeli film *Rebels Against the Light,* an Arab terrorist apologizes to his commander for shooting his gun with the excuse "I could not help myself: the Jew was right at the window."[30] Along with the need to prevent and respond to terrorist attacks, the IDF has had to patrol Palestinian cities and villages, a task whose frequency was reduced only as a result of the Oslo agreement. (Israeli soldiers still staff checkpoints along the complicated road system in the territories and, with the second Intifada, began to re-enter Palestinian population centers.) The enactment of a role alien to the

IDF—that of policing and riot control—would lead to a collective repugnance toward Intifada policies. This domestic reaction would in turn help to precipitate the Israeli policy shift toward the Palestinians leading to the Oslo agreement.

ISRAEL'S SECURITY ETHIC: OPERATIONAL MANIFESTATIONS

The IDF's defensive orientation has historically placed Israel within the broad camp of status-quo states—those that seek to preserve the distribution of territorial or other goods within the regional or broader international system. As Yitzhak Rabin has written, "[T]he basic approach which has characterized Israel's political and security concept since its establishment [has been] maintenance of the status quo."[31] Part of the reason for the rise of Israel's status-quo orientation within the "dominant" Labor-Zionist narrative outlined in chapter three has doubtless been instrumental; that is, the Israeli belief that the Arab-Israeli conflict cannot be solved by military means. Whether Israelis privately *desire* to alter the status quo in their favor (and an observer would be hard-pressed to find a citizen of most polities who would not want to increase their state's material prowess were the cost-benefit calculus deemed favorable) is not the issue here. Nor is a status-quo orientation necessarily contradicted by a grab for territory as a bargaining chip for peace, as was the case in the Six Day War where no Israeli government has since sought to annex the West Bank and Gaza Strip. Rather, the explicit goals that successive Israeli governments have harbored vis-a-vis the Middle East have almost exclusively been centered around maintenance of the territorial status quo. Israel acted more like a revisionist state during the war in Lebanon, when Israel lent military support to its choice of Lebanese president—Bashir Gemayel—and invaded its northern neighbor in an effort to drive the PLO and Syria out of Lebanon. It was this series of "revisionist" actions, coupled with the IDF's violent attempts at suppressing the Intifada, that led to the psychic dissonance that will be discussed in subsequent chapters.

In practice, Israel's status-quo orientation has led it to develop a military doctrine centered around deterrence.[32] This deterrence has been articulated to be primarily conventional in nature, although it is believed that by the mid-1960s Israel had already possessed the ability to produce nuclear weapons. Scholarship published from inside Israel during the early 1970s referred to Israel's nuclear status as embodying a "consensus [having] been reached in Israeli defense circles that Israel should continue its research and acquire the necessary knowledge to produce nuclear weapons, but that it should not be the first...to introduce weapons into the area, that is, develop a nuclear option."[33] As more contemporary scholarship makes clear in its assessment that Israel "probably possessed nuclear weapons since before the 1967 war,"[34] the so-called consensus regarding Israel's hesitance to be the first nuclear power in the Middle East either quickly broke down, was aimed at not fanning the flames of the Arab-Israeli security dilemma, or else was a veiled attempt by Israel to appear morally superior to its adversaries. Subsequent decades saw the existence of Israel's nuclear capability leaked to the press both inside and outside the country. This knowledge resulted in Israel's deterrent posture ultimately resting on its nuclear potential, yet the IDF was still trained to withstand an Arab onslaught through the use of conventional might. That is, given the inherent destructiveness of nuclear weapons, making them a last resort for almost any state, Israel would have to maintain a conventional deterrent and defensive posture all the while that it developed its nuclear deterrent.

A conventional deterrent stance has meant that Israel attempts wherever possible to hold onto its existing territory while proving through battlefield prowess that its borders are military inviolable and that any attempt to attack the state will cost the enemy dearly. Such military skill serves to prevent would-be aggressors from attacking, and has enabled Israel to secure the confidence of a great-power patron. Until 1967, Israel relied on France as its main arms supplier; after the Six Day War, when France turned away from the Jewish State, the United States filled this role, as it has continued to do until today. Paradoxically, however, Israel has had to restrain itself from using too much force so as not to provoke condemnation by its major patron.[35] The negotiations between the Israeli government and U.S. Secretary of State Alexander Haig prior to the 1982 war in Lebanon is a case in point. Prime Minister Begin came away perceiving that he had received a "green light" to launch the war, yet the invasion was ultimately condemned by the international community at large, as well as by the United States (i.e., once Israel went so far as to bomb Beirut and lay siege to the city). The intensification of the Cold War through another two decades following the 1967 war meant that Israel could be guaranteed American support if nothing else as a counterpoise to the Soviets arming the Arab states.

On those occasions when Israel *has* conquered territories (such as the West Bank, Gaza Strip, Sinai Peninsula, and Golan Heights won during the Six Day War), Israel has largely viewed these areas as a bargaining chip for future negotiations. While the West Bank has to date only been partially ceded to the Palestinians under the terms of Oslo, that agreement included the "return" of almost all of the Gaza Strip (though to the Palestinians, rather than to Egypt, from whom Israel won it in 1967). Israel returned the Sinai desert to Egypt in 1982 under the terms of the Camp David accords and accompanying peace treaty reached between the two countries in 1978–1979; this being the second time that Israel had returned that swath of territory to Egypt—the first being in 1957, following the 1956 Sinai Campaign. Similarly, Israel returned some fourteen villages to Lebanon in the aftermath of the 1948 war of independence and the accompanying cease-fire. Thus, while Israelis have historically bemoaned their lack of strategic depth, inherent in the IDF doctrine has been no outright attempt to expand Israel's borders—with the exception of the Golan Heights, which was conquered from Syria in 1967 and annexed in 1981. Even here, however, debate continues within Israel as to whether this strategic area should be the subject of peace negotiations with Syria. As discussed in chapter three, so central to Zionism was the idea of "normalization," that a status-quo-oriented IDF doctrine followed accordingly. Even the Lebanon War, Israel's most aggressive campaign to date, involved the holding on to the southern strip of Lebanon as an occupied buffer zone; there was no attempt to annex it nor would the desire have been there to do so among the Israeli public at large.[36] The debate over the future of the West Bank and Gaza Strip is a partial exception to this stand, as voices from the right have historically called for annexing the areas to Israel. However, the (left-of-center and centrist) Israeli establishment never embraced the idea of annexation, and even the central core of the right wing soon gave up their demands, as they did not want to dilute the Jewish character of the state; annexation would have meant granting citizenship to 1.5 million Palestinians, or else forgoing Israel's democratic character under an apartheidlike system.

The defensive nature of the IDF is also embodied in the lack of militarism as a value among soldiers and veterans of the forces, a characteristic that highlights the delicate balance between "defensiveness" and "warriorness." Referring to the relationship between the civilian and military spheres, militarism can be understood to be "the subordination of civil society to military values and the subordination of civilian control of the military for military control of the civilian."[37] Researching within the context of Israeli history specifically, Uri Ben-Eliezer defines militarism as "the viewpoint that organized violence, or war, is the optimal solution for political problems."[38] With this definition, it is easier for Ben-Eliezer to make the case that Israel is indeed a militaristic society, preferring, as it did, to attempt to solve many of its foreign policy conflicts by military means. However, in drawing on the former definition, I am emphasizing the normative aspects of militarism as a permeation of society on the level of day-to-day culture as well as within the realms of civilian decision-making, with the latter necessarily impinging on democratic functioning.

Understood in this way, it is evident that Israel does not exhibit the militarism of many states of the Third World, for instance, whose armed forces have become a substitute for participatory democracy, and whose military is glorified for the intrinsic aspect of violence that it suggests. Israeli officers eschew the accouterments of their counterparts in other Western militaries, such as gloves and brass buttons; and military parades have in the past been subject to domestic disdain.[39] While IDF parades were held sporadically until 1973, their planning and execution were not without domestic opposition, even from some segments of the elite. Since the early 1990s, Israel's Independence Day celebrations have been accompanied by an Israel Air Force air show over the coastline, without the formality of a street parade.[40] Israeli soldiers are known for their untucked demeanor; indeed, the claim to fame of the eleventh chief of staff, Rafael (Raful) Eytan (1978–1983), was to institute a "spit-and-polish" element into the forces. That this was a revolutionary concept within the IDF is illuminating. Senior commanders are often referred to by their nicknames, which may derive from their high school or army years. These appellations inevitably carry over into one's political career, in the event that the individual makes such a transition.[41] The 1992 elections saw thirteen members of Knesset (out of a total of 120) who held the rank of colonel or higher,[42] and two prime ministers to date—Rabin and Ehud Barak—have previously held the post of IDF chief of staff. Thus, while military figures have certainly garnered the respect of the voting public, it is not accurate to claim that in the Israeli case, the civilian sphere is permeated by the military to the detriment of democracy. This antimilitarism is even more striking in light of the essential role in Israeli society historically accorded the IDF.

Part of the antipathy toward military formalism likely stems from two quite disparate sources. The first, and perhaps more superficial, explanation is the culture of "straight talk" (dugri) characterizing Israeli social communication.[43] Israelis, as any tourist will tell you, are notorious for "stating their mind," a tendency that can lead to customer-service misunderstandings and other cultural clashes. With this social characteristic comes a disdain for formalism in general, an attitude that carries over into the ranks of the military. Thus, a culture that eschews militarism for its own sake will be hesitant to pursue force that is not seen as purely defensive in nature. And from a culture of "straight talk" comes another, attendant push toward doing only what is necessary to achieve one's goals. The backhanded route to solving the Palestinian problem that was the Lebanon War—Defense Minister Ariel Sharon's plan to invade Beirut and prop up a friendly Christian regime there—would resonate painfully within a collective devoted to "straightforward" foreign policy, even if those policies are not always "morally pure" in the absolute sense of the phrase. Other, somewhat controversial, actions taken by the IDF, such as the 1981 bombing of Iraq's nuclear reactor or the assassination of various PLO and Hamas leaders in the last three decades have not had nearly the same Israeli public backlash as did the Lebanon War and Israel's response to the Intifada.

Yet the more deep-seated, possible reason for the lack of militarism is a Jewish ambivalence toward the use of force, alluded to briefly earlier. The Jewish historical prototype was a physical weakling who focused on intellectual pursuits at the expense of more productive, nationally self-sustaining, concerns. When Jews did excel within their host societies, it was most often through financial acumen as middle-men for the ruling elites—such as the Court Jews in Germany and Austria of the seventeenth century who served as financiers to European aristocracy. While the Court Jews enjoyed privileges based on individual patronage relationships, this power was not sufficiently institutionalized to serve as a stable source of security for the Jews as a community.[44] As such, part of the Zionist transformation was the evolution from occupying positions within the middle class to creating a culture of laborers. As Ben-Gurion wrote to his children in 1935, "The people who are workers in the Land of Israel were not workers in the Diaspora. Their parents were landlords, shop-keepers, traders, members of the middle class. Only a few of them worked with their hands."[45] (While Ben-Gurion was likely thinking of the Eastern European Jews, neither were the Jews from Arab countries laborers in the traditional sense of a large-scale proletariat—either in the realms of industry or agriculture.)

Thus, as the early Zionists saw it, "Jewish Labour in Palestine...is our Bible and our creed."[46] This idea of focusing on the use of the body for attaining Zionist objectives underpins the emphasis on creating a warrior people capable of shaping its own fate. Whereas the folk tales of other cultures describe the prototypical independent woman who, in order to fulfill her father's destiny, dons a male guise to become a warrior, the Jewish Diaspora folk counterpart depicts a woman who masquerades as a male scholar in order to devote her life to Talmudic study.[47] This ambivalence toward force was exacerbated by the experience of the Holocaust, in which Jews were remembered as being led "like sheep to the slaughter." The memory of this passive period in Jewish history has encouraged Israel to adopt an activist stance in providing for its own

security, but it also carries with it a legacy of nonviolence that is difficult
to overcome. More minor symbols of the Holocaust, such as the use of
dogs for army missions, were considered by the IDF, but were ultimately rejected due to their Nazi associations. While European Jews
emerged from that experience committed to preventing any such occurrence from happening again, Israel has been careful not to glorify force
for its own sake. The senselessness of the destruction wrought on
European Jewry meant that Israelis would forever be concerned with
justifying every act of force in defensive terms.

This ambivalence did not rest on a repellence of physical strength,
however; on the contrary, Israelis knew from the outset that they must
be responsible for their own productivity and their own defense, a belief
that translated into a strong ethic of self-reliance. This ethic was reinforced by the great-power isolation that Israel had experienced up until
1967, with early British support for a Jewish state waxing and waning
through the Mandate period, and France doing its about-face in the mid-
1960s. Israel's reliance on its own defense capabilities has historically
been exemplified in part by the state's attempt to develop and nurture an
indigenous arms industry.[48] Declares Shertok in June 1948 with regard to
Jerusalem *per se*, "experience had shown us that we could not rely on the
help of the international world to guarantee the safety of Jewish
Jerusalem. The Christian world had not fought even for its own interests
in Jerusalem, and it was only Jewish forces that had stood between
Jerusalem and its enslavement by a Moslem ruler."[49]

While the skillful diplomacy of the likes of Herzl was valued during
the early expressions of organized Zionism during the late nineteenth century in Europe, ultimately Israelis tended to shun diplomacy as the ultimate means of statecraft, preferring to focus on pioneering efforts
combined with a military deterrent posture to achieve their goals in the
Middle East. The two approaches to foreign policy became known,
respectively, as "political Zionism" and "practical Zionism." The former,
embodied by Herzl and later Jabotinsky, was ultimately overshadowed by
the practical Zionism of Ben-Gurion, Chaim Weizmann, and eventually
Gush Emunim, the modern-day settlers' movement in the occupied territories.[50] However, diplomacy and force would continue to interact
uneasily within Israeli history, as the secret deal between Israel and France
in the lead-up to the 1956 war shows. As previously stated, while even
Western observers viewed this arrangement in unsavory terms, Israel has
never experienced a collective rejection of this war, such as it did during
the war in Lebanon and the Intifada. These examples underscore the
importance of the relationship between role-identity and the *polity's own
view* of its actions in precipitating a radical foreign policy shift.

Historically, with Britain not having been seen as a reliable patron for bringing about Jewish independence (notwithstanding the 1917 Balfour Declaration), neither was the United Nations seen as an effective guarantor of Israel's security, even though its members had narrowly agreed to partition Mandatory Palestine into Arab and Jewish states. The oft-cited 1955 quotation by Ben-Gurion encapsulates the Israeli disdain for the organization: "Oom-Shmoom" (UN-Shmu-en).

With this perceived need for self-reliance comes a reverence for initiative and leadership, with *rosh gadol* (literally, "large head") referring to someone who does not shy away from taking the initiative in a group (or army) context; and the celebrated battle call of *aharai*! (Follow me!) whereby the commander leads his troops into battle, rather than fighting at the rear. The words of a company commander during Operation Nachshon during the 1948 war, in which the commander knew what fate awaited him, have since been repeated in IDF officer training courses over the years: "All privates will retreat, all commanders will cover their withdrawal."[51] While Israelis tend to believe that this practice is peculiar to their own defense forces, this proposed exceptionalism is not necessarily substantiated in reality.[52] Nevertheless, the relevance of the belief that Israel is unique in its sacrifice of commanders, if necessary, for the sake of victory in battle, lies in the fact that the IDF security ethic is in part informed by it.

DEFENSIVE ETHIC, OFFENSIVE DOCTRINE

While the Israeli security ethic is a defensive one, the doctrine and tactics of the IDF are offensive, making Israel an illuminating case for understanding the relationship between military doctrines and security ethics. Others have termed the offense-defense distinction in the Israeli case an operational-strategic one.[53] While it is true that the IDF's strategy is defensive while its operations and tactics are offensive, the relationship between its defensive *goals* and offensive *means* cuts to the heart of Israel's national identity, and, as such, the package of goals and means (one being defensive, the other being offensive) can be thought of in security-ethic terms as embodying a "defensive-warrior" ideal. Were *both* goals and means to be defensive in the Israeli case, we would think of Israel as a "defensive-victim" state. Conversely, were both goals and means to be *offensive*, we would consider Israel to be an "aggressive-warrior" state. The distinction between defensive values and offensive operations is not lost on Israeli citizens, "who are profoundly convinced that the IDF is a definitely defensive instrument from the political and moral viewpoint."[54] This defensive security ethic is so deeply ingrained in the Israeli narrative, from centuries of victimization punctuated by occasional victories, that when the state's behavior during the events of the 1980s contradicted it, Israeli society experienced the cognitive dissonance discussed here. Were the distinction to rest only at the level of operations versus strategy, the reaction would have been confined to military circles alone (if having occurred at all), and would not have carried the universally affective weight that it did.

Israel's military doctrine (as a subset of its security ethic) favors quick and decisive battles due to Israel's comparatively small population base—where full-scale wars are fought by all males—and some women—of conscripted and reservist age in the country. While the regular forces consisting of almost all Israeli males aged 18–21 form the day-to-day face of the Israeli army, it is the reservists who compose the bulk of the fighting power in any given war. Moreover, the IDF aims to transfer the war as soon as possible to enemy territory, due to the geographic offense-defense balance between Israel and its Arab adversaries.[55] Given that Israel's territorial size is small and its width exceptionally narrow across its coastal center, IDF doctrine dictates that a battle fought on Israeli territory would be too risky to endure, as there is virtually no hinterland available to absorb the first strike.

Neither does this doctrine rule out offensive strikes when deemed to be preemptive or preventive in nature, such as was the case in Israeli military thinking in the lead-up to the 1956 Sinai Campaign and the Six Day War.[56] The focus on preventive and preemptive warfare serves another, more psychological purpose as well: the aspect of *resolve* necessary for any deterrent posture to appear credible and therefore to succeed. As Rabin told his colleagues in support of his proposal to strike, precipitating the Six Day War, "If we don't face that challenge, the IDF's deterrent capacity will become worthless. Israel will be humiliated. Which power will bother to support a small state that has ceased to be a military factor?"[57] Thus, despite Israel's ethic of self-reliance, essential to the Israeli deterrent stance has been an implicit assumption of great power backing; neither Israel's own credibility nor its possession of a strong patron could be guaranteed in the event that Israel were to passively stand by in the face of a perceived provocation.[58]

As previously noted, the final aspect of Israel's security doctrine dictated that the capture of territory by the IDF was seen as a bargaining chip to entice the Arab states to make peace with Israel. Following the Six Day War, as the one-million-strong occupied Palestinian population in the West Bank and Gaza Strip began to enter Israeli consciousness, the holding of territory as a strategic asset began to conflict with the

Israeli role-identity of being a defensive warrior led by a democratic regime. As Rabin recalls, "we had not gone to war to acquire territories."[59] Even on the strategic level itself, though, Israel's newfound territorial gains ended up being somewhat of a liability, despite the reduction of the ratio of its land to sea borders as having shifted from 4:1 to 2:1.[60] The increased strategic depth meant that Israeli military doctrine no longer exclusively emphasized the need to strike the first blow.[61] In part, this shift resulted in a lack of readiness on the part of Israel's defense establishment to respond to the two-front attack by Egypt and Syria in October 1973, an operation that precipitated the three-week long Yom Kippur War.[62] That war paved the way for criticism of the army by the media and the public in general, and resulted in a judicial body, the Agranat Commission, set up to apportion blame within the defense establishment for Israel's lack of preparedness. Ultimately, Israel's failure to anticipate the attack was ascribed to poor evaluation of existing data by the intelligence branch that was seen to suffer from the grip of a faulty "conception"—in the parlance of the day—of the willingness and ability for the Arab states to wage war against the Jewish state. In the end, the commission's report led to the resignation of the defense minister and the dismissal of the chief of staff. The Yom Kippur War clinched the "beleaguerment" aspect of Israel's role-identity, as Israel suffered huge war losses following the surprise attack by Egypt and Syria. One observer has written that so besieged have Israelis historically felt, that "the periods between wars have usually been seen as times of 'latent war.' "[63]

CONCLUSION

The IDF's security ethic, and the lessons that Israelis have drawn from their state's adherence to or defection from this ethic, are underpinned by the major narrative tropes discussed in chapter three. In particular, these are Israelis' historic belief that their country's relationship to the outside world is represented by the phrase the "few against the many," mirrored by the David and Goliath myth, and encapsulated in the grand historic transformation from a passive and victimized Diasporic people to a Jewry of Muscle. The universal conscription policy that the IDF has maintained, along with the military's active educational wing, has meant that every (Jewish) Israeli citizen has internalized these narrative tropes as personal history.

The operational manifestations of Israeli military doctrine, such as the need for self-reliance through a deterrent posture and the fighting of

quick and decisive battles on enemy territory are not at odds with the
security ethic suggested here. In fact, Israel's offensive doctrine easily
co-exists with a defensive security ethic. This suggests that much more
than merely preemptive warfare (as was the Six Day War), or even colo-
nial collaboration leading to preventive war (as occurred in the 1956
Suez Crisis engineered by Britain and France and the accompanying
Israeli-Egyptian Sinai Campaign) is needed to elicit the type of collective
cognitive dissonance that can lead to a large-scale policy shift. It also
indicates that an observer-perspective that purports to ascribe "aggressiveness" to a given military operation and hence to predict a cognitive
dissonance is misguided. Instead, it is crucial to understand the actor's
own interpretation of its actions. As a "nation in arms," Israelis are
primed to keep their sword sharpened—yet in the self-perceived interests of coexistence and peace. Only when a military operation is deemed
by the polity to diverge from these aims can we expect an eventual policy
shift to occur. The next chapter investigates one such operation: the 1982
Israeli-PLO war in Lebanon. This war was the first of two pivotal events
in the 1980s that led Israelis to experience a psychic tension between
their role-identity as defensive warriors and their security ethic of fighting only wars of no alternative, on the one hand; and their policy
actions, on the other. The second event—Israel's response to the first
Palestinian Intifada—would occur five years later.

Chapter Five

Israel and the Lebanon War

With the Israeli occupation of the West Bank and Gaza Strip a decade and a half old, in June 1982 Israel launched a war in Lebanon against the PLO and Syria, officially named Operation Peace for Galilee and informally called the Lebanon War—and in the process created the most concerted break with the Israeli security ethic to date. While the 1973 Yom Kippur War had exposed popular dissatisfaction with the competence of the IDF intelligence branch, the 1982 foray into Lebanon led Israelis to question the moral stature of the defense establishment and certainly the ability for a single personality—Defense Minister Ariel Sharon—to engineer a military operation that would leave 654 Israeli soldiers dead and 3,859 wounded, as well as a raw cleavage in the national consensus. In its break with Israel's role-identity, the goals and execution of the war—including the massacre of hundreds of Palestinians at Sabra and Shatilla for which Israel was found to bear indirect responsibility—initiated Israel on a soul-searching course that exposed its unconscious fears of becoming a violent aggressor. This process would ultimately culminate in the 1993 Oslo agreement with the Palestinians—but not before the outbreak of the Intifada five years later.

In three ways, the Lebanon War broke with Israel's defensive-warrior role-identity. Unlike the wars of Israel's past, at least as understood by the Israeli establishment, the Lebanon War was an offensive operation launched on what many Israelis saw to be a flimsy pretext, and it lacked an existential threat to be countered. Prime Minister Menachem Begin even called it a "war of choice," something that obviously clashed with Israel's security mandate of fighting only "wars of no alternative." Second, it had as one of its goals the meddling in the domestic politics of a neighboring state, as Israel backed its pick for Lebanese president. Third, the prosecution of the war represented a breakdown in intra-parliamentary relations, such that Israelis would later accuse Sharon of twisting the collective arm of the cabinet and the prime minister in order to fulfill his own far-reaching aims for the fate of Israeli-Lebanese-PLO relations. The Sabra and Shatilla massacre was the capping episode in a war that fractured the national consensus, and raised questions about the justness of Israeli warmaking that had never been asked before. Of course, none of these three charges would be relevant were it not for large swaths of the Israeli polity viewing the war in these terms, and experiencing a collective disjuncture between Israel's national identity and the government's actions. The continuing occupation of the southern part of Lebanon, that would continue, in some form or another, until May 2000 (and which had actually begun in 1978 with Israel's "Operation Litani"), further underscored the dissonance between the IDF as a defensive security organ versus an occupation force on the soil of a foreign country.[1] Writing as early as 1984, one observer went so far as to argue, on the basis of the IDF's perceived role as a defensive force, that "[i]t is highly unlikely that the IDF will be asked to sustain a long-term presence in Lebanon."[2]

While it became clear that the Israeli cabinet and even the prime minister were not always aware of events as they were taking place, the fact that the war unfolded as it did still allowed for a collective repugnance calling for a judicial investigation (specifically into the events surrounding the Sabra and Shatilla massacre) and a collective measure of guilt. Thus, whereas some have written about the war's centrality in precipitating Israel's eventual move toward peace with the PLO in terms of showing Israelis the limits of the use of force,[3] I argue that that analysis, while not untrue, nevertheless is insufficient. Israel did come to realize that neither the PLO nor Palestinian nationalism could be demolished through sheer military power. However, this conclusion alone does not explain Israel's decision to engage the PLO in a process of peacemaking. The Israeli-Palestinian conflict itself had to be painful enough to justify the material and symbolic losses to Israel inherent in any peace agreement. Judged against the likely costs of a peace settlement—a Palestinian state, shared sovereignty over Jerusalem, and a limited right of return for Palestinian refugees—the postwar status quo was not intolerable in material terms. At the war's end, the PLO was exiled from Lebanon to Tunisia—far from Israel's borders. Whatever threat the Palestinians continued to pose was not existential; the Palestinians and the PLO did not threaten Israel's existence in any meaningfully strategic sense. What *was* intolerable, however, was the *psychic tension* that Israelis experienced between their state's aggressive actions and its defensive-warrior role-identity. However, it would take another significant event five years later, the Intifada, to elicit the cognitive dissonance spurred by the emergence of unconscious fears about what Israel was becoming versus what it wanted to be: in the Intifada, not only did Israelis see themselves acting aggressively, but they became starkly aware of their country's attempt at suppressing another nation's call for sovereignty.

THE WAR

The Lebanon War was grounded in multiple goals, almost all the brain-child of Sharon executed with the more limited knowledge of Begin and his cabinet. According to Sharon's reasoning, Israel needed to invade southern Lebanon in order to push the PLO back out of shooting range of Israel's settlements in the Galilee region. The PLO had been launching guerilla attacks over Israel's northern border intermittently since 1968, a pattern that increased after the Palestinian expulsion from Jordan in "Black September" of 1970. While the actual distance to achieve this—as stated in Cabinet meetings and even in a memo sent by Begin to U.S. President Reagan—was forty kilometers, Sharon envisioned going far beyond this, in the process driving out Palestinian guerillas as well as the Syrian army that had been stationed in Lebanon since President Hafiz al-Assad's invasion in 1976, and ultimately meeting up with the Lebanese Christian forces outside Beirut to strike at the heart of the city. To cap off the operation, Sharon hoped to throw Israel's weight behind his pick for Lebanese president, Christian Maronite leader Bashir Gemayel, to ensure a Lebanese regime friendly to Israel. Israeli elites hoped that with Gemayel at the helm, Lebanon would sign a peace treaty with Israel, becoming the second Arab country—after Egypt—to do so.

Within these calculations, the Israeli government all but ignored the Palestinians as an autonomous political factor. The Israeli government hoped that by neutralizing Lebanon and driving back the PLO guerillas, suitable arrangements could be eked out in the West Bank and Gaza, allowing Israel to continue the status quo of occupation in the territories while the Palestinians engaged in a nominal form of self-rule, the nature and extent of which were to be determined by Israel. If successful, this plan could be considered the nail in the coffin of two previous attempts at establishing limited autonomy for the Palestinians in the territories. First, a system known as the Village Leagues, which was begun in the late 1970s under the first Likud government, installed pockets of local Palestinian leadership loyal to Israel. According to Menahem Milson, head of the Civil Administration in the West Bank in the years leading up to the Lebanon War, and who is identified within Israeli circles as a proponent of the Village League experiments, Sharon "lost interest in the Leagues" due to the Lebanon War, which also prompted Milson to resign his post.[4]

Second, and of more consequence for the Israeli-Palestinian conflict, the 1978 Camp David accords called for Palestinian autonomy arrangements in the West Bank and Gaza. Two years before the Lebanon War, however, the Camp David follow-up talks between Egypt and Israel regarding the fate of the Palestinians foundered on an overly strict definition by the Begin government of the extent of Israel's withdrawal from the territories under the terms of UN Resolution 242 (Begin thought that withdrawing from the Sinai Peninsula and part of the Golan Heights was sufficient), as well as what should constitute self-rule: Begin insisted on a local, population-based concept, rather than a territorially sovereign view of Palestinian autonomy.[5] From this it was clear to many Israelis that, through the launching of the Lebanon War, Israel was attempting to solve the Palestinian problem through military means.

The outcome of the war revealed mixed success for Sharon's goals. Israel ousted the PLO from Lebanon to Tunisia—the 15,000-member Palestinian force was forced to depart under U.S. supervision at the end of August 1982. Bashir Gemayel was indeed elected president, but was assassinated not long after—on 14 September 1983. And while the Syrians took heavy blows from the IDF, they remain in Lebanon to this day—effectively ruling over the shell of a state still haunted by its fifteen-year civil war (1975–1990). As for the Palestinians, the war did nothing to formally entrench Israeli control over the occupied territories, and ultimately only fueled the fire of Palestinian dissatisfaction, an impulse that would finally erupt in the form of the Intifada in December 1987.

To reach the goals originally set out in Sharon's war plans, Israeli contacts with the Gemayel family and their Phalangist forces had extended as far back as the mid-1970s, soon after the Lebanese civil war had begun. Christian-Muslim tensions had been inflamed by the rise of PLO activity in the country's southern region, creating a pocket of shared interests between Israel and the Phalangists. In 1970, King Hussein expelled the PLO from Jordan in a bloody clash that became known as Black September. The Palestinians fled to Lebanon, joining the 250,000 Palestinians refugees who had been residing in camps throughout the country since 1948.[6] The PLO soon set up a "state within a state" within the country's southern strip, an area that became known as "Fatahland," named for Arafat's wing of the PLO. Once the Lebanese civil war between the Christians and Muslims broke out in 1975, the PLO was able to step up its guerilla attacks into northern Israel, a pattern that led to Israel's launching of Operation Litani in March 1978.

There, Israel succeeded in establishing a "security zone" in southern Lebanon, three to five kilometers from the border. The IDF remained in that area for six months, until it was replaced by UNIFIL (the United Nations Interim Force in Lebanon). In July 1981, U.S. special envoy Philip Habib brokered an Israeli-PLO cease-fire. This represented the first negotiated settlement between Israel and the PLO, a precedent-setting event that would not be lost on the Israeli peace movement.

The actual trigger for the Israeli invasion of 6 June 1982, though, was the attempted assassination of the Israeli ambassador to London, Shlomo Argov, on the night of June 3; Argov was gravely wounded, but survived. It soon became clear to Israeli intelligence that the Palestinian Abu Nidal group, rather than the PLO, was behind the attack, and indeed Arafat disclaimed all responsibility on his organization's behalf.[7] Nevertheless, Begin "dismissed the information, saying, 'Abu Nidal, Abu Shmidal....They're all PLO.'"[8] Prior to this, there had been an exchange of shelling along the Israeli-Lebanese border. However, since the signing of the 1981 Israeli-PLO ceasefire, the PLO had "shown considerable restraint."[9] Even after the IDF had launched an air raid over PLO strongholds, followed by indirect shelling by the PLO into Israel in May 1982, Arafat declared to Begin, "You of all people must understand that it is not necessary to face me on the battlefield," and he implored him not to "send a military force against me."[10]

As early as 20 December 1981, Begin and Sharon, assisted by Chief of Staff Rafael Eitan, had attempted to woo the cabinet toward authorizing a full-scale invasion, presenting the ministers with a plan code-named Operation Big Pines. The operation would entail an all-out war against the PLO in Lebanon in order to reach the Beirut-Damascus highway and stop short of Beirut, but with the possibility of landing at the port of Juneih, north of the capital. The cabinet was stunned by the radicalness of the idea, and, in reaction to the vehement opposition by a number of cabinet ministers, Begin shelved the proposal. The war that Israel eventually launched in June 1982 was known to cabinet members as Operation Small Pines; although, through a series of *faits accomplis*, Sharon would ultimately push ahead with his initial plan. Tellingly, "Operational Small Pines" would become a phrase known only in military-history circles because the official name the Israeli government gave to the war was "Operation Peace for Galilee." Yossi Beilin, at the time deputy foreign minister, would later refer to the war's official name as "the most cynical use of the peace myth" by a leader of Israel throughout the country's history.[11]

The actual cabinet decision to invade Lebanon was taken on June 5—two days after the assassination attempt in London. In Begin's

words, the IDF was being charged "with taking all the northern settlements out of the range of fire of the terrorists concentrated...in
Lebanon," and that "in the course of implementing this decision, the
Syrian Army is not to be attacked unless it fires on our forces."[12] The
eventual war included a direct confrontation with Syria and a seven-
week siege on Beirut. During the war's initial stages, the Syrians too had
shown restraint. They had not sent reinforcements into the Golan
Heights, despite Israel's beefing up of its own presence there, and did
not initially send additional troops and materiel into the Bekaa valley.[13]
Nevertheless, the IDF ultimately attacked the Syrian forces on 8 June,
despite the fact that at that moment, in an address to the Knesset echoing
his own words three days earlier, Begin pledged that the IDF would not
attack Syria if the latter did not strike first. "We do not want war with
Syria. From this podium I call on President Asad to instruct the Syrian
army not to attack Israel's soldiers."[14] The actual Israeli siege of Beirut
began on 12 June and was led by Sharon and Eitan, without Begin's initial approval.[15] The siege involved cutting off the city's electricity and
water supplies, a move that not even Labor opposition member Yitzhak
Rabin objected to.[16] This hawkish stance would be echoed half a decade
later by Rabin's call to "break the bones" of the Palestinian protesters
during the Intifada.

One of the main criticisms of the war to emerge as the events
became clear to the public and policymakers alike was the lack of consensus even within the cabinet itself for how, precisely, the war should
be prosecuted. The most cutting critique is encapsulated in Shimon
Peres's description of the war, as contrasted with the 1956 Sinai
Campaign: "In 1956, [Defense Minister] Moshe Dayan had translated
[Prime Minister] Ben-Gurion's political policies into the language of a
military campaign against Egypt. In 1982, Sharon, in effect, demanded
that Begin do the opposite: that he translate Sharon's own military
designs into a political doctrine."[17] This perceived role reversal by the
defense minister vis-à-vis the head of state was reinforced by the perception that Sharon was acting in concert with Eitan to deceive the government. Ten years later, in the lead-up to the Oslo accords, this view had
not vanished from public memory. In a 1992 interview with Army
Radio, Eitan was still proclaiming his innocence against accusations that
he had attempted to mislead the prime minister.[18] Against Eitan's pleas,
one scholar has claimed that Eitan "openly admits that...in most cases
he [did] not correct one-sided information and biased impressions given
by Sharon" to Begin during the war.[19]

A related dynamic to that of civil-military relations in the war-fighting process is that of the relationship between tactics and strategy, as

well as between military strategy and political outcomes. Former Chief of Military Intelligence Yehoshafat Harkabi has pointed to the reversal of the proper relationship between these two sets of concepts in the case of the Lebanon War, charging that Sharon and Eitan set out to "'tacticize' strategy." In the process, the war failed to lead to two of their main goals: the establishment of a friendly, Christian regime in Lebanon, and the ousting of Syria from the country. These objectives, Harkabi insists, were "impossibly grandiose" and "mutually inconsistent" (the latter because installing a Christian regime would have fueled tensions between the confessional groups within the already precarious consociational parliamentary system, thereby preventing domestic stability).[20] Given the widely perceived strategic failure of the war, coupled with an exhausting three-year initial occupation of southern Lebanon immediately followed by a fifteen-year continuation of it in the form of the "security zone," Israelis were primed to reject the war in its totality—as an aggressive operation in which political goals did not suit military means. In the words of *The Jerusalem Post*'s military correspondent at the time, Israel behaved like a "bull in a china shop."[21] The dissatisfaction on the part of the Israeli public would come to a head, however, with the horrific events in September 1983 at Sabra and Shatilla, thus bringing to the fore unconscious counternarratives that elicited a widespread cognitive dissonance between the IDF's actions in the war and the polity's view of itself as a defensive-warrior fighting only "wars of no alternative" under the ethic of "purity of arms."

SABRA AND SHATILLA

While the missions of the war itself clashed with Israel's role-identity, bringing to light a *jus ad bellum* concern, the Sabra and Shatilla massacre—in representing the *jus in bello* dimension of just war theory— most strongly brought to the fore unconscious fears of adopting the role of the Jewish people's most hated victimizers. While other Arab-Israeli wars, namely, the 1956 Sinai Campaign, had been criticized by segments of the international community as representing revisionist attempts at forging a new status quo, the Lebanon War contained the first widespread realization—by others as well as by Israelis themselves—that the IDF's arms had been less than pure, at least by implication.

As the war was winding down in September 1982, the Phalangist forces (archenemies of the Palestinians and Muslims in Lebanon more generally), under the supervision of the IDF, were sent into the two refugee camps to conduct a mopping-up operation of the remaining

Palestinian militants. The Israeli leadership was keenly aware that by involving itself in this final bit of close-quarters battle with PLO fighters under the cover of civilian refugee camps, its image could be tarnished. Thus, as IDF Order Number 6, issued on September 16, stated, "The refugee camps are not to be entered [by the IDF]. Searching and mopping up the camps will be done by the Phalangists/Lebanese Army."[22]

On the evening of 16 September, 150 Phalangist soldiers entered the camps, aided by mortar illumination supplied by the IDF. IDF Brigadier General Yaron had warned the Phalangist commanders "not to harm the civilian population." Yaron later testified to the Kahan Commission that he "knew that the Phalangists' norms of conduct are not like those of the IDF and he had had arguments with the Phalangists over this issue in the past,"[23] a revealing indication of how the IDF perceived itself in the context of other militaries, particularly those of its neighbors in the Middle East. (Further comparisons between Israel and other, disdained, regimes—including Syria and South Africa—would be evident in the context of the Intifada, as Israeli elites questioned their state's behavior in the context of Israel's role-identity.) The events that transpired over the next thirty-six hours confirmed that while Israeli forces were not directly involved in the massacre, senior IDF officers received scattered indications that something unsavory was taking place, and did not ultimately intervene as they could have. One Israeli soldier overheard a Phalangist officer asking his commander (Elie Hobeika) over the radio what he should do with a group of fifty women and children whom he faced in the camps. Hobeika replied, "This is the last time you're going to ask me a question like that, you know exactly what to do." The officer who overheard this conversation, Lieutenant Elul, reported it to his superior, who then talked directly to Hobeika.[24]

Once the news was out that 700–800 Palestinians, including women and children, had been massacred, and that the Israeli public as well as the court of international opinion were questioning the integrity of Israel's army and its leadership, the Cabinet went on the defensive.[25] A September 19 government resolution stated that accusations of responsibility against the State of Israel were akin to "a blood libel against the Jewish state and its Government." It continued, "No one will preach to us moral values or respect for human life, on whose basis we were educated and will continue to educate generations of fighters in Israel."[26] Not only was the government concerned with absolving itself of responsibility, but it took pains to entrench its position as the leader of a state guided by moral considerations. The significance of the blood libel metaphor was not lost on the Israeli public that had centuries of religious persecution etched on its collective memory. Blood libels had emerged from medieval folklore, and became an unhappy staple of European Jewish life from the twelfth through the nineteenth centuries. In these two hundred documented cases, Jews were accused of killing Christians (often children) to use their blood in the baking of the ritual Passover *matzah* (unleavened bread).[27] It is these centuries of fending off false accusations of murdering hapless Christians that have helped to form Israel's unconscious fears of becoming a vicious aggressor, such that when they saw their actions as aggressive, the polity experienced the cognitive dissonance necessary to embark on a radically different policy course concerning its most intimate adversary.

In a speech to the Knesset a few days before the government resolved to establish a commission of inquiry into the massacre, Sharon emphasized the lack of culpability of his government in being less than truthful about events: "Nobody here is trying to hide anything. Our Government, like all our people, is sensitive to acts of terror, *more so than any other government or any other people* in the world."[28] In so stating, Sharon was emphasizing Israel's role-identity in contrast to the perceived roles of other states in Israel's regional environment. It is thus clear that the role-identity elaborated here is not only espoused by the left wing, but is celebrated across the sphere of Israeli leadership. Moreover, so intrinsic is the idea of fighting only "defensive" wars, that, despite the highest rate of conscientious objection ever before seen in Israel's history and the largest protest rallies to be launched by the Israeli peace movement, Sharon went so far as to call the Lebanon War a "war of defense."[29] As we will see, this inversion of the defensive-offensive logic was mirrored, in a slightly different form, by Begin.

In a parliamentary speech on the same day, then-Labor Party leader Shimon Peres attempted to counter the Likud position directly, in his declaration that "[w]e all confront this abominable act, which the rabbis said is the absolute antithesis of the traditions of Judaism...from all classes is heard a painful cry of disapproval. But the Prime Minister and the Defense Minister were struck dumb....The fate of Israel, David Ben-Gurion said, is dependent on its strength and its righteousness. Righteousness, not just strength, have to guide our deeds."[30] Here, Peres was implicitly calling to mind the importance of adhering to Israel's security ethic, the set of normative guidelines that interact with strategic considerations to place limits on how force ought to be used.

The government's attempt to shun discussion about Israel's role in the massacre was short-lived, however, as the Israeli public forced its country to stand the trial of self-scrutiny. Peace Now held a rally in Tel Aviv on 25 September to demand a state-led inquiry into the massacre. The event attracted 400,000 protestors, and marked the first time that members of the Labor Party (in this case Rabin and Peres) participated in a Peace Now rally in an official capacity.[31] The event would go down in the annals of the peace movement's self-regarded successes in mobilizing fully ten percent of Israel's Jewish population to protest the excessive use of force (in this case, in complicity rather than directly) by the IDF. The massacre had elicited widespread revulsion among the Israeli left; one Peace Now spokeswoman later would refer to the massacre as a "pogrom,"[32] drawing on the discourse of nineteenth-century persecution of Jews in Eastern Europe, and in turn associating Israeli actions with those of its victimizers. Perhaps more strikingly, the world-renowned Nazi-hunter Simon Wiesenthal, speaking from Vienna, declared that "Jews could not demand trials of Nazis suspected of murdering millions of fellow Jews in the Second World War and then not expect the criminals in Lebanon to be tried."[33] Not surprisingly, Israelis have tended to loathe comparisons between their actions (or those they are associated with) and the Holocaust. The fact that Wiesenthal, a prominent symbol of Holocaust victimhood and survival, chose to make such a comparison is telling. Even prominent Israeli social critics typically associated with the right, such as Yaakov Kirschen, creator of *The Jerusalem Post*'s satirical comic strip "Dry Bones," were quick to denounce Israel's role in the massacre. The day of Peace Now's rally, his cartoon read:

> When terrorists attacked from Syria, we blame the Syrians. When murderous infiltrators slipped in from Lebanon, we blamed the Lebanese.... When fedayeen goons came in from Egypt, we blamed the Egyptians. But when we send a bloodthirsty gang into a refugee camp, we blame everyone in the world except for ourselves. Whether it was omission or commission, we have got something to atone for this Yom Kippur.[34]

In response, three days after the rally, the Cabinet begrudgingly resolved to establish a commission of inquiry to investigate the events surrounding the massacre. In the course of its deliberations, the commission, presided over by Justice Yitzhak Kahan, met sixty times and interviewed fifty-eight witnesses before issuing its report on 7 February 1983. While Israel was not found to be *directly* responsible for the killings, the Kahan Commission's report emphasized the need to attribute *indirect* responsibility as well. In defending its mandate for pursuing judgments of indirect responsibility, the Commission stated:

> it should also not be forgotten that the Jews in various lands of exile, and also in the Land of Israel when it was under foreign

> rule, suffered greatly from pogroms... and the danger of disturbances against Jews in various lands... has not yet passed. The Jewish public's stand has always been that the responsibility for such deeds falls not only on those who rioted and committed the atrocities, but also on those...who could have prevented the disturbances.[35]

Here, even the highest institutions of the state were drawing on the Jewish historical memory of victimhood in the service of self-critique. It seems that only a state experiencing a collective emotional conflict between aggressive policy actions and a defensive role-identity would allow itself the liberty of calling on its weaker past (and indeed, the current threat to some members of its extended national collective, as suggested in the previous statement) in order to sanction its present actions. In the context of invoking historical narratives of victimization, the unconscious fears of becoming victimizers were all the more apparent.

Abba Eban of the Labor Party, former Israeli foreign minister, and at the time of the commission's report, opposition spokesman on foreign affairs in the Knesset, invoked a similar sentiment to that of the commission. In defending the decision to order an investigation, Eban asked,

> Were the Israeli soldiers in the vicinity merely by chance or were they, inconceivably, in liaison or contact with the Phalangists or even in some posture of command? The question gnawed at the very roots of Israel's conscience, and within a few days it was plain that *without some great cathartic release* the question would have a stifling effect. *Israeli life simply could not go on unless the release was sought.*[36]

The release that Eban cogently identified would come in the form of Israel's decision to abandon an attempt at solving the Palestinian problem by force, and instead embark on the Oslo process. Eban elaborates: "at the center of Israel's *image of itself* stands the Israel Defense Forces as the exemplar of those virtues that have not been swamped by the ethos of a pragmatic, modern, consumer society—the bright memory of ancient valor and modern sacrifice."[37] Once Israeli elites had identified Israel's actions in the Lebanon war as clashing with the state's defensive-warrior role-identity, a radical policy shift had to emerge to stave off the unconscious fears of becoming an aggressor.

The commission found that, in terms of indirect responsibility, a number of senior military and political personnel, including the prime minister, foreign minister, head of the Mossad, minister of defense, chief of staff, as well as three other senior military officers were in breach of the ethical code guiding Israel and its defense forces.[38] The commission declared that Minister of Defense Sharon "bears personal responsibility," and advised Begin to "consider whether he should exercise his authority under Section 21-A(a) of the Basic Law of the Government, according to which 'the Prime Minister may, after informing the Cabinet of his intention to do so, remove a minister from office.'"[39] Sharon ultimately resigned as defense minister in February 1983, but Begin kept him on as minister without portfolio. Since his term was nearing completion, Chief of Staff Eitan was permitted to sit out the period without renewal. Begin resigned in September 1983, and ended up secluding himself in his home under an evident depression, likely fueled by the death of his wife a year earlier, until his death in 1992. While Begin merely told government colleagues that "I can go on no longer," interviews around the time of his death indicated that the Lebanon War, and particularly the Israeli casualties, also spurred his decision. As his close friend Ya'acov Meridor told Army Radio in 1992, "I asked Begin in 1983 why he decided to step down. He told me, 'I could not face the daily anti-war vigils outside my home in Jerusalem,'"[40] a reference to the protests mounted across from the prime minister's residence in which activists held aloft placards tallying the mounting IDF casualties.

BEGIN'S NARRATIVE

While Sharon harbored particular policy goals and pursued corresponding strategies to achieve them, and while the war did not unfold in a way that represented coordinated planning at the cabinet level, the war's launching would not have been possible without a similar worldview held by Begin. A Holocaust survivor who lost his parents and older brother at the hands of the Nazis, Begin represented the Israeli narrative put forth by Jabotinsky's Revisionists. As discussed in chapter three, Revisionist Zionism existed uneasily alongside the dominant Zionist narrative that espoused the practice of restraint. By contrast, Revisionism advocated the use of unabashed force in securing the integrity of the Jewish state within a sea of hostile Arab neighbors. All this was to be enacted against a conception of Jewish particularism ("chosenness") and perennial isolation, with the underlying belief, drawn from the Old Testament, that the people of Israel represents a "nation that dwells alone." The Lebanon War in part reflected this understanding of Israel's place in the community of nations. As Begin reportedly said to U.S. Senator Daniel Patrick Moynihan during the Lebanon War, "I am a proud Jew. Three thousand years of culture are behind me, and you will not frighten me with threats."[41]

Intriguingly, Begin went so far as to defend the war by actually call-ing it a "war of choice." In a much-cited speech in August 1982 to the Staff and Command College, Begin stated that "there is no precept to fight only wars of no choice.... To the contrary, a free nation, which hates war, loves peace, and cares for its security must create conditions in which the choice will remain in its hands. And if a war must be waged, it should not be a war of last resort."[42] Begin's inversion of the "no-alternative" logic conveyed the idea that only by attacking first could Israel guarantee its own security: both for the short-term protec-tion of Israel's northern border by wiping out the PLO forces in Lebanon; and for Israel's long-term security interests through an even-tual peace agreement with the new Christian regime in Lebanon. While critics faulted Begin for altering "no-alternative" discourse to the point of meaninglessness, on closer inspection, it was an idea not wholly for-eign to the defense establishment. Similarly, Efraim Inbar points out that the distinction between a "no-choice war" and a "war of choice" is mis-leading. Decision-makers always have options other than attacking (or counterattacking, as the case may be), including passivity and surren-der.[43] So too is the distinction between preemptive/preventive war and aggression a slippery one. As Major General Yeshayahu Gavish noted about the Six Day War, "Our only 'choice' was to wait until they attacked. If we were to let ourselves come under surprise attack, we'd have to pay a great price. Thus, we had to attack first."[44] Transferring the battle to enemy territory once a war has begun, as well as conducting preemptive and even preventive strikes, have come to be the hallmark of Israel's military doctrine. Within Israeli discourse, neither preemptive nor preventive measures are considered to be outside the bounds of the security ethic, although many non-Israelis have viewed the 1956 Sinai Campaign (a preventive war that involved colluding with France and Britain) as ethically dubious.

Scholars of military affairs have agreed on a rough distinction between preemptive and preventive war (the former to address an imminent threat; the latter to destroy an enemy's potential war-fighting capabilities). Policymakers like Begin tend to view a threat that might be months or even years away as still within the sphere of "imminence," not because their temporal assessments are any different, but because their comfort zone relative to the expected time frame of threat is nar-rower. There are many explanations for this variance across decision-makers. This is not the forum to explore these systematically, but certainly Begin's personal history involving the Holocaust likely forms part of the story. On the collective level, the Israelis—both Labor and Likud strands—wanted to compensate for the victimization that had characterized Jewish history throughout the centuries. In addition,

Israel's geographic circumstances—a narrow coastal waistband with no hinterland—necessitate at least the rapid transfer of battle to enemy territory and at most a preventive strike. However, the Lebanon War, fought as it was in a northerly direction, did not threaten the central coast to the extent that it was endangered in the 1967 and 1973 wars.

Neither did Begin hesitate to exploit Holocaust imagery in promoting his policies, no less during the war. One popular joke during the period was that "we [Israelis] have no more blood left in our veins because Begin has spilled it all in his speeches."[45] Indeed, some observers have argued that the Holocaust was one of the themes that ushered Begin's Likud party into victory in the 1977 elections, after almost two decades of Labor rule; this victory was repeated in 1981, against the Labor Alignment led by Shimon Peres. Given that Israelis viewed the leaders of the Yishuv as not doing everything in their power to aid Holocaust victims, and given the experiencing of the 1967 and 1973 wars, both of which Israel faced as a vulnerable state, the Israeli public was ready for a political platform that overturned the Israeli establishment and spit in the face of perceived Arab aggression.[46] These themes, coupled with a policy of greater inclusion vis-à-vis Israel's historically underrepresented Sephardi population, helped to propel the Likud into power under Begin's leadership. The 1977 elections represented the first time that Labor (then called the Alignment) did not form the government, an outcome that became known as the "upheaval."[47] Moreover, the narrative that the Likud espoused and that a plurality of Israeli citizens endorsed was different from that of Labor. As discussed in chapter three, Jabotinsky's views certainly formed a part of the pallet of Israeli narratives; however, the main voice that had prevailed during the crucial first three decades of the state's existence, and that would subsequently be reinstated in the 1992 elections, was one that rejected the idea that Israel "is a nation that dwells alone" in favor of the view that Israel is a "nation like all others." The warmer relations that Labor's Rabin enjoyed with the United States compared to Likud leader Shamir's mistrust of the White House is an example of this. The idea of "chosenness" and the ethnocentrism that that implied was correspondingly muted by this view.

Thus, one way to situate the Lebanon War and the philosophy that it represented in the context of Israel's eventual policy shift toward the PLO was that while the 1977 and 1981 elections represented a break from the dominant voice, the 1992 elections—held after the Lebanon War had shattered the national consensus and after the Intifada had raged for almost five years—represented a return to the views of the state's founders. It was the closer identification by voters and the elite

with these narratives that in part represented the experiencing of a dissonance between policy and self-image, and the need to realign the two.[48]
Similarly, one observer has argued that holding the June 1992 elections
around the tenth anniversary of the Lebanon War was one of the factors
precipitating a rejection of the Likud in favor of Labor.[49]

REACTIONS BY GOVERNMENT OPPOSITION
AND THE PEACE MOVEMENT

The initial stage of the war saw a broad national consensus, as even the
Labor opposition lent its support. Defending the northern settlements
from attack was an apparently justifiable aim to shell-weary Israelis, 93
percent of whom, in a late June poll, considered the war justified.[50]
However, once the government expanded the operation to support
Gemayel's presidential bid, widespread dissent took hold. By October
1982, only 45 percent supported the war, and by December, only 34 percent did.[51] It had become clear to many that while the moral stature (particularly according to the right-wing view of the Zionist Revisionist
camp) of the operation may have been on Israel's side, the government
was not taking all necessary steps to avoid a costly war. As Begin reportedly said to his colleagues in the lead-up to the war, "Ben-Gurion used
to say that if you're *pursuing a policy that may lead to war*, it's vital to
have a great power behind you."[52] Israel had a strong tradition of "rally-
ing 'round the flag" in wartime, a trend that would make the controversy over the Lebanon War pivotal in bringing unconscious
counternarratives to the fore.

Although there had been some doves in Labor all along, notably the
younger generation led by Yossi Beilin (who would later pioneer the
Oslo talks as deputy foreign minister under Peres), and who viewed the
Lebanon War as a "disaster" from the outset, the Labor opposition generally supported the war's initial limited aims while condemning the
war's expansion, particularly the shelling of Beirut. Of the outright critics of the war, Yossi Sarid was the most prominent; he would later
become a pivotal member of the Meretz peace bloc that would join the
Labor-led government in 1992. Of the more mainstream Laborites who
criticized the war in a more limited way were Peres and Rabin. Finally, a
hawkish contingent within Labor supported the war much more forth-
rightly; these members, however, would eventually fade from public
view.[53] Much later, Beilin would reflect on the linkage between Israeli
nationalism and the IDF's foray into Lebanon: "The war was totally
unnecessary. There had been a cease-fire....Israel triggered the war.

Plus, the Israeli involvement with the Lebanese regime was lunatic."[54] Years later, Peres would reiterate his opposition to the war. "It was a war of *breira* (choice); this is something we were always against. If you have a choice, don't make war."[55] And when asked about the possible similarities between the Lebanon War and the American involvement in Vietnam, Peres was not loathe to compare the two events: "I don't like comparisons, because every event is an event in its own right. But if you mean that they were both 'bad wars,' then yes, the comparison holds."[56] In retrospect, Peres condemned the war for the effect it had on the Israeli psyche: "Israel's Lebanon War, which dragged on with a bloody and pointless occupation for nearly three years, gravely weakened the discipline and moral cohesion of Israeli society, because our soldiers did not know why they were fighting or what they were dying for."[57]

While not all Labor members, including Rabin and Peres, were as forthcoming in their criticism of the war at the time as were others, including Peace Now and segments of the IDF itself, the war would become an election issue a decade later. In the lead-up to the 1992 race, Meretz spokesman Yossi Sarid would condemn the war as a "wasteful, stupid and bloody chapter in our history that was aimed more at scaling down the Palestinians as a political entity than ensuring security for the north of Israel."[58] Similarly, Rabin would use his role in facilitating the withdrawal of troops from Lebanon as campaign fodder against the Likud during the 1992 elections.[59] Already in 1984, before the Israeli withdrawal to the eventual security zone that would remain in place until 2000, Rabin was condemning the Lebanon War as being "a war in the wrong place, at the wrong time and—with regard to the true problems of the Arab-Israel conflict—over the wrong issue." Rabin went on to add that "[i]n this sense, what happened to Israel in 1982 is no different from what happened to Syria in 1976,"[60] a reference to Syria's invasion of Lebanon. Since it was the mainstream of the Labor Party that eventually took the decision to move toward peace with the PLO, we can conclude that not only those with an outright dovish attitude are the ones who can propel a state toward a policy shift.

This break in the parliamentary consensus corresponded with the rise of multiple channels of protest, including preexisting peace groups and those created to protest the Lebanon War. Only two weeks into the military campaign, Peace Now took out a newspaper advertisement asking, "Why are we killing and being killed in Lebanon?"[61] On 26 June, the newly formed Committee for the War in Lebanon, which had evolved out of the Committee for Solidarity with Bir Zeit University, drew a crowd of 20,000 to their antiwar demonstration.[62] Soon after, on 4 July, Peace Now organized a rally drawing 100,000,[63] a considerable

size, though not as large as what would come in the aftermath of the
Sabra and Shatilla massacres two and a half months later. Nevertheless,
compared to the far left, Peace Now was slow to react. Writes movement
leader Tzaly Reshef years later, "We were torn between our patriotism
and our consciences, between a sense of loyalty to our comrades on the
front and a sense of historical responsibility to do 'the right thing.' "[64] In
addition to the newspaper advertisement campaign of 16 June and sporadic rallies, Peace Now sent letters to government ministers urging
them not to invade Beirut. The group also protested outside of the prime
minister's office with placards indicating the rising number of Israeli soldiers killed—the vigil that would in part lead to Begin's resignation, as
he himself would tell it. Ultimately, Peace Now viewed the war as being
outside the bounds of Israel's security ethic; years later, activists would
go so far as to affirm the justice of all of Israel's wars hitherto fought,
singling out the Lebanon War as a "war of aggression."[65]

It was this sort of attitude that drove home the idea that the mainstream Israeli peace movement was not one to advocate pacifism as an
intrinsic value, and thus was considered to operate within the bounds of
legitimate national security discourse. Another Peace Now activist and
former IDF chief educational officer described the war as one of
"choice" in his assessment that "we were not faced with military
threats."[66] Given the government's attempt to situate the war as a defensive measure against the shelling of the northern settlements, that an
army officer would go so far as to say that Israel was not threatened—
whether or not one agreed with the means used in Lebanon to expel the
PLO—suggests that the war was not serving a defensive purpose. The
words of Member of Knesset Naomi Chazan, of the left-wing Meretz
Party, supports this view of military force being acceptable within certain limits—the perspective that supposedly guides the IDF. "[The]
Lebanon [War] broke the consensus over the use of the IDF. I'm a
super-dove, but not a pacifist. The IDF should do what it's supposed to
do: defend Israel, not be used for political purposes."[67]

THE IDF

Short of the radical stance of conscientious objection (discussed later),
the soldiers in the field were faced with the difficult task of fighting a
war whose aims were neither always entirely clear to them, nor were
they wholeheartedly supported by the general public. Recalls Colonel
(Ret.) Yeshayahu Tadmor, "[During the Lebanon war,] I was in
reserves, and was sent, along with the author S. Yizhar...as

Information Officers. Our task was to meet with companies of soldiers and talk to them about the war...to make sure they acted in a humanitarian way, and to emphasize the need to have a moral fighting stance."[68] In that senior members of the IDF clearly felt the need to behave morally in the midst of war, later events, such as the army's complicity in Sabra and Shatilla, would propel the Israeli military and political leadership on a course of soul-searching.

While the early weeks of the war led to political quiescence among recruits, early July saw the first organized protest group emerging from the IDF. These soldiers returned from the front and set up a continuing vigil outside the prime minister's office, under the name "Soldiers against Silence." While they condemned the war and called for Sharon's resignation, the group stopped short of advocating refusal.[69] Yet the act of soldiers protesting a war in progress was unheard of in Israeli history.

Like the Intifada five years later, the Lebanon War saw soldiers subvert popular symbols to convey resentment toward the defense establishment and resignation to a fate they saw as unavoidable. In a satirization of a children's folk song ("Come down to us, airplane / And take us to the sky. / We'll soar up / To top of the trees / And will be / Like birds"), soldiers sang, "Come down to us, airplane / And take us to Lebanon. / We'll fight / For Sharon / And we'll come back / In a coffin."[70] As Yael Zerubavel notes, Arab-Israeli wars, particularly in the first few decades of the state, generated a plethora of commemorative poetry and folk songs. For the Lebanon War to spawn songs such as the one above, as well as "When we'll die / They will scrape us / With a scraping knife / Off the tanks' walls. / There are pieces there / Of burnt flesh / In the colors of / Red and black" indicate a strikingly different collective dynamic at play during the 1980s.[71] At the time of Israeli independence, folk poetry was celebratory and hopeful, even when addressing the theme of death in combat. In "The Silver Platter," Natan Alterman's oft-quoted 1947 poem whose refrain is featured in the Palmach museum in Tel Aviv, two youths approach a faceless crowd:

> Tired, oh so tired, forsworn of rest / And oozing sap of young Hebrewness—/ Silently the two approached / And stood there unmoving. / There was no saying whether they were alive or shot. / Then the nation, tear-rinsed and spellbound, asked, / Saying: Who are you? And the two soughed / Their reply: We are the silver platter / On which the Jewish State has been given you. / They spoke. Then enveloped in shadow at the people's feet they fell. / The rest will be told in the annals of Israel.[72]

The idea behind the IDF in the early years of the state was that, however sad, spilled blood was the necessary mortar by which the bricks of the state would be bound. IDF soldiers were seen as selflessly giving of themselves for the sake of Israeli progeny. The general feeling among Israel's senior military establishment was therefore that the Lebanon War clashed with Israel's security mandate. As Major General (Ret.) Yeshayahu Gavish (CO Southern Command during the Six Day War) said, "The Six Day War was an existential war. It was a real threat, as was 1948. It was a war of *ayn breirah* [no choice]. The Lebanon War, on the other hand, was a war of choice."[73] So too would later-IDF Chief of Staff Amnon Lipkin-Shahak describe the war, saying that it "led to a national debate; it was a war of *'yesh breira'* ("there is a choice")."[74] Ultimately, in defending a more nuanced policy of dealing with Palestinian stone-throwers, Dan Shomron, the IDF Chief of Staff during the Intifada, would declare, "After the 1982 Lebanon War, and all the domestic controversy it aroused, we could not get enough candidates to fill up our officers courses. We managed to keep the army intact and united despite controversy. It was no mean achievement. And we need to ensure solidarity for the future."[75] The discomfort experienced by the military and society with the war's aims would later be critiqued by a senior member of Israel's defense establishment who charged that "since the shock of the Yom Kippur War...every set of top brass in government and military circles has done its utmost to delegitimize war. The Lebanon War was called Operation Peace for Galilee and the [i]ntifada is called civil disturbances. The army and the politicians seem to have agreed to avoid seeking decisive outcomes."[76] While this critique emanates from someone advocating the *further* use of force, it is instructive that the Lebanon War is recalled in the same breath as the Intifada, as examples of hesitation on the part of decision-makers.

Neither were parents of soldiers wholeheartedly supportive of the war. As the battles continued, some actively protested an operation they deemed unjust. One such group, Parents Against Silence, was formed in July 1982 and served as a platform to condemn the war. Though its members did not advocate refusal, the group held demonstrations and vigils outside of the prime minister's office and the Ministry of Defense. One of the founders, Naomi Bentsur, recalled her motivation: "This was not like previous wars Israel had to fight. I called a few of my friends whose children were also in Lebanon and we decided to protest. We remembered the dictum 'When truth is silent, silence is a lie,' and decided to call our group 'Parents against Silence.'"[77] A father of a soldier killed during the war sent an open letter to the press in July 1982 asking the premier, "How many years would it have taken the Palestinian terrorists to kill or injure as many Israeli soldiers as [the government] did in the course of one week of this damnable war?"[78] (Palestinian guerillas killed 250 Israelis and wounded over 1,500 between

1971 and 1982.)[79] Years later, and just prior to Israel's pursuit of peace with the PLO, a mother of a fallen soldier petitioned the Israeli High Court to have the words "Operation Peace for Galilee" erased from her son's headstone. Hours before the court's ruling, the Defense Ministry relented, agreeing to the phrasing "fell in Lebanon." (Spiegel had wanted the words "Lebanon War" to be used; the Defense Ministry refused.)[80] Beginning with the Lebanon War and culminating with the Intifada, Israeli elites began to experience a collective sense of discomfort generated by the clash between their state's policy actions and its role-identity. Acquiescing to the grieving mother's request indicates that elites were confirming a view of that war as falling outside the bounds of Israel's security ethic.

Conscientious Objection

Perhaps most dramatic was the rise of conscientious objection, hitherto virtually unheard of in Israel.[81] Even the Israeli peace movement, while visible and active (particularly since the late 1970s), has rejected pacifism in and of itself. During the Lebanon War, selective refusal claims were not based on antiwar sentiment, but from a belief that this particular war clashed with Israel's role-identity. Given that the IDF's defensive ethic has been drilled into generations of soldiers, those called to Lebanon were able to contrast the apparent war aims with the stated IDF maxim of fighting only wars of "no alternative." As one analyst has written, reservists during the Lebanon War "gradually and painfully realized, in their words, that they belong to the Israeli *attacking* forces. Since they had never pledged their commitment to this army, refusal was possible."[82]

The organization at the helm was Yesh Gvul ("there is a border/limit"), founded a few years prior to the war to oppose the occupation in the West Bank and Gaza, and which would see a continuation of activity during the Intifada. While Peace Now was careful to distance itself from military refusal, preferring to ally itself close to the mainstream at the same time that it protested the goals of the war, it nevertheless refrained from condemning the objectors' movement: "Yesh Gvul is not our rival. In many ways they are a piece of our flesh and bones. Sharon and Begin have to be blamed for creating the circumstances which have pushed some people to feel that they have reached the limit.... But... as a collective, Peace Now is not ready to adopt disobedience as its official line."[83] During the summer of 1982, Yesh Gvul focused primarily on extending material and moral support to objectors in the Lebanon War. In July 1982 the movement sent a letter to the prime minister and defense minister, declaring, "We took an oath to defend the security and the welfare of the state of Israel. We are faithful to that oath. Therefore, we request you [*sic*] to permit us to perform our reserve duty within the borders of the state of Israel and not on the soil of Lebanon."[84] By the end of August, Yesh Gvul had collected over 250 signatures; by 1983, over forty reservists had been imprisoned for refusal, and by the war's end, 143 soldiers had refused to serve. Prison sentences varied from fourteen to thirty-five days,[85] and one-fifth of those jailed were officers.[86] Insiders estimate that more than 143 soldiers actually refused, since there were likely many cases of would-be refuseniks who were simply reassigned within their unit.[87] In the case of reservists, relationships between soldiers and their commanders had been entrenched over many years. This could lead to a scenario whereby a commander would accommodate a would-be objector by repositioning him, or perhaps where the soldier would be swayed by a sense of loyalty to his unit.

The most publicized case of objection during the war was that of Colonel Eli Geva. A member of the IDF elite, Geva was an enlisted officer and an armored-brigade commander; he thus could certainly not be considered a pacifist. Geva headed his command successfully during the first ten days of the war, but when his brigade was asked to lead the incursion into Beirut, he refused. He later offered to stay with his unit and serve as a regular tank driver, but Chief of Staff Eitan personally dismissed him from service.[88] Geva's refusal was rare in the Israeli context; prior to the Lebanon War, there had been only two other cases of refusal by commanders—both occurring in 1948. However, these cases appeared to rest on critiques of poor planning,[89] and less with regard to morality or the relationship between security ethics and operational mission. As Geva expressed it, "I thought that my responsibility to my men made my primary duty doing anything I could in order to try and prevent the decision to enter Beirut. My second reason was that moving into Beirut would have forced us to use massive firepower in order to secure our men's lives. Doing so would have caused vast destruction and loss of life. In my opinion this was morally unjustified."[90] The latter part of his statement reinforces the role-identity of Israel and its military as being a defensive force that is meant to follow the principle of "purity of arms." That is, while the loss of life could be morally justified in the context of defensive war-fighting, the idea of fighting an aggressive war that clashed with the IDF's security ethic made Geva, and others like him, view the inevitable deaths as ethically repugnant.

THE MEDIA AND POPULAR DISCOURSE

While critiques of the war became pervasive among members of the Labor opposition and the peace movement, the Israeli and international media helped to dredge up unconscious counternarratives and drive home the image of Israel as carrying out policies that clashed with the country's role-identity. While the Israeli media had traditionally refrained from criticizing the IDF—especially during wartime—the Yom Kippur war had exposed the conspiracy of silence to which the Israeli "conception" had given rise. The "conception" view holds that, after the Six Day War, Israeli policymakers had been under the sway of a misguided reading of the Arabs' willingness and ability to wage war on Israel, such that when Egypt and Syria attacked in October 1973, Israel was taken by surprise and only narrowly escaped defeat. The defense correspondent for *The Jerusalem Post* at the time of the Lebanon War, Hirsh Goodman, notes that a "new skepticism" toward defense policy arose in the wake of the 1973 war that contrasted with the close relationship that the IDF had previously enjoyed with the Israeli press, and journalists no longer treated the IDF as a "sacred cow."[91] Accordingly, during the Lebanon War the media did not hesitate to expose the government's policies as representing a controversial mission that broke the popular consensus. One prominent voice from the Israeli media, that of Jacobo Timerman, expressed it this way: "We are uneasy because in the fourth week of the war we cannot continue to deceive ourselves, and when we stop deceiving ourselves we begin to feel the shame—a strange and unreal sensation for a Jew, *this conception of oneself as a victimizer.*"[92] Timerman adds, "With all this [the Israeli's] identity has suffered a true shock, and now, out of necessity, he must rethink his very self."[93]

The same introspection that was occurring at the domestic level in Israel was mirrored by the Diaspora Jewish community. In the United States, where the majority of Jews are liberal-leaning and the most active of whom, in the 1980s, were products of the 1960s revolution, the nature of Jewish support for Israel became tinged with criticism as a result of the Lebanon War and intensified through the Intifada.[94] In France, three prominent Jews wrote an open letter that was later referred to only obliquely in *The Jerusalem Post* during the war, and which called for "the reciprocal recognition of Israel and the Palestinian people.... What is now essential is to find a political agreement between Israeli and Palestinian nationalism."[95]

By 1991, Israelis had come to revisit the war through popular artistic channels. Except for the 1985 IDF-made film entitled *Ricochets*, it took until 1991 for two Israeli feature-length films to emerge dealing with the war. Both *Cherry Season* and *Cup Final* offered backhanded critiques of the war. As Haim Bouzaglo, director of *Cherry Season*, noted, "Just as the big Vietnam movies in the U.S., like *Apocalypse Now*, didn't come out until some years after that war ended—and Lebanon was very much our Vietnam—I think we needed time to get over our initial trauma before being able to view the Lebanon War with any kind of perspective."[96] Given that *Ricochets* was produced by the IDF, it is not surprising that that film did not attempt a wholehearted critique of the war. However, *Cherry Season* and *Cup Final* both offered subverted narratives of the war; the latter condemning "the justice of the Israeli cause," and the former "portray[ing] Israeli justice as utterly irrelevant and the war as utterly perverse."[97] The training of a critical eye on an Israeli war in feature film contrasted sharply with the euphoria exemplified in what Ella Shohat calls the "heroic-nationalist genre" emerging in the wake of the 1967 war.[98] Unlike the Lebanon War, the Six Day War dredged up no collective conflict between Israel's role-identity and its military actions.

Still another form of discourse, that of critical historical scholarship—in Israel referred to as the "new historiography" or "revisionist history"—was beginning to take shape in the 1980s. Laurence Silberstein draws a direct link between the events surrounding the continuing occupation of the West Bank and Gaza Strip as well as the Lebanon War and the views held by a new generation of Israeli scholars.[99] According to Silberstein, the shattering of myths surrounding the use of the IDF for purely defensive purposes led to a general trend among some social scientists and historians to reexamine Israel's early history, including the origins of the Palestinian refugee problem, and the relationship between Israel and the Holocaust.[100] This trend suggests a heightened awareness of the contradiction between Israel's policies and its role-identity.

CONCLUSION

The Lebanon War ultimately revealed that a solid percentage of Israelis considered this war a "war of choice" beyond the confines of the preventive war versus absorbing-the-first-blow debate. And except for Begin, who attempted to use the phrase to his advantage, the Israeli polity was deeply uncomfortable with the notion of *choosing* to wage a particular war. Moreover, unlike the Six Day War or even the Sinai Campaign, both of which involved striking the enemy before it struck Israel, the operation in Lebanon was ultimately viewed by a significant portion of the population as contradictory to Israel's role-identity. This

view was reinforced by both the conduct of the war itself, and the political goals accompanying it, not simply by Israel's decision to strike first.
That is, the IDF's venturing into Beirut, a distance more than twice that
of the proposed invasion, including placing the city under siege, the massive destruction wrought upon Palestinian refugee camps and Lebanese
towns and cities, the government's meddling in Lebanese domestic politics, and the army's indirect involvement with the massacre at Sabra and
Shatilla led the polity to revile the state's actions north of its border.

On a deeper level, Begin considered the attack on Lebanon as an
inversion of centuries of Jewish persecution in the Diaspora. Cabinet
secretary Arye Naor described the prime minister's actions as striking "a
deep emotional chord; after all, the state of Israel had been established
specifically to put an end to the pogroms that made them [sic] the hapless victims." Viewed this way, the Lebanon War was not a break from
Israel's view of its own place in history, but was nevertheless contradictory to its security ethic. This tension between the Israeli historical narrative and Israel's role-identity penetrates the issue of why a state would
ever initially deviate from its role-identity to enact a policy dissonant
with it. We see here that a particular historical narrative leads to an array
of behavioral choices, each of which will elicit a particular reaction from
that same actor. In the Israeli case, a history of stateless victimhood
could lead, in the event of that nation's acquiring sovereignty, either to a
policy of aggression (to avenge past wrongs) or to a policy of restraint
(to bask in the moral glow of self-perceived justified sovereignty).
Throughout most of Israel's history, the latter course was the preferred
one. Begin represented the Revisionist Camp, a more radical version of
Zionism that espouses a more Manichean view of the Jewish narrative,
while employing looser constraints on the use of force to achieve security and political goals. While no people likes to consider itself 'at fault,'
the Revisionist Zionist school emphasizes the plight of the Jews as continually battling victimizers in their midst. The Lebanon War and the
PLO attacks over the northern border that preceded it were therefore
seen by Begin as the latest in a chapter of existential threats. From a
security perspective, these raids were clearly *not* a threat to Israel's sovereignty, given the weakness of the PLO as a fighting force. As discussed
in chapter three, this school was ultimately overshadowed within Israeli
national discourse by the more moderate Labor Zionism movement.
This latter current of thought prevailed in the 1992 elections under
Rabin and Peres, and propelled the peace process with the PLO to the
Oslo agreement. The next chapter examines the second major event in
Israel that resulted in the polity viewing itself as an aggressor despite its
self-image, and that would result in a policy shift on the part of Israel
toward the Palestinians: the Intifada.

Chapter Six

Israel and the Intifada

Like the Lebanon War five years earlier, the Intifada—the 1987–1993 Palestinian uprising in the West Bank and Gaza Strip—exposed Israelis' collective, unconscious fears of becoming an aggressor. As the uprising wore on, Israelis became aware that their defensive-warrior role-identity was being challenged by their military response to a people's revolt. Israeli power having steadily increased from the state's inception until the late 1980s while the Palestinians remained weak no doubt heightened this cognitive dissonance as the IDF attempted to suppress the uprising in the occupied territories conducted by mostly unarmed Palestinians. And by the fifth year of the Intifada, the disparity between Israeli and Palestinian power had sharpened, as the PLO lost two important sources of patronage—the Soviets, with the end of the Cold War and the disbanding of the Soviet Union, and the Arab Gulf states (particularly Saudi Arabia), as retaliation for the PLO siding with Iraq in the 1991 Gulf War.

That the Intifada in part propelled Israel toward peace is not intuitive from a strict material calculus. From a strategic point of view, the Intifada was not a direct military threat to Israel. It certainly did not (despite what many Palestinians may have wished for in private moments) embody an attempt at "politicide," the threat characterizing Israel's security environment since independence. Indeed, during the uprising, Rabin publicly stated that only 4 percent of Israel's defense budget was devoted to quelling the protests,[1] and economists noted in 1990 that the Intifada was costing only 1 percent of Israel's annual GNP, the equivalent of $400 million a year.[2] Messages from the Likud during this period reinforced the belief that the occupation did not entail significant costs for Israel.[3] And as Yossi Beilin wrote, "[t]he Intifada did not pose an existential threat to Israel, but it constituted a continuing nuisance, aggravated the sense of personal insecurity and seriously harmed Israel's image in the world." None of these descriptions—a "nuisance," "personal insecurity" or the harming of Israel's image—would predict a wholesale Israeli policy shift toward negotiating with the Palestinians from a strictly geopolitical perspective, particularly since the threat was confined to the occupied territories. Israelis could simply refrain from "wandering around the garages of Gaza," in Rabin's words, rather than pressing their government to make radical strategic and symbolic concessions that would likely lead to the creation of a Palestinian state.[4] Similarly, Israel had a long-standing policy of not negotiating with terrorists; thus, any "insecurity" that Israelis did feel owing to the situation in the occupied territories could not be expected to elicit negotiations on the part of Israel that would be seen to reward the PLO for whatever "semiviolent protest" the Palestinians were launching in the West Bank and Gaza.[5] Finally, the economy of the territories had become largely dependent on Israel, relying on it for 90 percent of the raw materials used for agriculture and industry; and, along with the Gulf states, for employment.[6] From a purely economic and strategic calculus, Israelis were arguably better off maintaining the occupation rather than being seen to give in to Intifada tactics.

Yet the Intifada clearly exposed the contradiction between Israel's defensive-warrior role-identity and its actions in the territories. As the occupation progressed, Israel was racked by an internal debate over the fate of the 1.5 million Palestinians living in the West Bank and Gaza. The situation was exemplified by what has come to be known as the "triangle dilemma" of democracy, Greater Israel, and the Jewish character of the state: Israel could have any two, but not all three. If it chose to annex the territories without granting citizenship to the Palestinians, Israel would fulfill the right wing's call for an expanded Israel, but would cease to be a democracy. If it did grant the Palestinians Israeli citizenship, the country would, within a few generations, no longer be demographically Jewish. Thus, for those opposed to annexation on democratic grounds, the Intifada led to, in the words of Uri Savir, an *"internal dissonance* between experiencing ourselves as a democracy on the one hand, and as occupiers on the other."[7] Echoing this sense of discomfort, Foreign Minister Shimon Peres' aide Avi Gil stated, "We understood that a solution wouldn't come about by force. We asked ourselves, what kind of Israel will this be? An apartheid state? Rule by oppression?"[8]

Why, indeed, did Israel decide to negotiate an end to the occupation if the Intifada was neither a great economic drain nor a geopolitical security threat; and instead, make the first genuine attempt at peacemaking with the PLO? Given that the uprising was widely considered to constitute a status quo that Israelis were loathe to continue, the Intifada—like the Lebanon War—must have had effects on the Israeli psyche that were not purely geopolitical in nature. Rather, the Intifada convinced Israelis that how they conceived of the state—Israel's defensive-warrior role-identity—had come into conflict with the Israeli response to these six years of street disturbances in the West Bank and Gaza. By the end of 1988, Arafat had renounced "all forms of terrorism" and "recognized Israel's right to exist."[9] Yet it took until 1993, and six years of the Intifada, for Israelis to seriously contemplate a shift in policy towards recognizing the Palestinians as a distinct nation. Israel's actions in suppressing the uprising brought about uncomfortable counter-narratives of aggression, leading elites to realize that their state's actions in the territories clashed with Israel's defensive-warrior role-identity. The ability of Israelis to contemplate their country's actions in terms of the discourse of apartheid, oppression and occupation reveals the power of unconscious counter-narratives—those that had been repressed during earlier years of arguably aggressive actions but had emerged due to a critical mass recognizing the contradiction—in propelling a policy shift.

Specifically, the Intifada challenged Israel's role-identity in three ways. Most importantly, large segments within Israel and within the international community saw the army's actions in responding to the uprising, and which led to multitudes of deaths and injuries among Palestinians, as being too harsh. Second, unlike in the Lebanon War, the army was playing the roles of riot controller and slapdash police force, tasks alien to the interstate-warrior aspect of its role-identity. Third, Israel, which was founded on the principal of self-determination, found itself suppressing another nation's attempt to achieve sovereignty. Coupled with the experience of the war in Lebanon, the dissonance between Israel's actions and its role-identity led Israel to take radical action to realign its policy stance with its self-image. This action would come in the form of peacemaking with the PLO in the early 1990s, with the moves toward Palestinian sovereignty that the Oslo agreement implied.

THE UPRISING AND ITS OUTBREAK

The Intifada—an Arabic word meaning "shaking off" (as a dog would shake off fleas, or a nation would shake off the 'yoke of oppression')—erupted on the heels of an 8 December 1987 traffic accident in which an Israeli truck swerved into a line of cars in the Gaza Strip, killing four Palestinians. Rumors quickly spread throughout Gaza that the collision had been intentional, and soon the territories erupted into large-scale protests, including rioting, general strikes, and the use of Molotov cocktails and homemade slingshots. Scenes of Israeli soldiers shooting into crowds, beating Palestinian protestors and chasing children through alleyways quickly became a staple of the evening news.

While most accounts treat the Intifada as a spontaneous outburst that took the Israeli military and political establishment by surprise, we are still left to wonder how blissfully ignorant of the situation in the territories the Israeli government actually was. Clearly, the six years of striking, rioting, and low-level violence that emerged from the grass roots were both unplanned and unexpected, with not even the PLO orchestrating the initial protests: Arafat's Fatah wing jumped on board only once the Intifada was in full swing. Yet what *had* been clear was that the political mood in the territories in the lead-up to the uprising was grim, if placid: While chief Oslo negotiator Uri Savir admitted that the Intifada "took us by surprise,"[10] then-Deputy-Foreign Minister Yossi Beilin referred to the uprising as an "expected surprise," arguing that the pre-Intifada situation reminded him of the apparent "quiet" that preceded the Yom Kippur War in 1973: "Things were all too silent, and that worried me."[11] Longtime Rabin aide Shimon Sheves recounted that the then-defense minister was not surprised by the Intifada, and that Rabin had previously referred to the situation in the occupied territories as akin to "smoldering coals."[12] Yet when the uprising broke out, Rabin was about to travel to the United States to negotiate an arms deal, and did not postpone his trip. Finally, one member of Knesset, Naomi Chazan, who is also a political scientist, stated, "It was totally expected. As a student of colonialism, this was clear to me."[13] Israel's main grievance with the Arabs has historically been their refusal to recognize Israel as a sovereign state; thus, that a member of the Israeli establishment chose to associate the situation in the occupied territories with anticolonialist uprisings illustrates the dissonance between Israel's role-identity as a peaceable state clamoring for its own place in the region and its behavior as a suppressor of the sovereign aspirations of another people.

It is not surprising that the military-political establishment was less than fully attuned to the mood among the Palestinians, for in the twenty years since Israel had captured the West Bank and Gaza Strip in the Six Day War, the state had attempted to implement a policy of benevolent rule, enabling Israelis to stave off the sense of dissonance that would result once the Palestinians revolted. Israel's so-called policy of benign occupation was initially enshrined in a 1976 program issued by then-Prime Minister Rabin, Defense Minister Shimon Peres, and Minister of Police Shlomo Hillel. The directive entailed that certain punishments—which eventually became rampant during the Intifada years, such as house demolitions and deportations—would be used sparingly, and only

as a deterrent for mass unrest.[14] These policies no doubt stemmed from a
collective desire among Israelis to see themselves as passively presiding
over the Arab states' Palestinian brethren until those states agreed to recognize Israel's existence. Similarly, the closer that Israel came to recognizing Palestinian nationhood, the sooner would Israel have to recognize
its role as an occupier—a role that clearly clashed with its defensive-warrior identity. Given that the mechanism for dissonance stems from
unconscious, fear-based counternarratives, it would take more than
simply acting as occupiers for Israel to come to terms with this role conflict. Rather, it would take the active suppression of the Palestinian
uprising, whereby Israeli soldiers found themselves in the position of
shooting unarmed protestors, demolishing their houses, and chasing
slingshot-bearing youth while the Palestinians, along with Israeli critics,
exposed the brutality of Israel's policies.

Another reason that elites were blind to the brewing unrest was
their only partly accurate belief that the Palestinians were faring better
economically under occupation than they had under Jordanian and
Egyptian rule (until Israel's 1967 victory in the Six Day War, Jordan had
occupied the West Bank and Egypt had possessed the Gaza Strip), and
perhaps—although this was not made explicit—better than they would
were Israel to withdraw. Glossy brochures printed by the likes of the
Jewish National Fund for foreign distribution showed the Palestinians as
fortunate beneficiaries of Israeli economic policy. Indeed, Israelis argued
that, since 1967, the Palestinians' personal income levels had risen—
along with the almost total disappearance of unemployment and, with
that, the levels of personal consumption. In general, economic growth
had been experienced in the territories at an even greater pace than that
which had occurred within Israel itself; the West Bank's GNP had
grown by 12.9 percent during the first ten years of the occupation, and
the Gaza Strip's had increased by 12.1 percent.[15] Yet Palestinian analysts
countered that the Israelis had neglected to develop important areas of
infrastructure, particularly in the spheres of transportation, communication, and education. They further argued that whatever economic benefits had accrued to the Palestinians were overshadowed by the creation
of a dependency economy whose chief export was unskilled labor.[16]
Among Israelis, the association of manual labor with Palestinians had
long ago led to the phrase "Arab work" to describe undesirable jobs
within Israel—one metaphor among many that would help to dehuman-
ize the enemy and therefore enable the aggressive counternarratives to
remain in the Israeli unconscious as long as they did. Whatever improve-
ments over the conditions imposed by Jordan and Egypt that Israel
could take credit for since 1967, there was no outright attempt—nor

could there be, given the enormity of the counterfactual—to argue that Palestinian economic conditions under Israel were better than they would be *were the Palestinians to govern themselves*—since the Palestinians were indeed not calling for a return to Jordanian or Egyptian rule.[17]

Thus, rather than presiding over a politically quiescent people silenced by the hum of new refrigerators, what was actually going on was arguably the beginnings of a "proletarian uprising," as Ze'ev Schiff and Ehud Ya'ari have termed it,[18] as the effects of refugee camp squalor and minimum-wage employment without security or benefits were lodging themselves in Palestinian consciousness. The economy of the West Bank and Gaza had largely depended on Israel, relying on it for 90 percent of the raw materials used for agriculture and industry, and, along with the Gulf states, for employment. (In 1988, revenue from work in Israel constituted 34 percent of the gross local product of the West Bank, and 70 percent in Gaza.)[19]

As long as Israelis viewed the occupation as mainly an economic issue, they would not absorb the full impact of the clash between their country's actions and its role-identity. A focus on salaries and consumer consumption served to obscure the notion that the occupation was humiliating the Palestinians on an *existential* level—a humiliation reminiscent of that experienced by the Jews during their years as precarious "guests" within the host countries of the Diaspora. It would take the actual uprising—which went beyond calls for economic rehabilitation to address the crux of Palestinian nationalism—to convince Israelis that their state's policies were clashing with Israel's defensive-warrior role-identity.

Likewise, the euphoria that Israelis had experienced in the aftermath of the Six Day War, both as a result of achieving a stunning victory over four Arab states on three flanks and from being reunited with such holy sites as the Western Wall and the tomb of the patriarchs, eclipsed the opportunity for a sober assessment of the Palestinian situation. Colonel (Ret.) Yeshayahu Tadmor, head of the IDF's information branch during the war, noted that "[t]he Intifada led to a strong realization of the moral problems inherent in the occupation; it brought it into our living rooms.... I think that the left and center of the Israeli public had lived as if in a slumber for many years." As a result of regaining the West Bank, "there had been a religious awakening.... Many of us liberals fell under this spell of messianism."[20] And while Peres viewed the Intifada more as a spontaneous "outburst" than something arising from a "plan," he conceived of the uprising as "growing into an 'intifada' out of anger and outrage."[21] That a senior official was attuned to the emotional side of the

Palestinian experience indicates that Israel had become aware of the humiliating aspects of the occupation—a crucial step toward experiencing the dissonance between actions and identity that would eventually lead to a radical policy shift.

POLICY RESPONSES

Whether or not Israeli elites had been completely unsuspecting that widespread protest might one day erupt in the territories, the IDF soon found itself ill-prepared to deal with the mass rioting that necessitated nonlethal, hand-to-hand combat. Because of the lack of riot-control training, initial IDF policies led to more deaths than would otherwise have occurred. Already in the first month of the Intifada, the United Nations Security Council (with the United States abstaining) passed a resolution condemning Israeli policies in the territories, particularly the use of live ammunition.[22] As one ex-military member observed, "the problem [was] no longer how to defend Israelis from being killed by Palestinians, but rather how to avoid, or at least minimize, the killing of Palestinians by Jews."[23] This sentiment echoes Golda Meir's statement blaming the Arabs for having made killers out of Israeli youth. However, with the proximity of the Intifada to Israeli consciousness, given that it was an ongoing struggle waged in towns and refugee camps rather than on a battlefield, a similar statement would take on a very different meaning within the Israeli psyche. While Meir's words served to villify the enemy, the military leadership during the Intifada wished to extricate itself from a psychically uncomfortable situation.

The IDF certainly possessed the resources to quash an adversary on a single front, no less one that was unarmed. Indeed, all of Israel's previous wars had displayed the military's might in the face of formidable, multifront battles. The Intifada lasted as long and led to as many casualties as it did precisely because the IDF was not morally comfortable killing civilians. As it stands, even the use of beatings (which likely led to fewer deaths than the use of live ammunition) clashed with the IDF's security ethic. Thus, the riot-control policies of attrition during the Intifada represented a concerted—yet failed—attempt by the Israeli military to adhere to its security ethic, as Palestinian casualties mounted in the face of Israeli repression.

In order to deal with the rising death toll, Israel soon mandated the use of rubber and then plastic bullets (metal bullets encased in rubber or plastic). However, even these were found to inflict serious injury, especially when fired at close range. Still other riot-control tools, such as dogs, had long ago been ruled out due to their Nazi associations. Yet the IDF's lack of riot-control preparation was not necessarily an oversight. Then-Chief of Staff Moshe Levi had specifically opposed this sort of training, fearing that the IDF would deteriorate into a "professional occupation force,"[24] thus illustrating the importance of Israeli soldiers' identity as interstate warriors rather than occupiers. This fear of lapsing into a contrary role echoes the self-proclaimed identity of the Israeli military as not being a "professional" one, despite the large cadre of career officers. Rather, Israelis have historically viewed the IDF as a necessary, defensive arm of an embattled country, fighting only wars of "no alternative." As General Nechemia Dagan, chief educational officer during the Intifada, stated, "There is no such thing as a 'professional solder' in Israel, in stark contrast to armies such as the French Foreign Legion. Even though I was in the army for 32 years, I never considered myself a 'professional soldier'... We do it because we have to."[25] Chief IDF psychologist Reuven Gal has observed a similar phenomenon, writing that IDF officers have historically shunned the label of "'career officer...preferring the perception that they were motivated by moral and national commitment rather than by occupational considerations."[26]

This widespread desire by the IDF to extricate itself from the quagmire of the uprising cannot be attributed to faulty planning: the lack of training for these sorts of situations was deliberate. Anything else would have validated Israel's presence as a "permanent" occupier rather than as a temporary custodian of the territories until such time as the Arab states were ready to seek peace. As long as the IDF let itself be "taken by surprise" by the mass Palestinian outburst, the counternarrative of occupier could remain safely in the unconscious. Once the Intifada wore on, however, this counternarrative came to the fore, forcing Israelis to confront the clash between their country's actions and identity.

In many ways, the evolution of Israel's Intifada policies embodied this attempt at keeping unpalatable counternarratives at bay. Efraim Inbar's analysis of the three stages of Israeli policy toward the uprising is helpful in illuminating this evolution.[27] In the earliest phase, Israel embraced a carrot-and-stick policy whereby politically quiescent towns received economic benefits. Among Israelis, this approach served to reinforce the idea that as long as the Palestinians cooperated with the situation of occupation that the Arabs had "forced on" Israel through decades of aggression, they would be duly rewarded. Once the uprising intensified, though, the IDF introduced the use of beatings. At the time of the Intifada's outbreak, Rabin was defense minister in a national unity government—a power-sharing arrangement between Likud and Labor. (Rabin would be replaced in 1990 by Moshe Arens of the Likud Party.)

By now, Rabin's directive to "break the bones" of the Palestinians is well known (though there is some controversy as to whether he actually uttered these words) and led to immediate revulsion by both the international community and the Israeli left wing.[28] Member of Knesset Naomi Chazan noted that the day Rabin said this was the day she joined Meretz—the peace bloc to the left of Rabin's Labor Party.[29] However, Chief of Staff Dan Shomron explained to soldiers that this method should be accompanied by "restraint and sensitivity," and that beatings should not be used as punishment.[30] While this policy outraged Israeli and especially international audiences, Rabin argued that, in contrast to using live ammunition against rioters, "Nobody dies of a beating."[31]

The adoption of these measures brings to light the most intimate form of Israeli-Palestinian relations under the rubric of conflict that Israel had yet experienced. The act of manual combat allowed the clash between a defensive-warrior role-identity and the actual role of occupier to become all the more apparent, particularly since Israeli military doctrine has traditionally focused on lightning strikes. This shift from deterrence to "compellence"—yet on an intercorporeal level—further brought to light the ill fit between Israel's role-identity and its policies during the Intifada, both in terms of the preference for post-hoc uses of force over deterrence, and in terms of proximity to the enemy. Night raids on sleeping couples, lethal games of hide-and-seek with children through alleyways, and commanding Palestinians to scrub nationalist graffiti off of cement walls were a far cry from the relative geographic and emotional distance afforded by air strikes and tank battles.

Eventually, the IDF shifted to a third stage of response: a policy of "attrition," including mass arrests, administrative detention, deportations, and the continuation of economic pressure. One explanation for Israel's reluctance to thwart the uprising in one fell swoop was fear of the Intifada's alternative: increased terrorism and a rise in support for the Islamic fundamentalist groups Hamas and Islamic Jihad.[32] Nevertheless, even if a more radical leadership had emerged in the territories, the Palestinians still would not have posed a grave military threat to Israel. What was more, the policy of attrition, as we will see, led to a profound tension between the military establishment and some right-wing members of government, who accused the military of going "soft" on the Intifada. However, the form that these policies took—collective punishment—helped to expose Israel's quelling of Palestinian attempts at furthering their sovereignty claims. Given the IDF's stark power advantage, that the Intifada was not quashed outright suggests that Israel was determined to preserve its "enlightened" image in domestic and international opinion. Ironically, the policies of beatings as well as collective punishment, while causing fewer deaths than the use of live ammunition targeted against specific protestors, rallied domestic Israeli and international opinion around the Palestinian cause more swiftly than would likely otherwise have occurred had television viewers not been subject to daily footage of soldiers assaulting unarmed protestors and destroying Palestinian property.

ISRAELI REACTIONS TO THE POLICY RESPONSE

Society

Abundant local and international media coverage brought the Intifada into the living room of every Israeli. And for families of regular conscripts and even reservists, stories of military excesses penetrated the realm of family narratives, just as they ricocheted off the walls of the discotheques frequented by soldiers on weekend leave. The most immediate impact of the uprising on Israeli political thinking was, as Mark Tessler points out, the reemergence of the Green Line (the 1967 cease-fire boundary dividing pre-1967 Israel from the West Bank and Gaza and Golan Heights) into Israeli consciousness,[33] an awareness that would be essential to any political settlement entailing some form of Palestinian self-government in the occupied territories. The territories were now seen as alien regions where soldiers were no longer defending the frontiers of Jewish statehood, but were fending off stones, burning tires, and graffiti by Palestinians clamoring for collective recognition. True, there were some Jewish populations to be defended within the West Bank and Gaza, namely, those in what have come to be known as "the settlements," but these areas then, as now, claimed a proportionately tiny population base (100,000 settlers versus 1.5 million Palestinians by the uprising's end), and, by the time of the Intifada's outbreak, had become not only an internationally controversial issue, but an internally divisive one as well.[34]

Of even more significance, the Israeli public wondered whether the IDF's Intifada policies accorded with its vision of Israel as a state. Israelis asked themselves, in the words of one journalist, "Is this what Israel is about? Chasing 14-year-old children in the alleyways?"[35] Hearkening to the deepest recesses of collective memory, some Israelis invoked biblical narratives to critique the occupation. As one journalist wrote, urging Israelis to engage in a process of soul-searching, "what matters is less the Geneva Convention than the Sinai Convention. According to that agreement, our stay in this country has a condition: 'Justice, justice you shall pursue.'" And, "when we weigh holding on to the territories, we have to look at the risk to our moral survival as well as to our physical survival."[36] Israeli nationalists have often used the Old Testament to justify nationalist policies, particularly with regard to extending Israel's hold over Jerusalem and the West Bank. For biblical tropes to be appropriated by voices on the left indicates that the master narrative of Exodus-Exile-Rebirth and Occupation-as-befits-the-extension-of-Jewish sovereignty was being challenged by Israelis questioning the singular interpretation of Jewish history and the lessons to be drawn from it.

In terms of Israelis' attitude toward the army, from 1986 to 1992, survey respondents said that the presence of the IDF in the occupied territories was having a "negative effect on the army's fighting ethic." In this case, where a score of 1 = negative and 7 = positive, responses showed a perceived worsening from a mean of 4.2 in 1986 to a mean of 3.2 in 1992, one year before Israel signed the Oslo agreement.[37] Similarly, 63 percent of respondents in a 1990 survey said that the national mood had worsened because of the Intifada.[38] Israel is a country profoundly attuned to the ebbs and flows of the "national mood," perhaps owing to the deep ideological commitment that propelled the founders to pursue independence. While Zionism has always contained a multiplicity of voices, that Israel came into being through such a self-conscious and articulate ideology means that political and emotional cleavages within the polity are considered at minimum an inflammatory irritant and at most a collective defeat. This, despite the old joke that in a room of ten Jews there will be eleven opinions.

While the uprising led to a heightened debate over the fate of the territories, Asher Arian concludes that, in general, while short-term attitudes among Israelis hardened, views regarding eventual policy outcomes softened.[39] Another study found that attitudes among Jewish Israelis toward negotiating with the PLO significantly moderated from 22 percent in 1978, to 37 percent in April 1990 (prior to the Gulf crisis).[40] Similarly, these respondents also increased their support for trading land for peace: 45–47 percent of Israeli Jews in 1986–1987 opposed withdrawal from any part of the West Bank, while by July 1990 the number had dropped to 35 percent.[41]

Ultimately, Israeli attitudes shifted rapidly enough to facilitate the coming to power in 1992 of a Labor government committed to bringing about a peace agreement with the Palestinians within six to nine months. As Arian states, "Those 1988 Likud voters who switched to Labor mentioned the Likud's settlement policy and the intifada more often as a factor in their vote decision than other groups of voters."[42] Finally, a May 1990 survey revealed that only 18 percent of Israelis advocated harsher measures, while 38 percent, and 30 percent of respondents who identified themselves as Likud supporters, supported greater restraint in the use of force.[43]

However, other evidence points to the right wing not experiencing the same direction of attitude shift that was overtaking the left during this period, and some commentators would go so far as to say that as the left wing moved leftward, the right wing moved rightward. For instance, 42 percent of Israelis surveyed in December 1990 reported becoming more hawkish since the Intifada broke out. However, while only 9 percent were "content" with the status quo, there was no overall policy consensus. Twenty-one percent favored the idea of "transfer" (forced removal of the Palestinians to the surrounding Arab states), while 25 percent supported the creation of a Palestinian "entity." Twenty percent wanted to withdraw only from the Gaza Strip; yet only 6 percent favored annexing "all or part" of the West Bank.[44] Thus, while Israeli society did undergo a polarization during the Intifada, it is possible that as more radical proposals entered the political discourse, the center and left increased their commitment to peace.

As would be expected, the Intifada period generated a plethora of plays and songs, many of which were harshly critical of Israeli policies. Two popular songs written during this period are particularly telling of the Israeli mood. One, Nurit Galron's "After Us, the Flood," describes Israeli day-to-day life in the midst of IDF violence against Palestinians.[45] Chava Alberstein, generally considered a mainstream entertainer, subverted a prominent aspect of the dominant narrative by recording her own version of the Passover song "One Little Goat" (*Chad Gadya*); criticizing Israel's treatment of the Palestinians. In response to the critique imparted by these songs, Israeli Radio banned them from the airwaves. While the supreme court overturned the order, they still were rarely played after that.[46]

One 1992 Israeli rock opera called "Samara" told the story of a Palestinian woman who is accidentally shot by soldiers, one of whom is then haunted by her ghost. In a telling commentary on the moral fault line running through Israeli society during this period, the last line of the play states, "There's no complete bad / and no perfect good; Only those who command/ and those who are ruled." Playwrite Hillel Mittelpunkt stated that "If we try to distance ourselves from the nightmare of what is happening out there, then we'll also end up alienated from everything else; both in our lives and in ourselves."[47] And in a shocking display of the role conflict Israelis were experiencing, in May 1989 the Center for Holocaust Studies at Ben-Gurion University held a conference on Holocaust Remembrance Day to investigate the relationship between Nazism and

Israeli policies in the territories. Along with apartheid, and justifiably so, Nazism has been an analogy that Israelis have been loathe to consider. Its exploration in a public forum—even though members of the audience were repulsed by the comparison—is therefore highly revealing.[48]

The Military

In any democracy, the military primarily enacts civilian orders and therefore should be viewed as a conduit for government policy. However, and as discussed in chapter four, the military and civilian branches may form a policy feedback loop, whereby a particular security ethic is created and nurtured. Moreover, the defense establishment may advise policymakers at particular decision moments, as was the case during the latter phases of the Oslo negotiations. Thus, the reactions of the military to the Intifada are relevant in both gauging and helping to shape the overall mood of the public, as well as, oftentimes, the specific security thinking of the elites. Given that Israel is a country with universal conscription, uniformed citizens form a significant part of the electorate; a majority of which would, in 1992, usher the Labor Party back into power on a platform of peace.

By all accounts, the Intifada took its toll on the spirit of a military trained to defend itself in the face of existential threats from the surrounding Arab states. In the few years between the outbreak of the uprising and the pursuit of the Oslo agreement, the Israeli media was rife with references to military morale being at an "all time low" in the history of the state.[49] In a society valuing warrior culture (albeit for defensive purposes), conscripts posted to the occupied territories expressed frustration with acting as "policemen" rather than "soldiers."[50] And as one reservist observed, "The army, as the more sophisticated soldiers put it, is an organization entrusted with training and preparing for an attack by the forces of an external enemy. Here we were being ordered to become a policing force, one charged with enforcing law and order."[51] That Intifada policy-deliberation was intrinsically linked to the fate of the occupied territories meant that the IDF was forced to play a part in what was essentially a political debate. As Rabin said in 1988, "You cannot saddle the IDF with a mission that is outside its proper function. The unrest in the areas reflects a problem that can only have a political solution."[52] Even more telling was the recollections of Eitan Haber, Rabin's bureau chief, of the prime minister's concern about the IDF's morale: "The indications of moral deterioration that had appeared as part of our rule over the Arabs in the territories led [Rabin] to recognize that we would not be able to continue to rule two-and-a-half million Palestinians against their will."[53]

Officers were caught in a three-pointed vortex of patriotism, morality, and self-protection. With frequent trials of suspected military
abuses, a running joke became "every officer wants a lawyer by his
side."[54] From 1987 through 1994, three hundred military personnel were
investigated, put on trial, or disciplined for abuses against Palestinians.[55]
Many officers became aware of the problematic situation of occupation
only once the Intifada was in full swing; others later claimed they saw
the warning signs at least slightly earlier, if not early enough. The dissonance between serving in the territories and Israel's defensive-warrior
role-identity became so acute that a 1990 interview with the head of the
IDF's manpower division revealed that reservists' having to serve in the
territories had become a cause for leaving Israel.[56] Moreover, Chief
Educational Officer Nechemia Dagan later reported that five years prior
to the Intifada, "I already said that what is happening in [the territories]
is very dangerous for Israeli society. It's not right to send 18-year-olds
after Palestinian children...it leads to the brutalization of Israeli society."[57] The relationship between brutality and warriorness is a delicate
one in warfare in general, and no less so in Israel, where the drive toward
being effective warriors is tempered by the desire to remain defensive in
mission and practice. Clausewitz neatly sums up the role of violence in
human nature as contrasted with the war situation: "In the soldier the
natural tendency for unbridled action and outbursts of violence must be
subordinated to demands of a higher kind: obedience, order, rule, and
method."[58] Thus, the defensive-warrior role-identity in large part mirrors a classical, Clausewitzian ideal of the soldier.

As a soldier, the most deliberate way to protest the government's
Intifada policies was selective refusal. Compared to other mass movements of conscientious objection, such as among American draftees
during the Vietnam War, the numbers in Israel were small. While
activists estimate that up to 2,000 soldiers engaged in selective refusal of
some sort, including 186 reservists,[59] some 200 were actually jailed.[60]
Loathe to lend legitimacy to this group, President Chaim Herzog point-
edly refused to meet with representatives of the organization *Yesh Gvul*
which supports conscripts who refuse to serve in the territories.[61]
Indeed, most Israelis view conscientious objection with suspicion, especially given the stamp of social mobility that completion of one's regular
military service bequeaths. (Although in recent years, this linkage has
been diminishing.) Stated General Dagan about conscientious objectors
during the Intifada: "There weren't many at all. It's supposed to be
against violence; but among those in Israel, there was more "political
objection" than "conscientious objection."[62] This view represents the
tension between the moral imperative of enacting (legal) military direc-

tives as a democratic citizen whose government has issued those policies, versus bringing an independent moral view to prevail over the choice of which legal orders to follow. Given the highly sectarian nature of the debate over the future of the territories, conscientious objectors are viewed as inserting political positions into the supposedly nonpartisan space enclosing the military as an arm of state policy. Nevertheless, in a country in which the military is considered one of the most sacred institutions of the state, and where conscientious objection was otherwise exceedingly rare, the fact that there were objectors of this sort was significant. One objector, an American-born reservist, emerged from his three weeks of military imprisonment with a book manuscript that was subsequently published by an American press. In it, he alludes to the unconscious forces that come to plague the conscience as a result of occupation policies: "Each actual person I meet is a potential Thou. If I behave toward someone in disregard of her being as human as I, then her humanity comes back to trouble me. It is she as a Thou who haunts me, the Thou whom I should have seen and did not."[63] Another reservist expressed the tendency for soldiers serving in the territories to become "an-other person (a certain 'other' to themselves)" since "reservists during their stint of duty are temporarily not themselves but people placed in...circumstances that in themselves may allow (or...demand) a certain type of behavior."[64] This dual position—of being both self and other concurrently—allows for the experiencing of unconscious fears that one is enacting a role anathema to one's sense of self.

Soldiers who asked for an audience with President Herzog during the Intifada to vent their feelings about serving during such a period of unrest told him that "It pains us to see what's happening to the army. We can testify that despite the calls for restraint, the 'exceptions are becoming the rule.'" And that "what we need now is [*sic*] authoritative leaders to remind us, day and night, that the people we are dealing with out there are human beings made out of exactly the same stuff as we are."[65] Israeli military observers noted during this period that the Intifada was resulting in "the brutalization of an entire generation of soldiers."[66] The tension between military violence and mass Israeli discomfort led to the popular characterization of Israeli troops during the Intifada as soldiers who "shoot and cry"—a phrase first uttered by recruits serving in the territories following the Yom Kippur War.[67] Among general infantry soldiers, there was a common sentiment that the means deployed to suppress the uprising were morally questionable. One soldier told the media, "You don't believe in what you're doing. It's no fun knocking on a door, pulling out a 50-year old man who could be your father, telling him to paint over a slogan."[68] One of the more peaceful forms of Palestinian protest, painting graffiti in the red, white, and green of the Palestinian flag was deemed by Israel to be illegal, and more than one Palestinian died by electrocution after being forced to climb a utility pole to remove a Palestinian flag.[69] Overall, in the words of one Israeli observer, the Intifada "dramatized the ambiguities between the roles of Israeli military force as an instrument of defense and as a means of domination."[70] At no time previously was the IDF in a position of direct and palpable control over another nation.

Out of concern for the potentially deleterious effects the uprising was having on soldiers, the IDF sent psychologists to the field. Among their findings was a warning of "the tremendous damage which will be done to the soldiers when they realize that their sacrifice was in vain."[71] The need to avoid this situation lends more credibility to the argument that the Israeli government pursued Oslo in part as a reaction to the cognitive dissonance between attempting to sustain a defensive-warrior role-identity and enacting occupation policies.

Through all of this, the IDF was the object of harsh criticism from the Israeli right, including cabinet ministers and lobbyists, who decried the military's refusal to achieve outright victory over the uprising.[72] Moreover, the IDF took a more moderate stance than even Defense Minister Yitzhak Rabin (himself of the Labor Party) was prepared to allow.[73] As a result, the IDF general staff took pains to protect its image, at times even relying on moral reasoning. For instance, Major General Yitzhak Mordechai (OC Southern Command) made a speech at Kiryat Arba (a Jewish settler town on the edge of Hebron, known for its extreme-right politics) in the presence of the prime minister, saying that "anyone who believed that the army would discard an entire system of values or tailor it to the demands of the 'war' that Israel was fighting in the territories was laboring under a grave delusion."[74] (Ironically, at the end of 1990, Mordechai would be tried for charges of issuing illegal orders of brutality, but was exonerated four years later.)[75] The IDF soon began issuing printed and oral directives calling for restraint in dealing with captured Palestinians, in order to uphold "our Jewish moral legacy" and "respect for human honor and human life."[76] Similarly, IDF Chief of Staff Dan Shomron reportedly threatened to resign if the army was forced to act against its "moral code."[77] On another occasion, Head of Central Command Major General Amram Mitzna declared, "Are you suggesting that we shoot women and children for throwing stones?... This is Israel, not Syria!"[78] This statement is highly illustrative of the role conflict that Israelis were experiencing, as they feared imitating an enemy they perceived to be among the most ruthless. One of the most prominent justifications for Israel not to have actively sought peace with the surrounding Arab states since the peace treaty with Egypt had been a crude Kantian logic deploring the absence of democracy among them.[79]

While Israelis have always resisted the colonialist label, other anti-colonialist struggles and attendant military atrocities were not far from the minds of the IDF leadership during the Intifada. As General Dagan later noted, "I knew about My Lai at the time that it happened, and about Algeria, and the British in the Faulklands. But as opposed to those events, our soldiers did the best they could. It's never a good situation, soldiers against civilians."[80] It is telling that an IDF officer was implicitly comparing the Palestinian nationalists to other, anticolonialist movements. Even during the Intifada itself, Chief of Staff Shomron publicly compared the uprising to Algeria and other anticolonial struggles.[81] This sort of comparison would have been unthinkable in the early years of the state, when isolated atrocities by the IDF, when they did occur, were swept under the rug, only to be faced forty years later. One example of such an attack was the 1956 IDF massacre of forty-nine Arab civilians at Kafr Kassem. While Israel has never officially apologized, in 1999 the Ministry of Education directed high school civics teachers to discuss the event in their classrooms.[82]

The Media

The Intifada was in large measure a battle fought for the media; images of Palestinian children facing down the barrel of an Israeli gun forced Israeli and international opinion to be moved by the uprising. In terms of government relations with the foreign press, it was not Israel's finest hour. This dynamic was magnified by the fact that the international press tended to broadcast a message more in keeping with the Palestinian "frame" of events than with that of Israel.[83] As Government Press Office head during the uprising, Yossi Olmert had no qualms about imposing censorship regulations. As he noted, "the need for censorship is one of the unavoidable aspects of the Israeli situation."[84] Israeli elites were well aware of the wide-reaching international sympathy being garnered by the Palestinians through the media. And as Rabin stated in 1989, "It is true that the intifada, as they call it, has had worldwide repercussions, has focused international attention on the Palestinian problem. Therefore, it also obligates us [to reach a settlement]."[85]

As for domestic reporting, the Intifada period exhibited two trends: one, the continuation of the tension between the Israeli press and the IDF; the other, the articulation of the already existing national mood. Arguments in favor of the latter have been made by Nir and Roeh, who

conducted a diachronic study of Israeli reporting of the Intifada.[86] They
found that in presenting the events of the Intifada, the Israeli press
merely reflected the existing collective consciousness. For instance, they
cite the tendency of the written press to mention Arab agency (in attacks
on Jews) more than the reverse. When a Jew was attacked, the article
would state that "An Arab has attacked a Jew;" whereas when an Arab
was attacked, the report would read that "An Arab has been attacked at
the hands of a Jew."[87] The tension between the Israeli press and the IDF
continued the trend that had begun after the Yom Kippur War and had
intensified during the war in Lebanon: Israeli journalists—in keeping
with the general mood enveloping the country—became more skeptical
of the way the IDF was being used as an instrument of defense policy.
One senior *Jerusalem Post* correspondent (who is known to hold left-
leaning attitudes toward the Israeli-Palestinian conflict) left the paper in
protest over what he saw as biased coverage. According to him, editorial
meetings were characterized by the sentiment of "How can we fuck the
army today?" In another account, the paper reported that soldiers were
puncturing the arms of stone-throwers with needles. When this was
found to be false (in this case, the punctures were found to have resulted
from drug abuse), the paper apparently refused to print a retraction.[88]
Whether or not the reporting of the paper was in fact biased, in the
words of the paper's then-publisher, Yehuda Levy, there was a "deep rift
that...existed between the Post and the defense establishment, caused
by the consistent support given by the Post to the Palestinians and the
harsh criticism of the IDF and the way it acted during the intifada."[89]

The Peace Movement

In interviews conducted by this author, the Israeli negotiators of the
Oslo agreement were virtually unanimous in claiming that the activities
of the peace movement had no impact on Israel's decision to pursue
peace with the Palestinians. Senior Peres aide Avi Gil went so far as to
claim that the peace movement had a hindering effect, if any, on Oslo.
The logic here is that if the Israeli public witnessed Israeli activists
protesting IDF policies in the territories, then the peace process would
be associated with a "fringe" element,[90] something that any government
seeks to avoid in garnering popular support for its policies. Nevertheless,
while elites might not be aware of a direct link between their policies and
the peace movement's activities, it is important to examine the nature
and extent of the movement's activities during the Intifada in order to
gauge its potential impact on public opinion more generally.

The general mood during the Intifada among the Israeli left, long the proponent of peace with Israel's neighbors, swayed between personal discomfort and a desire to see radical policy change. Said one self-declared member of the left, "If we looked too closely into the mirror, we'd leave [Israel]."[91] Not all members of the left refused to confront their government's policies directly. Some dealt with the contradiction between being part of a country with a particular self-image and the policies it was enacting by openly identifying with the Palestinians. As in the Lebanon War, Peace Now staged numerous protests, including one in which demonstrators displayed the names and photographs of all the children—Israeli and Palestinian—killed during the Intifada, prompting one activist to note that this contributed to a process of "humanizing the Palestinians."[92] Throughout the first two years of the uprising, Peace Now held what it called "A Day without Stones." Organizers succeeded in convincing West Bank Intifada committees to halt violent activities for one day. On these occasions, sanctioned by the army, Peace Now members met with Palestinian villagers. In the event that participants were detained by the IDF at roadblocks, they would hold the meetings across the checkpoint by megaphone.[93] The organization also urged soldiers to defy illegal and/or unduly brutal orders.[94]

In addition to Peace Now and Yesh Gvul, at least thirty different Israeli protest groups operated during the Intifada.[95] Women in Black, a Jerusalem-based movement, organized weekly vigils at busy intersections in which black-clad women held aloft placards demanding an end to the occupation. Two other groups focused on human rights; one, Rabbis for Human Rights, emerged from the American-based Conservative and Reform Judaism movements; the other, B'Tselem, was founded by a group of academics and members of Knesset and is still active in monitoring human-rights abuses by the IDF in the territories.[96] B'Tselem launched a number of activities, including handing out pamphlets and lobbying against house demolitions, administrative detention, and forced closure of Palestinian universities by the Israeli government. In a campaign against the IDF's use of rubber bullets, B'Tselem distributed rubber balls on street corners, with a note explaining that those children's toys are the same size as a rubber bullet. (The Hebrew term for "rubber bullet" is the same as for "rubber ball.") One of B'Tselem's cofounders notes the conflict between Israel's military strength vis-à-vis the Palestinians and its desperate policies involved in quelling the uprising: Precisely "because we're so strong, we don't have to be so weak as to use torture, administrative detention, house demolitions, etc."[97] Others, Hamizrach Le'shalom (The East for Peace) and Netivot Shalom

(Paths of Peace), increased their presence during the Intifada, and still other groups were founded during this period: Dai LaKibush (End the Occupation); Shnat Ha'Esrim Ve'Achat (The Twenty-First Year—i.e., founded twenty-one years after the occupation began in the wake of the 1967 war); and the Council for Peace and Security.[98]

Unconscious counternarratives reared their head within Israeli discourse during the Intifada. About the uprising, Peace Now founder Tzali Reshef writes, "It was Israel's Goliath pitted against the Palestinian David."[99] Years later, Yossi Beilin would note that "[t]he small, sophisticated, moral Israel of the 1950s and 1960s was transformed in the eyes of the young generation of television viewers from David into Goliath, while the stone-throwers became the modern-day Davids."[100] For Israelis to perceive themselves as holding the key to the Other's destruction shows the depth of the cognitive and emotional dissonance discussed here. In another reversal of a typical reaction to a collective uprising perpetrated by the adversary, another long-time Peace Now activist stated that "Peace Now defined the Intifada as a "war of liberation. I supported the Intifada."[101] For an Israeli to support an uprising targeted against her own country illustrates the depth of dissonance between Israelis' collective self-image and Israeli policy. No longer was the enemy waging a war of destruction against the state; instead, the Intifada was primarily being fought by self-declared "civil" means—despite the deaths and injuries that Palestinians inflicted on Israeli soldiers and civilians through violent protest actions.

A final example of the reversal of the dominant narrative that was occurring in Israeli consciousness was embodied in a slogan announcing a February 1988 Peace Now demonstration: "We demand that we, the people of Israel, be freed from the territories which have conquered us!"[102] This sentiment represents perhaps a third side to the Janus-faced relationship between conscious narratives and unconscious counternarratives: a recognition that the Other has been able to destroy the Self not physically (which would be the primary fear of a passive victim state, perhaps), but spiritually—the latent fear of a materially capable state that possesses a strong security ethic—as the defensive-warrior role-identity suggests.

Political Elites

For Israeli political elites, the Intifada represented the low point to which the twenty years of occupation had brought the country. More than the actual Israeli military response, the uprising symbolized the moral price of continuing the occupation. As Uri Savir said, "The Intifada exposed the illusion that you can have an 'occupation with a human face.' No occupation has a human face."[103] And Foreign Minister Shimon Peres declared, "We didn't have the right response. You cannot fire against children: a soldier against a child is a lost cause."[104] Yossi Beilin's thinking about the Intifada exposes the nuance inherent in the conflict. "We want to be benevolent, human and liberal, but you can't be, because of the stones. It's impossible to say, 'I'm the liberal guy who doesn't want to hurt you.' It was a Catch-22. There were some instances of cruelty. But generally the soldiers wanted to defend themselves; they hated being there."[105]

This view of the Intifada being a "Catch-22" exposes the contextual nature of the uprising and its significance for Israel. While international media focused on Israeli beatings and shootings, soldiers experienced themselves as being forced into a situation in which they could not act morally and defensively at the same time. Neither could they act in a way consistent with their self-image of being liberal, as Beilin put it. Witnessing the Palestinians agitating for sovereignty made Israelis realize that their state was enacting the role of sovereignty-suppressor, rather than defensive warrior. This illustrates the importance of others' actions in dredging up unconscious counternarratives and bringing about an ensuing cognitive dissonance between one's behavior and one's role-identity. Said chief Peres aide Avi Gil, "For the Israelis, what had been understood...was part of the propaganda fixation that the Palestinians were terrorists, murderers. Suddenly, the Israelis saw them differently: they saw a child standing bravely next to soldiers with guns. We realized that they're not murderers; not mafia; they want freedom. And they were prepared to take heavy casualties."[106] And as Rabin's Chief of Staff noted, "If a nation fights for its independence, no army can stop it."[107]

Ultimately, many more Palestinians than Israelis died during the Intifada. By December 1990, halfway through the six-year uprising, the IDF cited 623 Palestinians killed by security forces, as compared to 21 Israelis (9 of those being soldiers).[108] By the end of the Intifada in 1993, 1,200 Palestinians had been killed by Israeli soldiers, while 150 Israelis had been killed by Palestinians.[109] Such desperation clearly resulted from the Palestinian experience of "humiliation," as Savir put it. The problem lay, however, in the fact that "we [Israelis] didn't consider ourselves humiliators. Given the history of the Jewish people, it's not surprising that we overlooked what we were doing to the Palestinians." In fact, Savir notes that through the Intifada, "we gained respect for the Palestinians."[110] With Israel's role-identity being that of a "defensive warrior," the realization by elites that they were enacting the role of a "humiliator" brought to the fore some of the most despised unconscious counter-narratives—that the Jews, who had suffered at the hands of unwelcoming host countries for generations, were now humiliating others. This tension in turn led to a role conflict, and to the need to reconcile policy actions with self-image. Elites dreaded the same dehumanizing actions that both the active-duty soldier and the conscientious objector deplored. To humiliate is to deny the Other's humanity, something which the IDF, with all its defensive-warfare mentality, took pains not to do. As Colonel Tadmor noted about the IDF in the 1960s, "We were careful not to demonize the enemy. We said that we don't have the motive of hate or dehumanization. In a historical and political way, those who sit on the other side of the border are our enemies; that is a fact. [But at least we don't have to demonize them.]"[111] Similarly, suppressing the desire of the Palestinians for self-rule wrought a problematic dissonance on Israeli elites, who themselves represent what is considered a miraculous attempt at resurrecting Jewish sovereignty out of years of persecution. As Uri Savir told his Palestinian negotiating counterpart early on in the Oslo negotiations, "Israel has today a government that doesn't want to rule over your people. Human rights and occupation don't go hand in hand. We know that."[112]

Whether or not elites chose to deplore the actions of the military publicly, they at least did not shrink from articulating the discomfort in which they found themselves. As early as January 1988, Intifada atrocities were brought to light by members of Knesset, including Yossi Sarid and Deddy Zucker, both of the left-wing Citizens Rights Movement, in a letter sent to Defense Minister Rabin and widely distributed in the Knesset and among the press.[113] Rabin told Jewish lobbyists in 1989, "When you see the television, when you read the papers, when you hear the radio, bear in mind just how unpleasant it is for the soldiers and the border policemen who have to carry out this job, and for those who give them the orders, since it is very unpleasant for uniformed personnel to confront kids throwing stones and women demonstrators."[114] Two elements in particular are striking about this statement: first, Rabin's admission that this form of "warfare" would be unpleasant. Second, with all the bloodshed that Rabin himself must have witnessed, and which generations of Israeli soldiers certainly did, it is notable that an admission of "unpleasantness" was being used to describe the relatively bloodless tasks of riot control and policing.[115] Ultimately, these policies were not continued ad infinitum, as the Madrid peace talks would begin two years later, and the Oslo negotiations less than two years after that.

CONCLUSION

In its casting of the Israelis as brutal suppressors of national sovereignty, and as the most significant event directly preceding the opening of the Madrid and Oslo talks, the Intifada provides a powerful testing ground for the argument advanced here. Israel's defensive-warrior role-identity was severely challenged by the IDF's response to the Palestinian uprising. Ultimately, citizens and elites experienced a profound cognitive dissonance between their national role-identity and the military directives that soldiers were carrying out in the West Bank and Gaza Strip, as unconscious fears of becoming a vicious aggressor were brought to the fore. This chapter has attempted to illustrate the role of the masses, the media, and the peace movement in propelling elites to experience the dissonance. As channels for representation, these three groups enabled elites to look into the "mirror" that was essential for realizing the conflict between role-identity and behavior. Finally, as the immediate executor of Intifada policies, the attitudes of soldiers and officers during the uprising were also relevant in transmitting to elites an overall sense of despair at the status quo, ultimately propelling Israelis to replace their government with one running on a peace platform. The next chapter will survey the moves that Israel took toward peacemaking with the Palestinians in the 1990s, in the form of the multilateral Madrid talks finally giving way to the secret Israeli-PLO negotiations held in Oslo that would engender a multiyear peace process by the same name.

Chapter Seven

From Dissonance to Rightsizing—
Israel's Path to Oslo

The Intifada was four years old before the first-ever Israeli-Palestinian peace talks—in the form of the 1991 Madrid negotiations (held under Prime Minister Shamir's Likud government)—were inaugurated. The Madrid conference, which combined bilateral Arab-Israeli talks with multilateral task-force groups, soon foundered on the lack of direct Israeli-PLO contact, as Israel forbade participation of PLO members in the joint Jordanian-Palestinian delegation. It was therefore not until the secret talks of 1993 between small PLO and Israeli delegations in Oslo, Norway, that Israeli-Palestinian relations took a meaningful turn toward peace. This chapter will discuss the evolution of Israeli-Palestinian peacemaking efforts in the 1990s, by way of concluding the investigation of what led Israel to radically shift its policy stance toward the Palestinians and the PLO from one of conflict to compromise. Following an overview of the Madrid talks, including an outline of the key players and problems that prevented the talks from moving toward substantive policy outcomes, I will discuss the dynamics of the 1992 election, in which, for the first time since 1977, the Labor Party, headed by Yitzhak Rabin, regained power. The election was central in testing the desire of the Israeli public to shift its government's foreign policy course, as the Rabin government won the election on a pledge to reach an agreement with the Palestinians within six to nine months of taking office. Indeed, in conversations with his confidants after assuming power in 1992, Rabin emphasized that his main task as prime minister would be to reach a peace agreement with the Palestinians.[1] What led the Israeli public to seek out a new leadership that would shift the state's policy toward conflict resolution with the Palestinians, and what led the Rabin government to chart a course of peacemaking with the country's most intimate enemy? As I have argued in earlier chapters, this change was an integral indication that the polity had undergone a widespread attitude shift toward the Palestinians, which had resulted from the cognitive dissonance—and the attendant unconscious fears of becoming what the collective disdained—arising from the state's actions in the Intifada and the Lebanon War. The outcome of Rabin's pledge was a peace process that would significantly reshape relations between Israel and the Palestinians. This chapter will conclude with an examination of the evolution of the Oslo process, in turn drawing inferences about the relevance of the secret negotiating style for reaching agreement in the context of highly interested publics.

THE MADRID TALKS

With the conclusion of the Gulf War in which the United States had attempted to send a clear message to Iraq and other would-be revisionist states that aggression would be met with American military might, the Bush administration turned its eye to the Middle East. Under Secretary of State James Baker, the United States sponsored, along with Russia, a series of concurrent bilateral and multilateral Arab-Israeli peace talks in Madrid beginning in October 1991. The process was soon hobbled by a hawkish Shamir-led Likud government that withheld meaningful concessions and refused to negotiate directly with the PLO. In addition to multilateral groupings of Arab states and extraregional actors discussing issues relating to regional peace, Israel met directly with representatives from each of Syria and Lebanon, as well as a joint Jordanian-Palestinian delegation. According to Israeli stipulations, the Jordanian-Palestinian delegation was to have no members directly affiliated with the PLO, and delegates were required to be residents of the West Bank and Gaza Strip—neither from East Jerusalem, nor from outside of the immediate region. While followed to the letter, the law was immediately broken in spirit by the Palestinian half of the delegation that received daily directives from PLO officials in Tunis. The Israelis were well aware of this circumvention, but did nothing overtly to stop it. During a prime ministerial debate on the eve of the 1992 election, opposition leader Rabin made plain the contradiction between the Israeli government's policy and its practice: "If you check the so-called 'Jordanian-Palestinian delegation,' you will find a representative of the Palestinian diaspora and avowed PLO representatives, and you will see that there is a dialogue between the Palestinian delegation and Yasir Arafat."[2]

The Madrid peace talks soon shifted their location to Washington, and continued through the first half of 1993—effectively overlapping with the Israeli-PLO talks in Oslo. Yet since the Oslo talks were kept secret until August of that year, the timing would only become known publicly in the aftermath of the signing of the Declaration of Principles (DOP) on September 13. Little progress resulted from the Washington talks. Sessions in which delegates could not agree on procedural matters relegated the representatives to negotiating on sofas in the hallway. One such incident lasted three days, and resulted from disagreement over whether the Palestinians could be considered a negotiating unit independent from Jordan—a point of tension that embodied the crux of the Israeli-Palestinian dilemma. If Israel was to recognize the Palestinians as a distinct nation, then the inauguration of statehood would not be far behind. Ultimately, the parties reached a compromise: two tracks would be convened—one Jordanian, the other Palestinian.[3] Still, Israel's recognition of the Palestinians as a distinct nation would only come in the course of the Oslo talks.

On the substantive level, the content of the Madrid-Washington negotiations soon became circular. At one point, Peres aide Avi Gil deleted the numbering on the transcripts of a particular round and shuffled the pages. When he challenged his delegation to rearrange the pages into their proper sequence, the delegates could not.[4] Both Israelis and Palestinians emerged frustrated from the meager efforts at peacemaking. The talks foundered on issues ranging from the institutional basis for the conference—whether parties should refer to UN Resolution 242 calling on Israel to withdraw from territories occupied in the Six Day War—to the type of Palestinian elections that Israel would allow. When Arafat finally proclaimed in an interview with an Israeli news magazine that "We [the Palestinians] are not Red Indians. We are not looking to elect employees for the Israeli occupation,"[5] Israelis must have realized that they had not yet stopped playing the role of suppressors of another nation's sovereignty, a role that had become evident through the Intifada. (That same interview would be remembered, seven years later, by the editor of *The Jerusalem Report* as indicating to Israel that Arafat was a "necessary negotiating partner.")[6]

Despite its participation in the peace talks, the Likud government was by no means committed to reaching a settlement with the Palestinians. After losing the 1992 election to Rabin, Prime Minister Shamir even went so far as to openly admit that he would not have minded dragging out the negotiations for another ten years.[7] In addition to this intransigence, however, the Israeli government's refusal to negotiate directly with the PLO was perhaps the single biggest barrier to achieving meaningful peace. Though not yet ready to state so publicly, Rabin told Baker in March 1991—prior to Madrid—that Israel needed to negotiate with the PLO.[8] And only a few days after the convening of the Madrid talks in October of that year, the Labor Party passed a resolution revoking its refusal to negotiate with the organization.[9] However, it must be emphasized that while the Israeli willingness to deal with the Palestinians as a national entity as enacted at Madrid was a new phenomenon for the region, it still did not fully embody an Israeli recognition of the distinctiveness of the Palestinian nation. Thus, while Madrid was significant in ushering in a new phase of Israeli-Palestinian relations, it would take until Oslo for Israel to recognize the PLO as the consensual leadership organ of the Palestinians, and for the Palestinians to be recognized as a separate political actor.[10]

Furthermore, the Palestinians' forced inclusion in a joint Jordanian-Palestinian delegation at Madrid meant that Israelis could still propagate the "Jordan-is-Palestine" argument. This viewpoint, popular among segments of the Israeli right, held that since the Jordanian state is composed of a large number of Palestinians (some say a majority, but demographic data is publicly unavailable), the Jordanian government should be responsible for finding a solution to the "Palestinian problem." King Hussein's decision to disengage from the West Bank in July 1988, however, effectively eliminated the Jordanian option from the political landscape. The king's statement sent a strong message to Israel that he considered the Palestinians to be a nation in their own right, and that Israel would no longer be able to rely on him to eke out a joint settlement that would preclude the formation of a Palestinian state along Israel's eastern flank. It would take a few more years for Israel to fully embrace this logic, however. In sum, the 1992 elections were the first institutionalized expression, beyond the more ambiguous Madrid talks, of an Israeli desire to seek peace with the Palestinians. The Oslo talks that would be secretly convened six months following the elections were the first official Israeli acknowledgment of the PLO as the legitimate representative of the Palestinians, and of the Palestinians as deserving of recognition as a separate nation. The following section will discuss the dynamics of the 1992 elections that represented such a shift in Israeli thinking.

THE 1992 ELECTIONS

Of all of Israel's elections, the 1992 race for the thirteenth Knesset would come to be the most pivotal for testing Israeli attitudes toward the Palestinians and the fate of the territories in the wake of a five-year long Intifada, and ultimately in relocating the Israeli government onto a policy course committed to seeking peace with the Palestinians through negotiations with the PLO. A 1986 Israeli law had banned contacts by Israeli citizens with members of the so-called terrorist group,[11] yet 1993 saw the commencement of talks between the Israeli government and the PLO. (The Labor-sponsored bill overturning the law passed a preliminary reading in the Knesset as early as December 1992, and became law in January 1993—one day before the opening round of the back-channel talks in Oslo.) In order to understand the impetus for this fundamental policy change, we have to examine the 1992 elections that brought the Labor Party back to power.

It is important to recall that Labor had dominated the political scene from the inception of the state in 1948, until being unseated by the Likud in 1977 in what became known as the "upheaval." This long tenure of the Labor Party had prompted some observers to think about Israel as a single-party state in multiparty clothing. The 1984 and 1988 elections created "national-unity governments," a power-sharing arrangement whereby the prime minister's post, along with other top ministerial positions, rotated between both parties. But since 1977, the Labor Party had not enjoyed governing dominance, and policies vis-à-vis the Palestinians had tended toward the hawkish. That said, the initial push toward settlement-building in the territories had come under the purview of a Labor government following the Six Day War. Implicit in peacemaking overtures with the Palestinians, and explicit in the Oslo agreement, would be at minimum a freezing of settlement-building and at most an uprooting of settlements in favor of Palestinian autonomy over the West Bank and Gaza. Thus, it is not enough to say that the peace process came about because Likud was defeated by Labor in 1992. Rather, we must continue to ask what caused a wholesale Israeli shift from belligerency toward peacemaking with the Palestinians, such that the Israeli electorate would want to bring back a Labor government in the first place.

By April 1992, when the election campaign began, Israel's first self-declared "war of choice" had been fought—in the form of the 1982 Lebanon War; five years of violent and civil unrest had shaken the territories—in the form of the Intifada; an Arab-Israeli peace process had been proceeding lamely for six months; and the most unusual backroom political scandal to rock Israeli politics had just taken place, precipitating the surprising formation of Israel's most right-wing coalition government to date. The series of events in March 1990 became dubbed by Yitzhak Rabin and his supporters "the smelly affair," and involved Shimon Peres, Rabin's longtime rival for leadership of the Labor Party, negotiating an alliance with the ultra-orthodox parties Shas and Agudat

Israel—in return for helping to unseat the incumbent Likud government through a parliamentary vote of non-confidence. When Peres's new-found friends fled from the agreement, he was personally humiliated, and the Labor Party lost its parliamentary support. The episode resulted in the defeat of Peres to Rabin for party leadership in the Labor primaries, and in turn led to a particular spin on the 1992 election campaign.[12] As discussed next, the party was able to cast a past-chief-of-staff into the role of peacemaker, thus embodying the duality inherent in the defensive-warrior role-identity.

The 1992 election campaign pitted Rabin against incumbent Prime Minister Yitzhak Shamir, and hinged on foreign and domestic policy via a battle of personalities—likely by design in the case of the Rabin team, and by default in the case of Shamir. Both of these elements were ultimately underpinned by an overall clash of worldviews: these elections were won and lost along a fault line of Israel's self-image. In the parlance of the day, the narratives were articulated as a self-definition of Israel as a "nation that dwells alone" versus Israel being a "nation like all others."[13] Shamir, like Begin before him, propagated the former narrative and lost; Rabin championed the latter view and won. While Rabin promised peace with the Palestinians (yet on a backdrop of his own military prowess), Shamir glorified the role of war in bolstering the human spirit: the Likud's closing election rally in Tel Aviv featured Shamir declaring that "we need to accept that war is inescapable, because without this, the life of the individual has no purpose and the nation has no chance of survival."[14] The relevance of these disparate role-identity messages were by no means divorced from the particularities of Israeli peace and war policies; rather, these identities defined them. Those who viewed Israel as isolated within a sea of hostility saw less reason to make the concessions necessary to reach peace with its neighbors. Conversely, a perspective of Israel as being "a nation like all others" meant that it could afford to take the risks associated with peacemaking, and in fact that the goal of peacemaking was deemed essential to the Zionist vision. As Yossi Beilin later described his view of Israel's mission, "I believe that the implementation of the Zionist dream is normalization, and you can't have normalization without peace with your neighbors."[15]

However, on this note it is interesting that at one point in the campaign, Shamir chose to defend his government's efficacy by emphasizing the expansion of Israel's diplomatic ties, noting that thirty-five countries had "resumed or established relations" with Israel in the previous two years. Yet, almost in the same breath, Shamir declared that "[t]here is no PLO representative or anyone resembling the PLO within the Palestinian delegation" at Madrid.[16] The pairing of these statements suggests that Shamir was attuned to the dominant narrative of Israel's seeing itself as a nation like all others, and was appealing to that segment of the electorate that might otherwise prefer to support a Rabin-led initiative that would bring diplomatic ties not only with far-off states, but with Israel's immediate neighbors. While opposed to peace with the PLO, Shamir was therefore stressing his government's attainment of diplomatic relations with many other states. This need to stress—and indeed, achieve—diplomatic relations with others in the international system emphasizes the overarching theme of *normalization* that was central to the Zionist enterprise, and that was discussed in chapter three. That is, so essential to Zionist goals was the attainment of a "normal," sovereign status that an expansionist policy orientation would not be deemed essential to Israeli grand strategy; moreover, it may even exclude the more aggressive forms of Zionism, such as those embodied in the Revisionist movement.

In addition to highlighting the role-identity of Israel in the regional and global system, the 1992 elections hinged partly on competing personalities. Labor's election campaign described Rabin as a pragmatic man of security ("Mr. Security" became the nickname favored by pundits) who had led his country as chief of staff to the most glorious victory of Israel's past—in the three-front clash that was the Six Day War. Indeed, during these elections Labor preferred to focus on its leader rather than on the party as a whole. A recent Knesset vote had instituted direct election for prime minister, but this electoral innovation would not take effect until 1996 (ultimately being reversed in 2001). Still, according to Labor strategists, the party acted as if that personalistic-thrust to Israeli elections was already in effect in 1992.[17] The Labor Party slogan was "Israel is awaiting Rabin"—a play on the popular jingle prior to the Six Day War, "Nasser is awaiting Rabin."

The overall message of the Labor campaign was that Rabin would bring peace with security. One campaign advertisement declared that "security is us" and featured the faces of a number of ex-IDF officers who populated the ranks of the party list.[18] Though hawkish in his views, Shamir possessed neither the distinctive military history nor the quiet charisma held by his opponent. Still, Rabin was forced to confront the personal demons of his past: a short-lived nervous breakdown on the eve of the Six Day War, and allegations of alcoholism. The latter accusation he firmly denied, and he was able to divert public attention from concerns about his mental health by focusing on his achievements as chief of staff during that fateful week in June 1967. By all accounts, the Six Day War remains etched in Israeli collective memory as an exalted event and perhaps the most striking embodiment of Israel's role-identity as a defensive warrior. As Rabin told reporters in May 1992, "I do not have to continually dwell on one small segment of the results of a great war which I directed and for which I prepared the Army."[19] The Six Day War—which, conveniently for the Labor Party, was being remembered on its twenty-fifth anniversary on the eve of the elections—as well as Labor's campaign platform combining peace with security—underscored the crucial intersection between defensiveness and warriorness that defines Israel's identity. By contrast, the Lebanon War was dubiously celebrating its tenth anniversary during the same election campaign, a coincidence that, as indicated in chapter five, was used as election fodder by the left against the right.

Finally, issues surrounding both domestic politics and Israeli policy toward the Palestinians were intertwined in the course of the campaign, leading Israelis to favor a pro-peace policy in the territories. By reaching out to the economically disaffected in Israel, Rabin promised to bring peace with the Palestinians at the expense of ideologically motivated settlement-building. A May 1992 radio report summarized the Labor platform as "link[ing] our economic situation to a peace that provides security....The way to do it is to determine priorities. How...? Without investment in the territories."[20] A Peace Now report released days before the election added fuel to the antisettlement fire, with its claim that the Likud government had in fact been accelerating the level of building in the territories during the months of April, May, and the beginning of June.[21] That the settlement issue—even if cast as an economic one—became one of the fulcra on which the election rested supports the idea that Israelis did not view an expansionist state as meshing with their collective view of Israel's role-identity. That is, Rabin would never have tried to convince voters that spending had been too high for IDF training for short- or long-range border threats, for instance. Such a claim would have been political suicide; so essential is Israel's view of its own defensive might that only expansionist policies (such as settlement-building) were deemed fair play within the context of mainstream campaigning. And the Labor Party was clearly trying to appeal to mainstream voters.

The settlement issue had been a sticking point for U.S.-Israeli relations for some months, but, as mentioned in chapter one, Israel could have simply decided to freeze settlement-building rather than negotiate with the PLO leading to an autonomy framework, if fear of harming the U.S.-Israel "special relationship" was the primary motivation for peace-making with the Palestinians. Instead, however, the Labor platform called for far-reaching changes in the West Bank and Gaza, including a "promise to implement immediately autonomy in the territories," and a recognition that "Labor will be prepared for...territorial compromise in all sectors, in accordance with UN Resolutions 242 and 338. Labor promises to conduct 'real' negotiations with the Palestinian delegation."[22] Presumably, the reference to "real" negotiations was meant to contrast with the stalled Shamir-led peace process begun at Madrid. And while the party platform did not acknowledge the government's willingness to negotiate with the PLO directly, such a policy course soon evolved during the early months of 1993.

A June televised debate between Rabin and Shamir exemplified the differences between the two parties on the Palestinian issue. The Gaza Strip was long considered a liability in security, economic, and demographic terms by the center-left in Israel. This was exemplified by Rabin's September 1992 statement to a gathering at the Washington Institute for Near East Policy that he wished that Gaza would "sink into the sea"—but "since that's not about to happen, we must find a solution to the problem of the Strip."[23] The comment—more often quoted without the second half of the sentence—generated much controversy, especially among listeners attuned to Israeli complaints that their Arab neighbors, since 1948, hoped to "drive the Jews into the sea." Nevertheless, during the debate, the differences between the two parties on the issue of Gaza became clear. In response to the moderator's question that "the Intifada crossed the Green Line in recent months [a reference to terrorist attacks that had taken place within pre-1967 Israel] and reached the heart of the large cities. Many people...are asking, 'How can we go on living like this?'" and that "Many people ask what do we need with Gaza—the home of all these Arabs who murder people in Israel's big cities?" Shamir responded by asking, "Look, one can ask why Gaza? Why Judea and Samaria?...This is Eretz Yisrael."[24] Rabin, on the other hand, indicated Labor's willingness to withdraw from Gaza within an autonomy framework. "Then we will see fewer Gazans in our cities. I want the Gazans to stay in the Gaza Strip."[25] Such reasoning reinforced the idea of separation that was becoming popular among Israelis in early 1993, particularly following Rabin's decision to seal off the territories in the wake of terror attacks inside Israel. These sorts of sentiments also supported the idea that Israel was no longer comfortable playing the role of occupier, as that clashed with its defensive-warrior identity.

The IDF and the Intifada on the Eve of Elections

While the 1992 elections were not the first to be held during the Intifada, they were the first since Israel's political and military policies in responding to the uprising had become deeply internalized by Israeli

society. The 1988 elections, by contrast, were held less than a year after
the Intifada had erupted in December 1987, and therefore we can expect
the 1992 race to provide a stronger test of Israelis' attitudes toward their
government's Intifada policies. The previous chapter detailed Israel's
policies during the uprising and the reaction from disparate segments
within Israeli society. Still, it is useful to examine what events were
occurring in the territories on the eve of the 1992 elections, and the
nature of Israeli security discourse during those few months.

The first apparent theme relates to the nature of Israeli control over
the territories—whether they were seen as an integral part of Israel or
whether the occupation was viewed as a temporary measure until peace
arrangements could be reached with the Palestinians. The Greater Israel
stream on the right, exemplified by Shamir and Jabotinsky before him,
saw the holding of the territories and the establishment of settlements
there as not only necessary for Israeli security, but as a path to national
salvation. Accordingly, in April 1992, a heated parliamentary debate
erupted over the Likud's convening of a ceremony in which Shamir
"awarded Judea, Samaria, and Gaza Defender decorations" to honor
IDF soldiers who served in the West Bank and Gaza while defending
the Israeli settlements there. At the event, Shamir declared that "Judea,
Samaria, and Gaza are ours, and will remain ours forever and ever." In
response, Labor Secretary Micha Harish declared that "Shamir's
extremist statements once more prove that there is no difference
between Shamir, Beni Begin, and the Likud; and Rehav'am Ze'evi,
Ge'ula Cohen, or Rafa'el Eitan."[26] (The latter three politicians belonged
to parties on the far right; Ze'evi, as Tourism Minister, would be murdered in 2001 by members of the Popular Front for the Liberation of
Palestine.) Clearly, Labor and parties to the left represented an Israeli
role-identity that could not accommodate a view of itself as an occupier
or as an expansionist state. Voters in the 1992 elections accordingly sub-
scribed to that view.

Another security issue that rose to the fore in the lead-up to the
election involved the actions of the IDF undercover units—known as
Duvdevan ("cherry") and Shimshon (Samson)—charged with rooting
out suspected terrorists in the territories. As evidence that armed
Palestinians were being shot dead by IDF undercover troops, often at
close range, voices from within Israeli society began to critique these
policies on ethical grounds. Stated one editorial, "The army apparently
has not given much thought to the legality of the shooting, the moral
repercussions of these acts on soldiers in elite units, and the practical
effects on the course of the Intifada."[27] Soon after, the army was forced
onto the defensive. An Israel Television Network interview on April 30

featured a reporter asking Major General Dani Yatom, OC-central command, "Where is the thin line between freer shooting at suspects today and the moral aspect?" and telling Gen. Yatom that "[t]here is public criticism that the finger is too heavy on the trigger" in the territories.[28]

Following this interview, Lieutenant General Ehud Barak and Deputy Chief of Staff Amnon Lipkin-Shahak both criticized the report as misleading, and sought to publicly explain the IDF's shooting policy, citing the criticisms as falsely based. Lipkin-Shahak stated, "I do not think we have tried to whitewash anything. I think the military establishment has been very critical of itself, and I believe we inculcate in our soldiers the right military values. . . . Incidentally, the rules of engagement have not been changed; we have merely clarified them. We have not instituted a more liberal approach toward opening fire."[29] These sentiments were echoed at the civilian level, when Defense Minitser Moshe Arens denied the existence of an alleged shoot-to-kill policy, declaring, "I do not know that there is a military force anywhere in the world that is engaged in fighting terrorism that is observant to such an extent and is limited to such an extent by the regulations as are the Israel Defense Forces."[30] Still, a month later, the Israeli human rights organization B'Tselem issued a report criticizing these policies as "immoral and illegal."[31] Again, the IDF went on the defensive, with its spokesman stating "that the IDF does not uphold and will never uphold a policy—or a reality—of doing away with wanted men. The IDF is sensitive to human life, be it Jewish or Arab, no less than anybody else."[32] Israeli dissent regarding its army's policies in the territories had not abated, despite the attempts by senior IDF staff to defend their institution's image. Yet the fact that the IDF responded to the critiques in the way it did—that is, in emphasizing its "sensitivity to human life"—reflects the deep-seated internalization of Israel's role-identity as a defensive warrior, and the IDF's purity-of-arms security ethic.

Soon after, the International Committee of the Red Cross (ICRC) issued a statement condemning Israel's practice of interrogating Palestinian prisoners. Israel's ambassador to the UN in Geneva, Yitzhak Lior, responded by expressing "deep regret" over the statement, adding that "[a]t a time when untold suffering is being caused by internecine and international conflicts in many parts of the world, it seems extraordinary that the ICRC has seen fit to publish a critical statement on this . . . issue alone."[33] That Israel's ambassador chose to distance himself from the criticism by claiming that Israel was being unfairly singled out reveals the depth of the country's discomfort with accusations stemming from its "international mirrors." Here, Israel was not denying the allegations, only regretting that they were being exposed by an international body with which Israel had a "tradition of cooperation and understanding."[34]

A final security issue in the lead-up to the elections exposed the face of an aggressive Israel that was surprised at its own capacity for vengeance. On 24 May, a Gazan Palestinian murdered a young girl, Helena Rapp, in the Israeli coastal town of Bat Yam. In the wake of the murder, the left-wing Meretz bloc (which would win a solid 12 seats in the subsequent elections) condemned the murder at the same time that it criticized the government "for continuing with the Likud's policy of taking over the administered territories," thus "playing into the hands of Palestinian terrorists and murderers"[35]—a clear suggestion that the government was perhaps indirectly responsible for the murder. And when segments of the Israeli public began calling for "death to the Arabs," with thousands of Bat Yam residents protesting and throwing stones and other debris at police, Likud Justice Minister Dan Meridor called on Israelis to "stop the call [of death to the Arabs] which, according to him, is reminiscent of terrible voices of the past."[36] Like the discourse surrounding Sabra and Shatilla, Meridor's reproach brings to consciousness Israelis' unconscious fears of becoming an aggressor similar to the multitudes of anti-Semitic persecutors throughout history to which Jews were subject.

Though having occurred after the elections, it is still useful here to examine an additional security issue that would come to the fore in the wake of the new government's assumption of power, but before the Oslo talks got under way in earnest: this was Rabin's December 1992 decision to expel 415 Hamas activists to Lebanon following the killing of eight Israeli soldiers in twelve days, including the kidnaping and murder of a border-guard soldier, Sergeant Nissim Toledano. An action embroiled in international controversy, the move led to the Palestinian decision to boycott the Washington talks, with Syria following suit. (The Palestinians did not return to the table until the following April.) The backlash that resulted from the deportation also prompted criticism from Rabin's own allies. Since Lebanese Prime Minister Rafik Hariri surprised Rabin by refusing to admit the deportees into the country, the media showed footage of the activists residing in makeshift encampments in the midst of a Lebanon winter. Yossi Beilin later dubbed the expulsion "one of the government's worst mistakes."[37] While Rabin had declared to the Knesset that "the same hand that is stretched out in friendship will pull the trigger against terror," his coalition partners—including some in his own party—viewed the act as too extreme. Environment Minister Yossi Sarid, from the left-wing Meretz bloc, criticized the deportation for not being accompanied by sufficient overtures to the Palestinians, particularly with regard to the government's refusal to talk directly with the PLO. "Expelling the Hamas people was only half the job; and a half-done job is worse than doing nothing at all," Sarid stated.[38] Ultimately, the Rabin government decided to shorten the duration of the expulsion.

Clearly, the criticism leveled against Rabin by his coalition partners stemmed in part from their frustration at the exclusion of the PLO from the Washington talks. According to one news analysis at the time, thirteen of the government's eighteen ministers favored negotiating with the PLO at this point.[39] Ultimately, of course, it would be learned that the Labor government was making inroads with the Palestinians in a back-channel setting. But the critiques surrounding the hesitance to recognize the PLO indicates a wholesale shift among significant segments of the Israeli polity toward making peace with the Palestinians. Since the PLO was recognized to be the only actor on the Palestinian side that would be able to reach a settlement, Israelis were aware that without talking directly to the PLO, a peace agreement would not be attainable.

Eventually, the expulsions and political backlash that followed had at least one positive effect on Israeli willingness to offer the Palestinians the territorial concessions necessary for peace. After further terrorist incidents in March 1993—ones inside the Green Line—Rabin decided to seal off the West Bank and Gaza, precluding Palestinian day laborers from entering Israel. While the so-called "closure" (a policy that would be repeated many times) aroused the wrath of international public opinion and fomented frustration in the territories where 120,000 Palestinians were prevented from reaching their jobs, Israelis were, for the first time, exposed to the possibility that the West Bank and Gaza may not be part of Israel forever. In addition to the Rabin government's public works initiatives that provided 40,000 jobs for Palestinians in the territories, the "separation" of the two areas from Israel meant that Israelis could now begin to contemplate a withdrawal, perhaps even leading to the establishment of a Palestinian state.[40]

The 1992 Party Platforms

In order to assess the significance of the Labor victory in the 1992 elections, it is also useful to investigate the various party platforms and messages delivered in the course of the election campaign. A brief look at three parties on the right—the Likud bloc, the National Religious Party (NRP), and Moledet ("homeland")—provides a good illustration of the position that would be overridden by Labor's vision of ending the occupation and granting the Palestinians autonomy. Conversely, examining the platforms of two prominent factions on the left—Labor and the Meretz bloc—helps us identify the precise message that was delivered by Israeli voters on election day. As for the Likud, Prime Minister Shamir stated at the party's opening election rally that "in the upcoming elections, the struggle will be over 'the future nature and character of Eretz Yisra'el'" (the Land of Israel). He added, "Several more years of Likud rule, and there will no longer be any mention of a Palestinian state."[41] Further to the right, the NRP—a staple of Israeli coalition governments throughout the decades of Israeli parliamentary history—declared its support for "the imposition of Jewish sovereignty on all of Judea, Samaria [the West Bank], and the Gaza Strip as the political aim of the State of Israel," and stated that it opposed the establishment of a Palestinian state.[42] Thus, it is clear that the right-wing was comfortable enough with the status quo to advocate a continuation of it. At the most extreme on the Israeli right stood Moledet, whose ballot symbol was the Hebrew letter "tet"—advocating the forced "transfer" of Palestinians from the territories into neighboring Arab states. A Moledet election advertisement stated that "settlers in Judea, Samaria, and Gaza live in terror and serve as targets for the Intifada's thugs, yet...our glorious army is being maimed and castrated."[43] The use of the castration metaphor invokes the idea that military prowess in the Zionist context is equated with masculinity; the nineteenth-century call for Zionism to give birth to a New Jew, a "Jewry of Muscle" is indicative of this drive. Still, at the policy level, these voices would be silenced by that segment of Israeli society that saw its army's actions in the territories as more psychologically distressing than was the implication that the IDF's sword was being blunted. And even at the level of electioneering, not all right-wing ideas were accommodated into the pantheon of lawful discourse: both the Kach party (founded by Rabbi Meir Kahane) and Kahana Chai, its offshoot, were disqualified from running election lists due to the parties' antidemocratic and racist overtones.

On the left, and as previously discussed, the Labor Party championed a course of moderation toward the Palestinians, promising "territorial compromise in all sectors, including the Golan Heights," as well as a "commitment to implement autonomy within 'the shortest possible time' (within six to nine months)."[44] This six-to-nine month promise would be perhaps the most prominent campaign bequest to the thirteenth Knesset, and was a phrase that would be remembered by Israelis throughout the entire Israeli-PLO peace process. Further to the left, the Meretz bloc—a new left-wing grouping composed of the three previously existing, smaller parties Ratz (the Citizens' Rights Movement), Mapam and Shinui—presented the voters with a tricolored promise of opposing the ultraorthodox and "religious coercion," supporting "peace initiatives," and pursuing the "rule of law."[45] It was these left-leaning messages that had the most impact at the ballots during the 1992 elections.

The Results

On 23 June, 77.4 percent of Israelis went to the polls, a voter-turnout rate slightly lower than previous elections, but still consistent with the country's near-80 percent rate throughout the decades. The Labor Party, winning 44 of the Knesset's 120 seats (compared with the Likud's 32), was asked to form the government. It joined with Meretz (12 seats) and the Sephardi, Orthodox Shas party (6 seats), providing for a bare-majority coalition of 62 seats. While Shas had historically been known to be dovish, the party's political activities came to focus more on social issues than on issues of territory and security. It was Rabin's choice to join with Shas; it would not have been necessary to do so to round out the coalition, as the Labor Party could have joined with the two smaller parties on the far left instead—the Communist Party, also called Hadash (an Arab-Jewish mix garnering 3 seats) and the Democratic Arab Party (2 seats). However, it was important to Rabin to maintain the impression that he had a Jewish backing for his peace policies, and so Shas and Meretz it was.

On the right, along with Likud's 32 mandates, was Tzomet's surprising 8 (up from 2 seats in 1988); Moledet with 3 (up from 2); the more moderate, but still rightist, NRP, with 6 (an increase of one seat from 1988); and United Torah Jewry, with 4 (compared to 2 in 1988). This suggests that indeed the right wing was not forgotten in the 1992 elections. However, the shift back to a Labor-dominated Knesset from fifteen years of Likud rule indicates that Israelis were hungry for a sweeping change.

THE RABIN GOVERNMENT PURSUES OSLO

The Rabin-led Labor government represented a worldview that stood in stark relief to that of its predecessor. In his opening address to the thirteenth Knesset in July 1992, Rabin declared, "It is no longer correct that all the world is against us. It is upon us to escape from the sense of isolation that has held us in its grasp for almost fifty years. It is upon us to join the voyage towards peace and international cooperation...for if we do not, we will be left alone at the station."[46] Reversing the Likud-held view that "the whole world is against us," in the words of an Israeli song

popular after the Six Day War, Israel was prepared to join the family of
nations by making the peacemaking overtures necessary to secure itself a
more welcome place in the international community, and within the
region itself. Fourteen years earlier, the Camp David Accords had stag-
nated following Begin's reluctance to implement Palestinian autonomy
measures, and then successive Likud governments' commitment to
staving off Palestinian independence. Now, on his first day as prime
minister, Rabin was openly declaring his willingness to abide by the
spirit of the agreements reached between Begin and Sadat in 1978. As he
said to the Knesset on the day of his inauguration, "We are convinced
that not enough has become of talks with the Palestinian residents of the
territories, in order to reach what, to my mind, Israel has committed
itself to: Palestinian self-rule, or autonomy. Not municipal autonomy,
this they almost have, but self-government, according to what is laid out
in the Camp David accords."[47]

In many ways, Madrid was a necessary backdrop to the eventual
substantive talks that were conducted in Oslo. Madrid served in part as a
forum for confidence-building between Israel and the Palestinians, as
when Shimon Peres asked PLO member Abu Ala (who was a chief
member of the PLO's Oslo delegation) to remove a certain PNC dele-
gate from Madrid. When he complied, Peres recalls, "I knew we would
be able to talk business together."[48] The Madrid process also initiated the
Israeli public and government alike into the idea of negotiating with the
Palestinians. However, it was not until the Oslo process that Israel
acknowledged the PLO as a formal negotiating partner. Without the
glare of local and international media, Israeli and PLO negotiators were
able to reach substantive agreement on a settlement between the two
peoples. And while polls revealed that a solid 62 percent of Israelis were
in favor of the Oslo agreement in the wake of the signing of the DOP,
Israeli elites did not have to worry that negotiation leaks would lead the
process astray as it was unfolding.[49]

The Israeli-Palestinian peace process that would become known as
Oslo had its genesis at an April 1992 lunch meeting at a Tandoori restau-
rant in Tel Aviv between soon-to-be Deputy Foreign Minister Yossi
Beilin; Terje Larsen, director of the Fafo Research Institute in Norway;
and Dov Randell, a member of the Trade Union Confederation in Israel.
Visiting Israel to research the living standards of the Palestinians, Larsen
believed that serious efforts at negotiation could not occur without PLO
representation. In this vein, he offered his institute as a venue for secret
talks between Israel and the Palestinians. Once Labor won the elections,
Beilin, with the knowledge of Foreign Minister Peres, began the process,
albeit unofficially.

The first Israeli negotiators to sit with members of the PLO were not elected officials; they were two academics, Ron Pundak, director of the Economic Cooperation Foundation, a non-profit organization dedicated to Israeli-Palestinian conflict resolution; and Yair Hirschfeld, a Middle East historian at the University of Haifa. In addition to Larsen, the Norwegian team of facilitators included Foreign Minister Torvald Stoltenberg—who would be replaced in April 1993 by Johan Jorgen Holst; Holst's wife Marianne Heiberg, an academic; Larsen's wife, Mona Juul, also an officer in the foreign ministry; and Jan Egeland, Norway's deputy foreign minister.

The Palestinian team was led by Ahmed Qurei (better known as Abu Ala), the PLO's so-called finance minister. A relative unknown within Israeli governmental and intelligence circles, Abu Ala was in close contact with Mahmoud Abbas (Abu Mazen), who had been in charge of the PLO's unofficial contacts with Israel for the previous five years. (Each of these men would eventually serve as Palestinian prime minister once Arafat agreed to lessen his hold over the Palestinian Authority a decade later.) Ala was joined by Maher el Kurd, an economic advisor to Abu Ala and Arafat, and Hasan Asfur, a political advisor to Abu Mazen.

On the Israeli side, at first only Hirschfeld and Pundak, who remained in close contact with Beilin throughout the initial rounds, participated. Confining the team to nongovernment representatives meant that those Israeli officials who did know about the back channel could feign ignorance to the press when necessary. Moreover, the initial rounds served as useful exploratory sessions for each side to glean the intentions of the other. Israel elevated the talks to official status only in May 1993, at that time bringing in Uri Savir, director general of the Israeli foreign ministry. The final addition to the Oslo team was Yoel Singer, an Israeli lawyer who had been practicing in Washington at the time; he joined the talks in June.

The Oslo venue and the fact that Israelis were negotiating with the PLO was kept secret almost right up until the signing of the DOP in September 1993. While the press was curious, the best they could do was to release red herrings—such as a July 1993 report that Health Minister Efraim Sneh was meeting with PLO officials under the auspices of Egypt's good offices.[50] While Beilin knew about the talks from the outset—and indeed helped orchestrate them; he only let Peres in on the details in February 1993—after the second round held in Sarpsbourg on February 11–12.[51] Peres, in turned, informed Rabin, who loosely gave his political rival a green light to continue with the talks. In the meantime, Rabin asked his private pollster to feel out Israeli public opinion on a Gaza-Jericho plan—the proposal that ultimately became the backbone of the Oslo agreement. That is, Israel would withdraw from all of the Gaza Strip, plus one location in the West Bank (which was decided to be Jericho) in order to enable the Palestinian Authority to establish a foothold in that territory, until such time as the fate of the rest of the West Bank was decided on. These polling efforts in February 1993 found 51 percent of Israelis in favor of such a plan, and only 37 percent against.[52]

Thus, until the negotiations were made public in August, Rabin, Peres, and Beilin were the only Israeli government officials aware of the Oslo talks. As for how much other parties knew, in March the Norwegians decided to hint to the Palestinian delegation at Oslo that the Israeli side now had official backing. That same month, Egypt was informed, as was U.S. Secretary of State Warren Christopher. However, the PLO refrained from informing the Palestinian delegation at the Washington talks.

THE DECLARATION OF PRINCIPLES

The Oslo agreement took the form of the Israeli-PLO Declaration of Principles that laid out a plan for peacemaking over the next five years, and that was signed on the White House Lawn on 13 September 1993. The agreement, signed by Shimon Peres and Abu Mazen, contained provisions on the goals and framework of the subsequent negotiations, Palestinian elections, the nature of the jurisdiction in question, and the timeline for transitional negotiations to give way to talks about final-status issues. The latter issues would include the status of Jerusalem, questions relating to the repatriation of Palestinian refugees, the fate of the settlements, and issues of security and borders—including the ultimate status of the West Bank and Gaza Strip. In the short-term, authority over education, culture, welfare, health, tourism, and taxation was to be transferred to the Palestinians.[53] While the Palestinian Authority would establish a police force of its own, responsibility for the security of the settlers, as well as the borders of the territories would be left to Israel—at least in the short term. However, the IDF would redeploy from Palestinian population centers within the territories. Moreover, as indicated in the "Gaza-Jericho First" plan, Israel would withdraw from virtually all of the Gaza Strip (although the fate of the Jewish settlements would be decided later), as well as the town of Jericho in the West Bank. The IDF indeed withdrew from Jericho on 13 May 1994, and from two-thirds of Gaza on 17 May (4,500 settlers remained), enabling Arafat to return to the strip where he established the new headquarters of the

Palestinian Authority.[54] Given the many crucial issues left for the later stages of the peace process, the DOP stipulated that "permanent status negotiations will commence as soon as possible, but not later than the beginning of the third year of the interim period," a schedule that was eventually abandoned.

CONCLUSION

In his speech at the September signing ceremony on the White House lawn, Rabin told the Palestinians, "we are destined to live together on the same soil in the same land," and that "[w]e, like you, are people; people who want to build a home, to plant a tree, to love, live side by side with you in dignity, in affinity, as human beings, as free men."[55] At long last, Israel was indicating its recognition of its mortal Other as akin to itself. As the forty-five years of warfare and mutual demonization between the State of Israel and its Palestinian neighbors had given way to efforts at peacemaking, Israelis and Palestinians were doubtless contemplating a vision of a new future. Israeli strategic analyst Ehud Ya'ari captured the complexity inherent in the Israeli-Palestinian peace process when he described Oslo as "a divorce where you wake up each morning in the bed of your former wife."[56] Given the geographic and economic contours of the Middle East core, it was clear that Israelis and Palestinians were bound to live side by side. Yet, by the early 1990s, the question had become whether that coexistence would take the form of occupation or separation. There was no doubt that the intimacy inherent in the occupation had shaken the moral foundation of Israel, leading to deep discomfort among large swaths of the occupation. In the words of Meretz MK Naomi Chazan, "The most obvious democratic way to achieve peace is through the creation of a Palestinian state. The occupation is undemocratic and un-Jewish. If your independence relates to subjugating another people, you'll never be Jewish. As Jews, we should know this, [since]...to subjugate another people is antithetical to Jewish history and to Jewish life."[57] Israel's actions during the Lebanon War and the Intifada had dredged up the counternarratives of oppression versus oppressor. For the first time, Israel consciously found itself on the other side of this divide—a position that needed to be realigned in order for the Israeli polity to maintain its identity of being a defensive warrior adhering to its security ethic.

Chapter Eight

Conclusion

The Israeli-Palestinian peace process that began with the 1991 Madrid conference and continued in earnest with the secret Oslo track in 1993 represents a striking example of conflict resolution, one that has consumed scholars of the region for the last decade. Israel's path has been a long road from Golda Meir's claim that there is no such thing as a Palestinian—because she, a Zionist emigre from Milwaukee to pre-1948 Israel, was "a Palestinian"—to the exchange of letters of mutual recognition between Israel and the PLO signed on 9 September 1993 and capped by the famous handshake between Israeli Prime Minister Rabin and PLO Chairman Yasser Arafat on the White House lawn. Observers have reveled in the obvious physical discomfort that Rabin exhibited in the second before that demonstration of diplomatic intimacy, as U.S. President Bill Clinton appeared to nudge the two men together. Yet it was precisely this discomfort that renders Israel's decision to shift policy course with the Palestinians so surprising and worthy of exploration.

In this book, I have developed a sociopsychoanalytic model to explain why Israel decided to seek peace with the PLO when it did, and in the process have suggested insights into other cases of potential and actual conflict resolution. In outlining a typology of six role-identity types that encapsulate state- and non-state actors across the international system through time, I have argued that if a state (or other political unit) acts in discordance with its role-identity, unconscious counternarratives will come to the fore prompted by the holding up of a "mirror" to the face of elites by international and/or domestic actors, necessitating a radical realignment of foreign policy with national self-image.

In Israel's case, centuries of persecution in the Diaspora had led to entrenched narratives of Jews playing victim to ungracious anti-Semitic hosts. The return to Zion thus enabled the Jews to attain "normalization," first by becoming masters of their own fate, and then by taking their place among the community of sovereign nation-states. In the

157

process of this rebirth, the Zionists sought to (re)create a Jewry of Muscle, a prototype that stood in stark contrast to the pale and withered Diaspora scholar-counterpart, but that hearkened back to the days of Jewish sovereignty in the ancient Land of Israel. Land-based settlement represented a vehicle for this transformation from passiveness to activeness, just as the sharpening of the Jewish sword for defensive purposes reflected a collective need for the Jews to protect themselves in their homeland. The most important bequest of normalization was therefore the intrinsic drive toward achieving and maintaining sovereignty and sovereign recognition. In part because sovereignty had been difficult for the Jews to attain since their exile two thousand years earlier, and recognition from the surrounding Arab states was almost nonexistent until the 1990s, Israel became a defensive-warrior state with attendant status-quo goals in the Middle East. While privately Israelis may have envisioned expanding the frontiers of their state—and certainly there were voices within the polity who did so publicly—essential to the Zionist narrative was the idea of defending the right of the Jews to live within secure borders, rather than seeking to necessarily expand or proselytize. The trope of normalization therefore helps to explain the rise of Israel's defensive-warrior identity.

Moreover, the existential threat of politicide that Israel historically faced from its Arab neighbors meant that a consensus soon developed in Israel around the idea that Israelis would be forced to unify around the goal of self-defense to stave off national annihilation. While all states seek security and longevity, not all governments are in a position to demand an active commitment from its citizens to be psychically and physically consumed with this task. In Israel, universal conscription and a lifetime of reserve service force security issues to dominate the national agenda. This situation has also meant that the IDF's security ethic has permeated national discourse, both lay and civilian. Therefore, when Israel deviated from its role-identity in the 1980s, Israelis were poised to experience the clash on an immediate and collective level.

By the early 1990s, broad segments of Israeli society were experiencing their state as an aggressor, a role that clashed with the country's defensive-warrior role-identity. Faced with voices from the peace movement, conscientious objectors, the domestic and foreign media, as well as the prodding of outside actors, including the United States, the Diaspora Jewish community, and the Palestinians themselves, Israeli elites were forced to reconcile the dissonance between Israel's identity and its actions. The preceding discussion shows that the *domestic* versions of the mirror (i.e., elements within society who critiqued state policies) turned out to be more important than critiques issued by outside actors.

However, actions taken by the adversary (the PLO in the Lebanon War; the Palestinian people in the Intifada) were crucial in leading Israel to play a role that did not mesh with its role-identity in the first place.

As Israel embarked on its first self-declared "war of choice" in Lebanon, culminating in a siege of Beirut followed by the IDF's indirect involvement with the Sabra and Shatilla massacre, Israelis feared that they had become members of a state enacting aggressive policies as part of a war whose goals were anathema to Israel's role-identity. Five years later, the actions that the Palestinians took during the Intifada, whereby their mostly civil protests pitted Israeli guns against Palestinian youth, prompted Israelis to realize that their government's policy of occupation clashed with the country's identity that entailed fighting only "wars of no alternative" under the maxim of "purity of arms." These events, and the unconscious fears that were brought to the fore, resulted in a painful dissonance for large segments of the polity. The result was Israel's extension of an olive branch to the PLO.

Admittedly, not every single Israeli citizen experienced a sense of dissonance between the state's actions and its role-identity. However, I have attempted to sketch a picture of the Israeli state as being guided by what I have called a dominant voice, and which roughly corresponds to the culture of Labor Zionism created and sustained primarily by the Ashkenazi elite. Toward the Arabs, the Labor Zionists—embodied first in the Hagana—had traditionally advocated a policy of restraint, as opposed to the Revisionist Zionist's call for unbridled militarism. What was therefore important, was that this segment, above all, experienced the contradiction between the state's actions and its identity, in turn bringing to light unconscious fears about what the state was becoming, and leading to a corresponding policy shift toward peace. Never—prior to the Lebanon War and the Intifada—had the IDF seen a concerted movement toward conscientious objection, and never before had the war aims of the state been publicly critiqued by large segments of the polity. The widespread protests that Israelis held during the Lebanon War reflected this rent in the national fabric, as Israel's unified security face now boasted a split lip. During the Intifada, Israelis squirmed at the unconscious counternarratives that were now coming to haunt them. A nation of defensive warriors had been turned into riot controllers and policemen battling unarmed Palestinians, many of whom were children. All of this added up to a deeply experienced cognitive dissonance at the collective level. To realign this dissonance, the state was forced to take radical action, which took the form of peacemaking with the enemy most salient to this story of role-identity and role clash: the Palestinians.

While conflict resolution is necessarily a multiparty endeavor, my approach has focused on Israel's decision to engage the PLO, rather than on the PLO's own overtures or responses in kind. This choice of scope can be justified based on a reasoned interpretation of the puzzle. That is, given that Israel was materially so much more powerful than the Palestinians, and given that Israel already was a state while the Palestinians were seeking sovereignty, it is indeed less obvious why Israel would be prepared to make the territorial and symbolic concessions necessary for a peaceful outcome to the conflict. Conversely, assuming they were to gain an autonomous state in the West Bank and Gaza Strip, the compromises that the Palestinians would be required to make were arguably much less from a material perspective. The Palestinians would have to recognize Israel's right to exist and, in doing so, implicitly renounce a claim to the whole of Palestine. Yet, given the existing status quo in the region in the early 1990s, this would not be a difficult choice to make from a strategic point of view. (Though the choice would admittedly be painful on a symbolic level.) Finally, I make no claims for my model to explain cases in which the party was so weak relative to the adversary that the former had nothing to lose. There, a strict materialist explanation might indeed be sufficient. There too, however, the case would be less bewildering.

Moreover, my investigation has focused only on the relationship between two "spaces" in the typology (defensive warrior and aggressive victim). With the same attention given to the type of ethnographic data that enables us to determine a given role-identity (otherwise we risk the tautology of inferring identity from behavior), further research could be devoted to investigating the causes and consequences of interaction between other role-identity dyads in the typology. Some preliminary examples might be Israel's nuclear deterrent posture against Iraq and Iran (defensive warrior vs. aggressive warrior); Nazi Germany's Holocaust against the Jews (aggressive warrior vs. passive victim); or a comparison of Canada's decision to send troops to the 1991 Gulf War with Canada's opting not to join the U.S.-led coalition against Iraq in 2003 (passive defender vs. aggressive warrior).

PSYCHOANALYSIS AND INTERNATIONAL RELATIONS REVISITED

A by-product of this book—in addition to shedding light on the important phenomena of conflict resolution and radical foreign-policy change—has been the introduction of psychoanalysis to the existing streams of international relations theory. In doing so, I have attempted to demonstrate both the utility and accessibility of psychoanalytic theory to the study of international action. Although the ontology of mutual-constitutiveness between actors is shared with constructivism in international relations, psychoanalytic theory, as I have presented it here, provides explanatory leverage for the *mechanisms* by which action comes about and by which a course of action is changed. Thus, while cognitive theory or various applications of constructivism could predict that role conflict would lead to a behavioral shift, psychoanalytic theory suggests that this conflict is psychically unbearable because of unconscious fears that are brought to the fore, and that are made conscious by the holding up of the metaphorical "mirror" of domestic and international critique. A justification for why psychoanalysis is necessary to this story suggests that other scholars might explore the utility of psychoanalysis and other motivational theories for explaining and predicting international outcomes. Further research bridging international relations with psychoanalysis would be useful to determine whether more attention should be devoted to training the next generation of international relations theorists in the maxims of psychoanalytic theory—just as an understanding of the basic principles of micro-economics, and the cognitive biases inherent in perception, to cite two examples, have become a requirement for engaging in contemporary international relations conversations. The inclusion of streamlined psychoanalytic theory in the training of international relations scholars would require a better understanding of the nature and function of the unconscious, as well as the role of emotion in explaining and predicting international action. Where psychoanalysis *has* been employed within international relations (and the cases are few), the treatments have often been too antiquated to have encompassed either contemporary psychoanalytic theory or contemporary international relations theory, or else have emerged from scholars not necessarily engaged in the latter.

I have also tried to show that conflict resolution, as a field of scholarship that has largely grown up separately from international relations theory, can benefit from the latter. Although the relationship between conflict resolution and international relations theory has not been self-conscious enough to generate the same sort of impassioned debate that has characterized the relationship between area studies and comparative politics, for instance, it is nevertheless an important one that needs to be considered more directly. Conflict resolution as a discrete field of inquiry is one that has mostly been avoided by international relations theorists, perhaps because much of international relations theory takes place at arm's length from policy prescription, and conflict-resolution

scholars—many of whom have been reared within the theoretical traditions of European "peace studies" that have largely been insulated from
the central debates within an American-dominated international relations field—have avoided the theoretical questions that have defined
international relations theory since the end of World War II, most of
which view the state as a member of a highly structured state system. My
project therefore seeks to bridge this gap, with the assumption that identifying processes of conflict resolution greatly aids in understanding
interstate conflict more generally—whether low-level conflict, state-
sponsored terrorism, or full-scale war; and that international relations
theory—with its claims about how international actors are positioned
and the range of policies that are likely to ensue given these material or
cultural configurations—can contribute to understanding how conflicts
are resolved at the micro-level.

WHITHER THE MIDDLE EAST?

That the Israeli-Palestinian peace process has been halted in the midst of
four years of violence in the region emphasizes both the puzzling nature
of the case and the importance of understanding it. The severing in relations between the two parties in September 2000, following the failed
Israeli-Palestinian peace talks at Camp David in July of that year and the
outbreak of the second Palestinian Intifada, indicates just how nonauto-
matic was the shift from conflict to compromise in 1993. And understanding why the actors ever did come to the table can help us arrive at
policy prescriptions that might stem the tide of bloodshed now consum-
ing the region.

The last four years have represented the lowest point in Israeli-
Palestinian relations since the Oslo agreement was signed over a decade
ago. Clearly, neither a policy shift from conflict to compromise nor even
the reaching of a peace agreement can guarantee a long-term peace settlement. However, the argument advanced in this book for addressing the
question of policy change and conflict resolution can illuminate the
events of these past few years—particularly Israel's harsh response to
this current Intifada. The Palestinians, under Arafat, rejected the most
generous Israeli proposal to date—at Camp David II in July 2000,
presided over by President Clinton. There, among other things, Israel,
under Prime Minister Ehud Barak, for the first time indicated a willingness to share sovereignty over Jerusalem with the Palestinians. The
future status of Jerusalem remains one of the most sensitive issues in the
Israeli-Palestinian conflict. Israelis therefore saw the violence launched

by Palestinians on 28 September 2000, following a provocative visit by then-opposition leader Ariel Sharon to the Temple Mount, as constituting a breach of trust, and a return to the tactics of the first Intifada. Yet this time, the violence has not been confined to the occupied territories, but has taken the form of scores of suicide bombings within the heart of pre-1967 Israel: by March 2004, 472 Israelis had been killed in fifty-three suicide attacks during the Intifada, and an additional seventy suicide bombings were thwarted as their bombers were en route to planned attacks.[1] Moreover, this terrorist phenomenon has garnered wide support among the Palestinian population, indicating that violence within Israel's borders no longer emerges from Islamic extremist sentiments alone. As of April 2001, 76 percent of Palestinians polled supported suicide operations, compared to only 24 percent supporting the same in May 1997.[2] Since Israel had professed a desire to end the occupation, and had indeed embarked on the Oslo peace process, Israelis have perceived the Palestinian violence as hateful and unjustified. Polls conducted in December 2000 revealed that 61 percent of Jewish-Israelis blamed the Palestinians for the recent setbacks in relations between the two peoples, and while only 20.5 percent of Israelis "perceived the Palestinians as violent" in December 1999, by December 2000 the number had more than doubled—to 46 percent.[3]

In general, while some members of the Israeli left protested the Israeli crackdown, including 600 reservists who were jailed for refusing to serve in the territories (another 2,500 went absent without leave),[4] these domestic critiques have been quiet and sporadic, and indeed the conventional wisdom has been that this second Intifada has decimated the Israeli peace movement. Israeli novelist and peace activist Amos Oz attributes this trend to the Israeli public's having lost "its trust in the sincerity of the Palestinians regarding the two-state solution."[5]

Increasingly, Israeli analysts are viewing the occupation as something that Israel has only a limited ability to end. As Ze'ev Schiff has recently written, the IDF "has found itself in a bear hug without the ability to release itself on its own," and "the IDF has had this reality forced upon it for decades and there are no real signs of a substantial change in the foreseeable future."[6] And while Israelis have largely maintained their willingness to engage in an Israeli-Palestinian peace process (69 percent of Israelis in February 2003 still favored talks with the Palestinians), the current Intifada has led even more Israelis (79 percent in February 2003) to believe it "impossible to renew contacts in the present situation," in particular with Arafat continuing to maintain a "substantial political role."[7] Yet one year later, Israeli war-weariness appeared to have been translated into a willingness to contemplate negotiating not only with the Palestinian Authority (still at 69 percent), but also with Israelis' most feared non-state enemy, Hamas. In response to the question, "Would you support or oppose Israel holding negotiations with Hamas on a cease-fire or a peace settlement, even though this organization is responsible for murderous terrorist attacks," 54 percent of respondents said they would support talks—yet that number declined to 48 percent in the immediate aftermath of a terrorist attack in Jerusalem. On support for the Oslo agreement itself, only 22 percent of Israeli Jews still heavily (8.5 percent) or somewhat (13.9 percent) favored Oslo. Almost half was somewhat (14.3 percent) or heavily (29.8 percent) opposed to the peace agreement, while 18.7 percent identified themselves as being in the middle.[8]

Yet as the Intifada progresses with no visible hope for the large-scale concessions required by Israel to entice the Palestinian back to the table (nor any serious effort by the Palestinian Authority to rein in the militants), more Israeli voices have reemerged to critique the ongoing occupation. One *Ha'aretz* columnist has decried the moral corruption resulting from occupation and the expanding Israeli settlements in the territories, claiming that, "[w]ithout [the] lies [of the government], it would be impossible to talk about peace with the Palestinians for 36 years while at the same time seizing more and more Palestinian land."[9] Soon after, in December 2003, selective refusal entered the ranks of the air force, as twenty-seven reserve and active duty pilots refused orders to bomb Palestinian cities as the Israeli practice of "targeted assassinations" has become more frequent (most notably the March 2004 killing of Hamas spiritual leader Sheikh Ahmed Yassin)—leading to multiple civilian deaths. Stated one captain, "In the beginning, we were pilots who believed our country would do all it could to achieve peace. We believed in the purity of our arms and that we did all we could to prevent unnecessary loss of life. Somewhere in the last few years it became harder and harder to believe that is the case."[10] And in a critique launched from the most prominent Israeli circles, in November 2003 four former internal security service (Shin Bet) chiefs issued statements harshly critical of Sharon's policies, while calling for Israel to withdraw from Gaza. Remarked Ami Ayalon (head of Shin Bet from 1996 to 2000), "We are taking sure, steady steps to a place where the State of Israel will no longer be a democracy and a home for the Jewish people."[11]

Part of the increased frustration among Israelis, despite more muted criticism about the IDF's handling of the Intifada than occurred during the first Intifada for the reasons previously stated, stems from a great deal of policy inertia by the Sharon government. Chief among the faults cited by Sharon's critics are his continued moves to expand settlement-construction in the territories, although, as of late 2004, Sharon and his security advisors were contemplating a unilateral Israeli withdrawal from Gaza (though under this plan, Israel would retain a slim corridor along the Egyptian border), including dismantling almost all of the settlements there—home to 7,500 Israelis—along with up to one-fifth of West Bank settlements.[12] Yet progress toward resuming serious efforts toward peace has clearly been slow. Now, with Arafat's death in November 2004, we may see the emergence of a new Palestinian leadership more amenable to Israelis who had largely lost faith in Arafat's credibility as a negotiating partner. (As this book goes to press, Mahmoud Abbas has won the January 2005 Palestinian presidential election, and indeed initial steps toward Israeli-Palestinian reconciliation are being made, as Sharon and Abbas appear to have reached a cease-fire agreement.)

To this end, former Israeli and Palestinian officials—led by former Israeli Justice Minister Yossi Beilin and former Palestinian Minister of Information and Culture Yasser Abed-Rabbo, and signed by a score of other Israeli and Palestinian political, security, and cultural elites—launched a citizen's peace initiative in December 2003 that became known as the Geneva Accord. This document attempted to build on the spirit of negotiation that seemed to permeate the January 2001 Israeli-Palestinian talks at the Egyptian resort town of Taba, but from which an agreement was never reached due to the February 2001 elections in which Sharon won a landslide victory over Barak.[13] While neither Israel nor the Palestinian Authority have sanctioned the Geneva agreement, with Sharon even referring to the drafters as "traitors," the plan has garnered widespread domestic and international attention, and could, potentially, serve as a template for the resumption of peace talks should the U.S.-sponsored "road map" fail. (The details of the road map are discussed later.) Eschewing the process-oriented approach of the road map and especially of Oslo, the Geneva initiative calls for a nonmilitarized Palestinian state to be established in 97.5 percent of the West Bank (the remaining 2.5 percent refers entirely to areas around Jerusalem) and all of Gaza with reciprocal Israeli land-trade arrangements near the Strip and the southern West Bank, with Israeli settlement property to be transferred to the Palestinians and the removal of Israeli military forces and settlers within thirty months; access to Palestinian airspace for IDF training purposes; shared sovereignty over Jerusalem with access guaranteed to all holy sites (with Israel to receive sovereignty over the Western half, Jewish neighborhoods within East Jerusalem, and traditional Jewish holy sites, and Palestine to control the Arab neighborhoods in the eastern half as well as Islamic holy sites); and Palestinian refugees to give up the right of return to within Israel, though they may emigrate in unlimited numbers to the nascent Palestinian state. (Israel would contribute toward an international fund for resettlement.)[14] It remains to be seen whether subsequent Israeli-Palestinian negotiations will draw on the principles of this unofficial accord.

What, then, would the findings of this study suggest at the level of policy prescription? The Bush administration had originally taken a less active role toward Middle East peacemaking than had President Clinton's foreign-policy team. However, recent months have shown Bush taking more of a lead in brokering peace, beginning with pressuring Arafat to reduce his own power by creating a new prime minister's post (held by Abu Mazen followed by Abu Ala when the former resigned amid tension with Arafat), and then sponsoring, in April 2003, along with the so-called Quartet (the United States, UN, EU and Russia), a "road map"—stipulating the cessation of terrorism, a freezing of settlement-building, and the dismantling of settlements built since March 2001, Palestinian political reform including the drafting of a constitution, the holding of open elections, and the establishment of a Palestinian state—that could serve as a framework for renewed negotiations if and when the parties return to the table.[15] Yet certainly the Bush administration's current War on Terrorism has distracted the American foreign-policy establishment from taking a more proactive approach in the Israeli-Palestinian nexus, particularly given that Israel's struggle has largely become defined (by the Israeli government and concomitantly by the United States) as an antiterrorism one.

The findings presented in this book suggest that if a state contravenes its role-identity, a cognitive dissonance will result, forcing it to realign its policy stance with its self-image. Yet the current uprising has suggested to Israelis that even once the government makes concessions, their partner in peace revolts from the process and reverts to violence. This dynamic partly explains Israel's harsh response and the ensuing so-called cycle of violence that has overtaken the region. Therefore, it would seem that in order for the peace process to be reinvigorated, both sides have to be reassured of the other's good faith. An honest broker, such as the United States—which has generally been seen throughout the peace process by both Israelis and Palestinians as such—needs to prod each side back to the table with clear conciliatory goals in mind. The Palestinians must be encouraged to halt the violence, particularly against civilians and particularly within pre-1967 Israel, and Sharon needs to reiterate his country's willingness to reach a final settlement that will include meaningful negotiations on the highly sensitive final-status issues—including Jerusalem, the settlements, and the fate of the Palestinian refugees. This sort of policy prescription assumes that what is most relevant is the parties' own respective view of the situation. Acknowledging Israel's perception that the Palestinians have bitten the hand that feeds them, so to speak, will help Israelis place trust in the continuation of the peace process.

Conversely, a third-party facilitator would have to validate the Palestinians' frustration that the peace process has stalled, and that the timeline outlined in the Declaration of Principles has not been adhered to. The issues of settlements and refugees are two areas in which Israel can be pressed to take action, which in turn would alleviate some Palestinian concerns. Specifically, the United States should press Israel to freeze settlement-building and consider uprooting settlements in the most sensitive areas, including those surrounding Jerusalem. There is already a precedent for this in Israeli history, when the Likud government under Prime Minister Begin forced residents in the Sinai Desert to evacuate their settlements in 1982, as Israel completed its final withdrawal from the peninsula under the terms of the Israeli-Egyptian peace agreement. That a Likud government presided over this domestic crisis presents an important legitimating function for the ability of subsequent Israeli governments—Likud or Labor—to do the same.

Moreover, Israel should be encouraged to acknowledge the symbolic importance of the Palestinian right of return—another of the outstanding final-status issues, and another of the sticking points that emerged from Camp David II—even if this acknowledgment does not entail an actual wave of immigration to pre-1967 Israel. A wholesale Palestinian immigration to within Israel proper would certainly upset the demographic balance from a Jewish perspective and is virtually unacceptable to Israelis. Yet from an identity point of view, the right of return for Palestinian refugees displaced in the 1948 war embodies the crux of the Arab-Israeli conflict and the competing Israeli and Palestinian historical narratives and corresponding role-identities. Israelis view Zionism as a movement to restore Jewish sovereignty, and, as previously discussed, to achieve normalization from a parasitic existence within host countries. That the Zionist experiment involved the displacement of another people—whether or not this was intentional—did not fit with the Jews' vision of themselves. Yet this displacement was such an unavoidable part of the establishment of the Jewish state that it would not clash with Israel's role-identity the same way that the state's actions in the Lebanon War and the Intifada would. This suggests a policy paradox: Israel should be encouraged to acknowledge the Palestinians' *symbolic* right of return, yet doing so would implicitly lay blame on the most basic core of the Zionist vision. Thus, perhaps Israel could issue a statement acknowledging the

Palestinians' historical rights to the land *alongside* the Jews' claim, with the actual policy entailing a limited right of return—based on family-reunification criteria—within pre-1967 Israel and a much more generous (if not unlimited) return policy for refugees who wish to immigrate to an incipient state in the West Bank and Gaza Strip, on the basis that the area can sustain them economically.

In more general terms, an observant third party could notice when a conflict is ripe for resolution based on a society openly reexamining some of the myths that had defined it, or protesting the state's involvement in wars based on moral grounds. Thus, the Lebanon War, where conscientious objection took hold across the military for nearly the first time, followed by the Intifada, where this trend continued, represented a moment of introspection on the part of Israelis that suggested that the state might be ready to come to terms with the enemy. Similarly, the rise of revisionist history within Israel during the 1980s suggested that the narratives of state-formation that had nurtured Israeli identity and guided foreign policy through the first few decades of Israel's existence were being challenged. It is not surprising, therefore, that at this point, Israeli elites were willing to reconsider their policy stance toward the Palestinians. A third-party mediator could therefore help to propel the parties toward peacemaking when these shifts within society become evident.

In addition, the arguments advanced here suggest that members of conflict dyads may be better poised to predict a shift in policy orientation by their adversary, and to respond in kind. To do this successfully, a state must be attuned to the domestic workings of its adversary, including attempting to gain a foothold on the narratives that drive the other's raison d'etat. The difficulty of this task—particularly when attempting to analyze "closed" societies—is softened somewhat by the paradox of authoritarianism. That is, many authoritarian states rely on explicit rhetoric to consensus-build and strengthen the legitimacy of what are often precarious regimes. This rhetoric gets transmitted to the masses in the form of narratives that shape and whittle historical memory. For many of these regimes, the historical struggle against colonialism provides the pillars on which their legitimacy rests. Thus, a postcolonial state that advances imperialistic goals might eventually come to realize that it is enacting a role contrary to its self-image as a "beleaguered" or "anticolonial" state. In the case of democracies, where access to the press and other communication is much freer, it is clearly easier for an observer to investigate the narratives of the former. A similar logic may apply to warring factions within the same state—such as Protestants and Catholics in Northern Ireland—where the narratives of one group often represent the inverse of those of the other.

POSTSCRIPT: IDENTITY AND
INTERNATIONAL RELATIONS

The story of Israel's decision to pursue Oslo suggests that identity is a relevant factor in international relations, a claim that has defined the constructivist agenda since its emergence in the discipline in the late 1980s. Like other constructivists, I have attempted to show that material factors are mediated by cultural understandings. The question that has therefore recently consumed international relations scholars is whether collective identity "matters" (in the academic parlance of the day), rather than whether it exists at all. In evaluating the most likely alternatives for the case of Israel's decision to seek peace with the PLO, I have found that a strictly materialist explanation is insufficient. The missing determinant is identity, and specifically the emotional reaction that results when policy actions do not adhere to a state's self-image.

Given the centrality of security to the Israeli condition, we might even conclude that the more important are territory and force, the more important are identity-related factors. That is, given that Israeli foreign policy has centered around the attempt to stave off existential territorial threats (as opposed to other states who might be more concerned with issues of trade or immigration; or drought or disease), and given that Israeli narratives reflect this quest, the collective identity of the citizenry will naturally be defined by issues of security. When this identity is challenged by the state's actions in the security realm, an acute sense of dissonance arises. This perspective lends credence to the central claim of constructivism: that power must be viewed in the context of shared understandings. It is not that material power is unimportant; the case of Israel shows that it is—at both the conscious and unconscious levels, at the levels of self-image, policy action, collective reactions, and policy shifts. More important, though, is the way that that material reality has been interpreted by society, as well as the ethical and ideational limitations placed on the use of force. By drawing on the rich and nuanced tradition of psychoanalytic theory, this book has attempted to bolster the explanatory power of constructivism, to further our understanding of identity creation and policy change, and perhaps to help us help warring others to take one more step toward the table.

In addition, one of the central contributions of constructivism in international relations has been to disengage culture from race or ethnicity, and rather to look at it as the entire universe of meaning systems that exist and are advanced within a particular social or political group. In adopting this ontology, this book responds to the recently issued maxim—current in contemporary area studies thinking—that "[n]either the strategies and calculations of groups and governments nor the attitudes and behavior of ordinary citizens can be adequately understood without a knowledge of the context within which these actors reside."[16] In so doing, I hope to strengthen the contribution of culturally oriented international relations theorists to area-studies-informed scholarship. That is, while area studies scholars who have bridged that literature with rational choice approaches have been lauded for escaping the confines of culturally specific explanation, there is a need for the constructivist turn in international relations theory to reach area studies as well. In some senses, and as with conflict resolution scholars and international relations theorists, these two traditions have been passing like ships in the night: until recently, the best constructivist work did not attempt empirical research, and those area-studies scholars liberated from the chains of cultural reductionism and Orientalism mostly have not looked to the ontology offered by the new social theory tradition within international relations.[17] Furthermore, much of the area studies-political science debate has been played out between historians and students of comparative politics, or among members of the latter group only. International relations theory has been slow to appreciate the nuance of area studies, and certainly area studies has often neglected the explanatory paradigms offered by international relations theory. By employing a "thick," ethnographic explanation of Israeli identity and policy, I have attempted to bridge these two traditions.

Notes

ONE. INTRODUCTION

1. Peter Liberman, "The Spoils of Conquest," *International Security* 18, 2 (Fall 1993).

2. For the original formulation of the distinction between international politics and foreign policy, see Kenneth Waltz, *Theory of International Politics* (Reading: Addison-Wesley, 1979).

3. Theo Farrell, "Constructivist Security Studies: Portrait of a Research Program," *International Studies Review* 4, 1 (Spring 2002).

4. David Makovsky, *Making Peace with the PLO: The Rabin Government's Road to the Oslo Accord* (Boulder: Westview Press, 1996), p. 11; and Charles D. Smith, *Palestine and the Arab-Israeli Conflict*, 3rd ed. (New York: St. Martin's Press, 1996), p. 322.

5. I thank Hein Goemans for suggesting this reasoning. For a theoretical elaboration, see H. E. Goemans, *War and Punishment: The Causes of War Termination and the First World War* (Princeton: Princeton University Press, 2000).

6. As suggested in the author's interviews with Israeli journalist David Makovsky, 19 October 1999, Jerusalem, and Director-General of Rabin's Prime Minister's Office Shimon Sheves, 25 November 1999, Tel Aviv.

7. *Israel Television Network* (in Hebrew), 6 May 1992 (FBIS-NES-92-089; 7 May 1992).

8. As Avner Yaniv writes, "Israeli policymakers tended to attribute Iraq's attitude not to genuine devotion to the Arab cause—certainly not to any real concern for the Palestinians—but to the cynical ambitions of Iraqi leaders or, at most, to an abiding rhetorical commitment that Iraqi governments could defy only at their peril." Yaniv, "Israel Faces Iraq: The Politics of Confrontation," in Amatzia Baram and Barry Rubin, eds., *Iraq's Road to War* (New York: St. Martin's Press, 1993).

9. Ziva Flamhaft, *Israel on the Road to Peace: Accepting the Unacceptable* (Boulder: Westview Press, 1996), p. 95. Both Makovsky and Susan Hattis Rolef

argue that the United States had no direct influence on Israel's decision to pursue Oslo. See Makovsky, *Making Peace with the PLO*, p. 130; and Rolef, "Israel's Policy Toward the PLO: From Rejection to Recognition," in Avraham Sela and Moshe Ma'oz, eds., *The PLO and Israel: From Armed Conflict to Political Solution, 1964–1994* (New York: St. Martin's Press, 1997), p. 268.

10. Robert J. Lieber, "U.S.-Israel Relations since 1948," in Robert O. Freedman, ed., *Israel at Fifty* (Gainesville: University of Florida Press, 2000).

11. *Israel Television Network* (in Hebrew) 28 March 1992 (FBIS-NES-92-061; 30 March 1992).

12. Makovsky, *Making Peace with the PLO*, p. 114.

13. Shimon Peres, *Battling for Peace: A Memoir* (New York: Random House, 1995), p. 261.

14. *Hadashot* (in Hebrew); report by Aharon Klein and Menahem Horowitz, 27 May 1992, p. 3. (FBIS-NES-92-103; 28 May 1992) (emphasis added).

15. Jack S. Levy, "Learning and Foreign Policy: Sweeping a Conceptual Minefield," *International Organization* 48, 2 (Spring 1994).

16. See Alastair Iain Johnston, "Thinking about Strategic Culture," *International Security* 19, 4 (Spring 1995); and Elizabeth Kier, *Imagining War: French and British Military Doctrine between the Wars* (Princeton: Princeton University Press, 1997).

17. Strategic culture resembles an additional competing explanation: that of organizational politics. However, the evidence in the Oslo case—namely that the military itself was not determinative in forcing the policy shift—likewise challenges this perspective.

18. Leon Festinger, *A Theory of Cognitive Dissonance* (Stanford: Stanford University Press, 1957, 1968).

19. Ibid., p. 18; see also Eddie Harmon-Jones and Judson Mills, "An Introduction to Cognitive Dissonance Theory and an Overview of Current Perspectives on the Theory," in Harmon-Jones and Mills, eds., *Cognitive Dissonance: Progress on a Pivotal Theory in Social Psychology* (Washington, DC: American Psychological Association, 1999), p. 15.

20. See Elliot Aronson, "Dissonance Theory: Progress and Problems," in Robert P. Abelson et al., eds., *Theories of Cognitive Consistency: A Sourcebook* (Chicago: Rand McNally, 1968); I. Sarnoff, "Psychoanalytic Theory and Cognitive Dissonance," in Abelson, et al., eds., *Theories of Cognitive Consistency: A Sourcebook*; and William J. McGuire, "Resume and Response from the Consistency Theory Viewpoint,"in Abelson, et al., eds, *Theories of Cognitive Consistency: A Sourcebook*.

21. Lowell Dittmer and Samuel S. Kim, "In Search of a Theory of National Identity," in Dittmer and Kim, eds., *China's Quest for National Identity* (Ithaca: Cornell University Press, 1993), p. 4.

22. These criteria are drawn from Stephen Van Evera, *Guide to Methods for Students of Political Science* (Ithaca: Cornell University Press, 1997), pp. 77–88.

23. For arguments against viewing Israel as "exceptional," see Michael N. Barnett, ed., *Israel in Comparative Perspective: Challenging the Conventional Wisdom* (Albany: State University of New York Press, 1996).

TWO. PSYCHOANALYSIS AND INTERNATIONAL RELATIONS

1. See Kenneth Waltz, *Theory of International Politics* (Reading: Addison-Wesley, 1979); Alexander Wendt, "Anarchy Is What States Make of It: The Social Construction of Power Politics," *International Organization* 46, 2 (1992); and Jonathan Mercer, "Anarchy and Identity," *International Organization* 49, 2 (1995). Theo Farrell notes the strategic decision that many constructivists have taken to contend with realism on its own turf. Farrell, "Constructivist Security Studies: Portrait of a Research Program," *International Studies Review* 4, 1 (Spring 2002).

2. For a perspective on psychoanalysis that is informed by quantum physics, see Maxwell S. Sucharov, "Psychoanalysis, Self Psychology, and Intersubjectivity," in Robert Stolorow, George Atwood, and Bernard Brandchaft, eds., *The Intersubjective Perspective* (Northvale: Jason Aronson, Inc., 1994).

3. "Introduction," in Stolorow et al., eds., *The Intersubjective Perspective*, p. ix.

4. James M. Goldgeier, "Psychology and Security," *Security Studies* 6, 4 (Summer 1997), p. 145.

5. Alexander Wendt, *Social Theory of International Politics* (New York: Cambridge University Press, 1999), p. 276.

6. See Alexander L. George and Juliet George, *Woodrow Wilson and the Colonel House: A Personality Study* (New York. Dover Publications, 1964); and Vamik D. Volkan, "Psychoanalysis and Diplomacy: Potentials for and Obstacles against Collaboration." Unpublished manuscript, University of Virginia, 1998.

7. See Randall Schweller, "Neorealism's Status-Quo Bias: What Security Dilemma?," *Security Studies* 5, 3 (1996); and Janice Gross Stein, "International Cooperation and Loss Avoidance: Framing the Problem," in Janice Gross Stein

and Louis W. Pauly, eds., *Choosing to Cooperate: How States Avoid Loss* (Baltimore: Johns Hopkins University Press, 1993).

8. See Jonathan Mercer, "Emotion and Identity," unpublished manuscript, Harvard University (1999); and Neta C. Crawford, "The Passion of World Politics: Propositions on Emotion and Emotional Relationships," *International Security* 24, 4 (Spring 2000).

9. Thus, while political scientists such as Bruce Jentleson have shown that such phenomena as the domestic support for the use of force depend on the values of the polity, psychoanalysis can illuminate why domestic audiences come to hold the values that they do. See Jentleson, "The Pretty Prudent Public: Post Post-Vietnam American Opinion on the Use of Military Force," *International Studies Quarterly* 36, 1 (March 1992).

10. See Fred Vollmer, "Intentional Action and Unconscious Reason," *Journal for the Theory of Social Behavior* 23, 3 (1993); and Morton A. Kaplan, *System and Process in International Politics* (Huntington: Robert E. Krieger, 1957, 1975), pp. 253–270.

11. In addition to Vollmer (op. cit.), see Jim Cheesman and Philip M. Merikle, "Distinguishing Conscious from Unconscious Perceptual Processes," *Canadian Journal of Psychology* 40, 4 (1986); Joel Weinberger and Lloyd H. Silverman, "Testability and Empirical Verification of Psychoanalytic Dynamic Propositions Through Subliminal Psychodynamic Activation," *Psychoanalytic Psychology* 7, 3 (1990); Robert F. Bornstein, "Implicit Perception, Implicit Memory, and the Recovery of Unconscious Material in Psychotherapy," *The Journal of Nervous and Mental Disease* 181, 6 (June 1993); and Philip M. Merikle, "Psychological Investigations of Unconscious Perception," *Journal of Consciousness Studies* 5, 1 (1998).

12. Sheldon Stryker and Anne Statham, "Symbolic Interaction and Role Theory," in G. Lindzey and E. Aronson, eds., *Handbook of Social Psychology*, vol. I (New York: Random House, 1985), p. 328.

13. For a similar view, see Peter L. Callero, "Toward a Sociology of Cognition," in Judith A. Howard and Peter L. Callero, eds., *The Self-Society Dynamic* (Cambridge: Cambridge University Press, 1991).

14. Vamik D. Volkan, "Psychoanalysis and Diplomacy: Potentials for and Obstacles against Collaboration," unpublished manuscript. University of Virginia, 1998.

15. Alexander Wendt, "Collective Identity Formation and the International State," *American Political Science Review* 88 (1994).

16. Sociologists are divided along this issue, with Weber being a proponent of individualism and Durkheim favoring holism. For a classic articulation of the methodological individualist position, see J. W. N. Watkins, "Social Phenomena

Result from the Activities of Individual Agents," *British Journal for the Philosophy of Science* 8 (1957).

17. This section draws extensively on Alexander Wendt, *Social Theory of International Politics* (New York: Cambridge University Press, 1999), pp. 193–245.

18. See Michael A. Hogg, Deborah J. Terry, and Katherine M. White, "A Tale of Two Theories: A Critical Comparison of Identity Theory with Social Identity Theory," *Social Psychology Quarterly* 58, 4 (1995); and Mercer, "Anarchy and Identity."

19. Gabriel A. Almond and Sidney Verba, *The Civic Culture* (Boston: Little, Brown, 1965).

20. See Sigmund Freud, "Group Psychology and the Analysis of the Ego," in vol. 18 of *The Standard Edition of the Complete Psychological Works of Sigmund Freud* (London: Hogarth Press, 1955); and C. G. Jung, *The Archetypes and the Collective Unconscious, 2nd ed.* (Princeton: Princeton University Press, 1968).

21. For a summary of the latter, see Lloyd Sandelands and Lynda St. Clair, "Toward an Empirical Concept of Group," *Journal for the Theory of Social Behaviour* 23, 4 (1993). See also Mary Douglas, *How Institutions Think* (Syracuse: Syracuse University Press, 1986); Margaret Gilbert, "Modelling Collective Belief," *Synthese* 73 (1987); and Herbert Blumer, "The Methodological Position of Symbolic Interactionism," in Blumer, *Symbolic Interactionism: Perspective and Method* (Berkeley: University of California Press), p. 17.

22. See Martha Finnemore, *National Interests in International Society* (Ithaca: Cornell University Press, 1996); Margaret E. Keck and Kathryn Sikkink, *Activists Beyond Borders: Advocacy Networks in International Politics* (Ithaca: Cornell University Press, 1998); and Richard Price and Nina Tannenwald, "Norms and Deterrence: The Nuclear and Chemical Weapons Taboos," in Peter Katzenstein, ed., *The Culture of National Security: Norms and Identity in World Politics* (New York: Columbia University Press, 1996).

23. See, for instance, Yael Zerubavel's cursory statement that pre-state Jewish society retained the Masada myth within its "collective conscious," while harboring "feelings of longing and loss" within its "collective unconscious." Zerubavel, *Recovered Roots: Collective Memory and the Making of Israeli National Tradition* (Chicago: University of Chicago Press, 1995), p. 119. See also Paul Connerton's brief mention of the value of studying unconscious processes of collective memory. Connerton, *How Societies Remember* (Cambridge: Cambridge University Press, 1989), p. 1.

24. Jung, *The Archetypes and the Collective Unconscious*. For an international relations treatment of the U.S.-Soviet relationship during the Cold War

that draws on Jung's archetypes, see Jerome S. Bernstein, *Power and Politics: The Psychology of Soviet-American Partnership* (Boston: Shambhala Publications, Inc., 1989).

25. Rodney Bruce Hall, *National Collective Identity: Social Constructs and International Systems* (New York: Columbia University Press, 1999).

26. Wendt, *Social Theory of International Politics*, p. 227.

27. For a discussion of roles versus role-identities, see Wendt, *Social Theory of International Politics*, p. 259; and Hogg et al., "A Tale of Two Theories," p. 256.

28. See Wendt's discussion of four types of identity in *Social Theory of International Politics*, pp. 224–233.

29. Lowell Dittmer and Samuel S. Kim, "In Search of a Theory of National Identity," in Dittmer and Kim, eds., *China's Quest for National Identity* (Ithaca: Cornell University Press, 1993), p. 14.

30. Joseph Lepgold and Timothy McKeown, "Is American Foreign Policy Exceptional? An Empirical Analysis," *Political Science Quarterly* 110, 3 (1995), p. 382.

31. Philip Blumstein, "The Production of Selves in Personal Relationships," in Howard and Callero, eds., *The Self-Society Dynamic*. See also Wendt, *Social Theory of International Politics*, p. 259; and Hogg et al., "A Tale of Two Theories," p. 256.

32. William H. Sewell, Jr., "Introduction: Narratives and Social Identities," *Social Science History* 16, 3 (Fall 1992), p. 483. See also Donald E. Polkinghorne, *Narrative Knowing and the Human Sciences* (Albany: State University of New York Press, 1988); and Michael N. Barnett, "Culture, Strategy, and Foreign Policy Change: Israel's Road to Oslo," *European Journal of International Relations* 5, 1 (March 1999).

33. Benedict Anderson, *Imagined Communities* (London: Verso, 1983, 1991).

34. Edward S. Herman and Noam Chomsky, *Manufacturing Consent: The Political Economy of the Mass Media* (New York: Pantheon Books, 1988).

35. This view of counternarratives is not to be confused with the idea of "revisionist history" or "counterculture." See, for instance, Michael Barnett's definition of counternarratives as altered readings of history. Barnett, "Culture, Strategy, and Foreign Policy Change."

36. James Fentress and Chris Wickham, *Social Memory* (Oxford: Blackwell, 1992).

37. Helen Epstein, *Children of the Holocaust: Conversations with Sons and Daughters of Survivors* (New York: Bantam Books, 1979).

38. See Connerton, *How Societies Remember*; and Volkan's claim that groups revisit personal traumas according to an internal, unconscious calendar. Vamik D. Volkan, "Psychoanalysis and Diplomacy: Part II—Large-Group Rituals." Unpublished manuscript, University of Virginia, 1998.

39. Others, such as K. J. Holsti, Naomi B. Wish, and Marijke Breuning, have introduced state typologies, though without attempting to combine capabilities and resolve with a focus on ethical constraints, a factor that has become increasingly prominent within security studies. See Holsti, "National Role Conceptions in the Study of Foreign Policy," *International Studies Quarterly* 14, 3 (1970); Wish, "Foreign Policy Makers and Their National Role Conceptions," *International Studies Quarterly* 24, 4 (1980); and Breuning, "Words and Deeds: Foreign Assistance Rhetoric and Policy Behavior in the Netherlands, Belgium, and the United Kingdom," *International Studies Quarterly* 39 (1995). On ethics and security, see Ward Thomas, *The Ethics of Destruction: Norms and Force in International Relations* (Ithaca: Cornell University Press, 2001); and Mira Sucharov, "Security Ethics and the Modern Military: The Case of the Israel Defense Forces," *Armed Forces & Society* 31, 2 (Winter 2005).

40. Barry Posen, *The Sources of Military Doctrine: France, Britain, and Germany Between the World Wars* (Ithaca: Cornell University Press, 1984), p. 50.

41. Randall Schweller, "Neorealism's Status-Quo Bias: What Security Dilemma?" *Security Studies* 5, 3 (1996).

42. An example of such a universal cognitive bias is the "fundamental attribution error," in which we understand negative actions by others to be a function of their disposition, but attribute our own negative actions to the situation. We therefore blame others for misdeeds while absolving ourselves of responsibility in similar contexts.

43. Peter J. Burke, "Attitudes, Behavior, and the Self," in Judith Howard and Peter Callero, eds., *The Self-Society Dynamic* (Cambridge: Cambridge University Press, 1991), pp. 192–193. For laboratory support for the phenomenon of role and role-identity alignment, see William B. Swann, Jr., and Craig A. Hill, "When Our Identities Are Mistaken: Reaffirming Self-Conceptions Through Social Interaction," *Journal of Personality and Social Psychology* 43 (1982), as cited in Peter J. Burke, "Identity Process and Social Stress," *American Sociological Review* 56 (1991), p. 839.

44. Donna M. Orange, George E. Atwood, and Robert D. Stolorow, *Working Intersubjectively: Contextualism in Psychoanalytic Practice* (Hillsdale: The Analytic Press, 1997), pp. 7–8.

45. Leon Festinger, *A Theory of Cognitive Dissonance* (Stanford: Stanford University Press, 1957, 1968), quotations from p. 2 and p. 3.

46. A good example of a cognitive treatment of such a shift (distinct from the cognitive-emotional process advanced here) is Janice Gross Stein, "Political

Learning by Doing: Gorbachev as Uncommitted Thinker and Motivated Learner," in Richard Ned Lebow and Thomas Risse-Kappen, eds., *International Relations Theory and the End of the Cold War* (New York: Columbia University Press, 1995). Because she argues that Gorbachev only developed his cognitive schema *while in power*, Stein's treatment falls to one end of the learning theory spectrum. A slightly different type of analysis would advance the idea that the leader in question experienced events that challenged his or her *previously held* cognitive maps. For example, see Janice Gross Stein's discussion of peacemaking in "Image, Identity, and Conflict Resolution," in Chester A. Crocker and Fen Osler Hampson with Pamela Aall, eds., *Managing Global Chaos: Sources of and Responses to International Conflict* (Washington, DC: United States Institute of Peace, 1996). However, neither of these views necessarily admits a role for emotion or for the concept of a collective self.

47. Burke, "Attitudes, Behavior and the Self," p. 199. See also Peter M. Gollwitzer and Robert A. Wicklund, "The Pursuit of Self-Defining Goals," in Julius Kuhl and Jurgen Beckmann, eds., *Action Control: From Cognition to Behavior* (Berlin: Springer-Verlag, 1985).

48. Mordechai Bar-On, "The Historians' Debate in Israel and the Middle East Peace Process," in Ilan Peleg, ed., *The Middle East Peace Process: Interdisciplinary Perspectives* (Albany: State University of New York, 1998).

49. See Audie Klotz, *Norms in International Relations: The Struggle Against Apartheid* (Ithaca: Cornell University Press, 1995); and Martha Finnemore, *National Interests in International Society* (Ithaca: Cornell University Press, 1996).

50. A useful summary of this dynamic is provided in John W. Crayton, "Terrorism and the Psychology of the Self," in Lawrence Zelic Freedman and Yonah Alexander, *Perspectives on Terrorism* (Wilmington: Scholarly Resources Inc., 1983).

51. See Erik Erikson's discussion of the "sameness" of identity over time. Cited in Dittmer and Kim, "In Search of a Theory of National Identity," p. 4.

THREE. THE ISRAELI SELF

1. Yossi Beilin, *Israel: A Concise Political History* (New York: St. Martin's Press, 1992), p. 146.

2. Myron J. Aronoff, *Israeli Visions and Divisions: Cultural Change and Political Conflict* (New Brunswick: Transaction Publishers, 1989), pp. 20–24.

3. The importance of the collective over the individual in Israeli culture is discussed in Yaron Ezrahi, *Rubber Bullets: Power and Conscience in Modern Israel* (New York: Farrar, Straus and Giroux, 1997).

4. Beilin, *Israel*, p. 149.

5. Amos Elon, *The Israelis: Founders and Sons* (New York: Penguin Books, 1971, 1981), p. 34.

6. Tamara Cofman Wittes, "Symbols and Security in Ethnic Conflict: Confidence-Building in the Palestinian-Israeli Peace Process, 1993–1995," Ph.D. diss., Georgetown University, 2000.

7. In 1894, the French military found Captain Alfred Dreyfus, a Jewish officer in France, guilty of treason. After suspicions that Dreyfus had been framed out of anti-Semitic motives, and the publication of an open letter by Emile Zola, Dreyfus was finally exonerated in 1906. For the French, the affair led to a wariness of the military; for Theodor Herzl (the founder of modern Zionism), the Drefyus trial emphasized the idea that Jews, even in "civilized" Western Europe, were not safe from anti-Semitism, and that the founding of a Jewish state was imperative.

8. Shlomo Avineri, *The Making of Modern Zionism: The Intellectual Origins of the Jewish State* (New York: Basic Books, 1981).

9. See Yael Zerubavel, *Recovered Roots: Collective Memory and the Making of Israeli National Tradition* (Chicago: University of Chicago Press, 1995); and Alan Dowty, "Israeli Foreign Policy and the Jewish Question," *Middle East Review of International Affairs* 3, 1 (March 1998; internet edition).

10. IDF official website—IDF Spokesperson (accessed on 18 June 2003) http://www.idf.il/english/doctrine/doctrine.stm.

11. In Shohat, *Israeli Cinema*, p. 62.

12. Speech to the Jerusalem Economic Conference (4 April 1968); cited in Michael Brecher, *Decisions in Israel's Foreign Policy* (New Haven: Yale University Press, 1975), p. 326.

13. Gil Merom, "Israel's National Security and the Myth of Exceptionalism," *Political Science Quarterly* 114, 3 (Fall 1999).

14. IDF Official website—IDF Spokesperson (accessed on 11 October 2000) http://www.idf.il/english/doctrine/doctrine.stm.

15. Ministry of Education file 4767/22/6 (1966), Israel State Archives, Jerusalem.

16. Aviezer Ravitzky, "Peace," in Arthur A. Cohen and Paul Mendes-Flohr, eds., *Contemporary Jewish Religious Thought: Original Essays on Critical Concepts, Movements, and Beliefs* (New York: Scribner's 1987), p. 686.

17. This view was articulated by Israel's fifteenth (1995–1998) chief of staff, Amnon Lipkin-Shahak. Author's interview; 16 March 2000, Jerusalem.

18. David Ben-Gurion, *Letters to Paula* (Pittsburgh: University of Pittsburgh Press, 1971), pp. 217–218.

19. Cited in Ariel Levite, *Offense and Defense in Israeli Military Doctrine* (Boulder: Westview Press, 1989), p. 31.

20. Ephraim Kishon and Dosh (Kariel Gardosh), *Woe to the Victors!* Trans. Yohanan Goldman (Tel Aviv: Ma'ariv Library, 1969).

21. Summary of meetings between M. Shertok, Count Bernadotte, and assistants (Tel Aviv, 17–18 June 1948), reprinted in Yehoshua Freundlich, ed., *Documents on the Foreign Policy of Israel, vol. 1, 14 May to 30 September 1948* (Jerusalem: Israel State Archives, 1981), p. 184.

22. Kishon and Dosh, *Woe to the Victors!*

23. Michael I. Handel, *Israel's Political-Military Doctrine* (Cambridge: Center for International Affairs, Harvard University, 1973), p. 64 (emphasis in original).

24. Gerald M. Steinberg, "A Nation that Dwells Alone? Foreign Policy in the 1992 Elections," in Daniel J. Elazar and Shmuel Sandler, eds., *Israel at the Polls, 1992* (Lanham: Rowman & Littlefield, 1995).

25. Alexander Wendt, *Social Theory of International Politics* (New York: Cambridge University Press, 1999).

26. M. Herskov, R. Levana, and Z. Malchiel, eds., *Our Country's Ports: A Study Booklet* (Jerusalem: Sald Child and Youth Foundation), Israel State Archives, Jerusalem, File1409/1853/2.

27. Yet, in Jewish thought, the idea of chosenness can be interpreted as either a duty (the Maimonidean view) or as a privilege (the view of Judah Halevi and Abraham Isaac Kook), with the attendant notion of having a "Jewish soul" through observance of the commandments. See Henri Atlan, "Chosen People," in Cohen and Mendes-Flohr, eds., *Contemporary Jewish Religious Thought*, pp. 55–59.

28. Martin Van Creveld, *The Sword and the Olive: A Critical History of the Israeli Defense Force* (New York: PublicAffairs, 1998), p. 87.

29. When asked about his decision to use a biblical passage in this speech, Rabin's speechwriter, Eitan Haber, dismissed the question with a "I've written 400 speeches; do you expect me to remember?" More than just a flippant response, what this lack of a reply seems to suggest is that biblical references are so pervasive in the Israeli psyche as to render them unproblematic in contemporary discourse. Author's interview with Haber, 16 November 1999, Tel Aviv.

30. Letter from David Ben-Gurion to President Truman (16 May 1948), reprinted in Freundlich, ed., *Documents on the Foreign Policy of Israel, vol. 1, 14 May to 30 September 1948*, p. 12.

31. Yitzhak Rabin, *The Rabin Memoirs* (Berkeley: University of California Press, 1979, 1996), p. 7.

32. Golda Meir, *My Life* (New York: Dell Publishing Co., 1975), p. 21.

33. Uri D'vir, Yael Levin, and Michael Chen, *Roads in Our Country: A Study Booklet* (The Sald Child and Youth Foundation, Jerusalem), p. 16 (emphasis added).

34. "We Are Fellow Pioneers," from "Songs Appropriate to Kindergarten," Ministry of Education File 4765/21/6, Israel State Archives, Jerusalem.

35. Meir, *My Life*, p. 44.

36. See Edward N. Luttwak and Daniel Horowitz, *The Israeli Army 1948–1973* (Cambridge: Abt Books, 1983); and Van Creveld, *The Sword and the Olive*, pp. 155–156.

37. Quoted in Elon, *The Israelis*, p. 45. Similarly, a chapter in Golda Meir's autobiography is titled "I Choose Palestine." Meir, *My Life*, pp. 49–70.

38. See Meir, *My Life*; and Ben-Gurion, *Letters to Paula*, p. 241.

39. "We Have a Land," in *Songbook: Grade 5* (Jerusalem: Israel Ministry of Education and Culture, division for the teaching of music, 1970), p. 52.

40. "Shech Abrek," from *Hora: Songs and Dances of Israel; Oranim Zabar Troupe Featuring Geula Gill* (New York: Elektra Records).

41. Shohat, *Israeli Cinema*, p. 32; and Elon, *The Israelis*, pp. 168–172.

42. Ben-Gurion, *Letters to Paula*, p. 193 (emphasis in the original).

43. Meir, *My Life*, pp. 11–12.

44. Max Nordau, "Muskeljudentum," *Juedische Turnzeitung* (June 1903), trans. J. Hessing, reprinted in Paul R. Mendes-Flohr and Jehuda Reinharz, *The Jew in the Modern World: A Documentary History* (New York: Oxford University Press, 1980), pp. 434–435 (quote from p. 435). See also David Biale, "Zionism as an Erotic Revolution," in Howard Eilberg-Schwartz, ed., *People of the Body: Jews and Judaism from an Embodied Perspective* (Albany: State University of New York Press, 1992).

45. For instance, the 1956 prize for best attendance awarded by the Winnipeg Talmud Torah junior congregation was a book entitled *The Jew in American Sport*. Author's interview with Max Sucharov, 7 November 2000, Arlington, VA.

46. Author's interview with General (Res.) Nechemia Dagan, 3 January 2000, Jerusalem.

47. Mark Tessler, *A History of the Israeli-Palestinian Conflict* (Bloomington: Indiana University Press, 1994), pp. 55–56.

48. Theodor Herzl, "A Solution of the Jewish Question," *The Jewish Chronicle* (17 January 1896), pp. 12–13; reprinted in Mendes-Flohr and Reinharz, *The Jew in the Modern World: A Documentary History*, pp. 422–427, particularly p. 425.

49. The sections in this chapter on Tel Hai, Bar Kochba, and Masada owe extensively to the work of Yael Zerubavel who discusses the role of these events in creating and sustaining Israeli collective memory; and those of David and Goliath and the Holocaust draw on the work of Ruth Linn. See Zerubavel, *Recovered Roots;* and Linn, *Conscience at War: The Israeli Soldier as a Moral Critic* (Albany: State University of New York Press, 1996).

50. Ve'David," from *Shalom! Oranim Zabar Israeli Troupe* (New York: Elektra Records).

51. From *Ma'ariv* (20 October 1989), cited in Linn, *Conscience at War*, p. 162.

52. The IDF's reasons for shifting away from the use of Masada for these induction ceremonies appear to have been largely logistical, with the added impetus that the armored corps leadership preferred a site that was more specific to the achievements of tank warfare. The new site chosen was Latrun. See Nachman Ben-Yehuda, "The Masada Mythical Narrative and the Israeli Army," in Edna Lomsky-Feder and Eyal Ben-Ari, eds., *The Military and Militarism in Israeli Society* (Albany: State University of New York Press, 1999), pp. 80–81.

53. The Goldstar advertisement is reprinted in Amnon Dankner and David Tartakover, *Where We Were and What We Did: An Israeli Lexicon of the Fifties and the Sixties* (Jerusalem: Keter Publishing House, Ltd., 1996), p. 22 (in Hebrew).

54. Ben-Yehuda, "The Masada Mythical Narrative and the Israeli Army," pp. 76–80.

55. See, for instance, Nachman Ben-Yehuda, *The Myth of Masada: Collective Memory and Mythmaking in Israel* (Madison: University of Wisconsin Press, 1995); and Daniel Bar-Tal, *The Masada Syndrome: A Case of Central Belief*, Discussion Paper 3 (Tel Aviv: International Center for Peace in the Middle East, 1983).

56. Tessler, *A History of the Israeli-Palestinian Conflict*, p. 13.

57. Ministry of Education file 4765/21/6, Israel State Archives, Jerusalem.

58. Elon, *The Israelis*, p. 137. However, Zerubavel notes that the available historical evidence actually supports the view that Trumpeldor did in fact utter the famed phrase, with the Russian curse theory having been largely fabricated in Israel as a countermyth. See Zerubavel, *Recovered Roots*, p. 160.

59. "The Night of the Eleventh of Adar," *Songbook for Grade 5* (Jerusalem: Israel Ministry of Education and Culture, the division for the teaching of music, 1970), p. 25.

60. Zerubavel, *Recovered Roots*, p. 91.

61. Zerubavel notes the paradoxical relationship between the actual loss of Tel Hai and its commemoration as a symbol of "successful defense" and "no retreat." *Recovered Roots*, p. xviii.

62. Linn, *Conscience at War*, p. 142.

63. Ibid., p. 3.

64. Nurith Gertz, "From Jew to Hebrew: The 'Zionist Narrative' in the Israeli Cinema of the 1940s and 1950s," in Dan Urian and Efraim Karsh, eds., *In Search of Identity: Jewish Aspects in Israeli Culture* (London: Frank Cass, 1999), p. 177.

65. Hannah Arendt, *Eichmann in Jerusalem: A Report on the Banality of Evil* (New York: Viking Press, 1963).

66. The United States became Israel's main arms supplier after the 1967 war when France, hitherto its central patron, reversed its Middle East policy.

67. Edward W. Said, *Out of Place: A Memoir* (New York: Alfred A. Knopf, 1999), p. 142.

68. Cable sent by Moshe Shertok (later Sharett), head of the Jewish Agency, to Nachum Goldmann, president of the World Jewish Congress (24 May 1948). Reprinted in Freundlich, ed., *Documents on the Foreign Policy of Israel, vol. 1, 14 May to 30 September 1948*.

69. Figures cited in Eliot Cohen, Michael J. Eisenstadt, and Andrew J. Bacevich, *'Knives, Tanks and Missiles': Israel's Security Revolution* (Washington, DC: The Washington Institute for Near East Policy, 1998), p. 148.

70. M. Shertok to N. Goldmann (15 June 1949). Reprinted in Freundlich, ed., *Documents on the Foreign Policy of Israel, vol. 1, 14 May to 30 September 1948*, p. 162.

71. Rabin, *The Rabin Memoirs*, p. 45.

72. For an historical overview, see Van Creveld, *The Sword and the Olive*, pp. 77–82.

73. The exact figure remains a subject of scholarly and political dispute: estimates range from 500,000 to over 900,000. See Tessler, *A History of the Israeli-Palestinian Conflict*, pp. 279–280.

74. See, inter alia, Benny Morris, *The Birth of the Palestinian Refugee Problem, 1947–1949* (Cambridge: Cambridge University Press, 1987).

75. Letter from M. Shertok to N. Goldmann (15 June 1948), reprinted in Freundlich, ed., *Documents on the Foreign Policy of Israel, vol. 1, 14 May to 30 September 1948*, p. 163.

76. Summary of meetings between M. Shertok, Count Bernadotte, and assistants (Tel Aviv, 17–18 June 1948), reprinted in Freundlich, ed., *Documents on the Foreign Policy of Israel, vol. 1, 14 May to 30 September 1948*, p. 184 (emphasis added).

77. M. Shertok to M. Comay (22 July 1948); reprinted in Freundlich, ed., *Documents on the Foreign Policy of Israel, vol. 1, 14 May to 30 September 1948*, p. 374.

78. Author's interview with Shimon Sheves, chief of staff under Prime Minister Rabin, 25 November 1999, Tel Aviv.

79. Reprinted in Rabin, *The Rabin Memoirs*, p. 391.

80. The Balfour Declaration stated that "His Majesty's Government view with favour the establishment in Palestine of a national home for the Jewish people, and will use their best endeavours to facilitate the achievement of this object, it being clearly understood that nothing shall be done which may prejudice the civil and religious rights of existing non-Jewish communities in Palestine, or the rights and political status enjoyed by Jews in any other country." Reprinted in Walter Laqueur and Barry Rubin, eds., *The Israel-Arab Reader: A Documentary History of the Middle East Conflict* (New York: Penguin Books, 1984), p. 18.

81. Cited in Tessler, *A History of the Israeli-Palestinian Conflict*, p. 173.

82. Van Creveld, *The Sword and the Olive*, p. 41.

83. Letter from M. Shertok to E. Bevin (16 May 1948), reprinted in Freundlich, ed., *Documents on the Foreign Policy of Israel, vol. 1, 14 May to 30 September 1948*, p. 12.

84. Ben-Gurion, *Letters to Paula*, p. 124.

85. Another example of constructive ambiguity was the difference between the French and English versions of United Nations Resolution 242 issued in 1967. The English version called for "withdrawal of Israel's armed forces from territories occupied in the recent conflict;" while the French version said *"des territoires."* Israelis have interpreted this to mean *some of* the territories, while the Arab states [and Palestinians] have historically called for an Israeli withdrawal from all of the West Bank and Gaza Strip, as well as the Golan Heights and Sinai Peninsula—the latter of which was returned to Egypt in 1982.

86. Van Creveld, *The Sword and the Olive*, p. 62.

FOUR. THE SECURITY ETHIC OF THE IDF

1. There are 900 war monuments in Israel. Tamar Vital, "Homage to the Heroes," *The Jerusalem Post* (5 June 1992), p. 16.

2. Although men and women are subject to military service at age eighteen (three years for men; two for women), until recently only men could serve combat functions. A 1993 supreme court ruling followed by a 2000 amendment to the Defense Service Law opened the ranks of combat to women.

3. For a discussion of the history of these groups, see Martin Van Creveld, *The Sword and the Olive: A Critical History of the Israeli Defense Force* (New York: PublicAffairs, 1998), pp. 45–62.

4. Zeev Sternhell, *The Founding Myths of Israel: Nationalism, Socialism and the Making of the Jewish State* (Princeton: Princeton University Press, 1998), p. 35.

5. For a discussion of Ben-Gurion's policies vis-à-vis the Palmach, see Edward N. Luttwak and Daniel Horowitz, *The Israeli Army 1948–1973* (Cambridge: Abt Books, 1983), pp. 72–74.

6. Ze'ev Schiff, *A History of the Israeli Army: 1874 to the Present* (New York: Macmillan, 1985), p. 60.

7. Creveld, *The Sword and the Olive,* p. 81.

8. See Yaron Ezrahi, *Rubber Bullets: Power and Conscience in Modern Israel* (New York: Farrar, Straus and Giroux, 1997).

9. Author's interview with past-chief of staff Amnon Lipkin-Shahak, 16 March 2000, Jerusalem.

10. Opening page remarks by Chief IDF Rabbi Shlomo Goren, in the *Passover Hagadah for the Soldiers of the Israel Defense Forces* (Israel: The Chief Military Rabbinate, 1964) (in Hebrew).

11. Uri Savir, *The Process: 1,100 Days that Changed the Middle East* (New York: Vintage Books, 1998), pp. 176–178.

12. Reprinted in Amnon Dankner and David Tartakover, *Where We Were and What We Did: An Israeli Lexicon of the Fifties and the Sixties* (Jerusalem: Keter Publishing House, Ltd., 1996), p. 21 (in Hebrew).

13. "The Educational Activities of the IDF" (IDF Chief Educational Officer, circa 1960) (in Hebrew).

14. Israel Tal, "Israel's Doctrine of National Security: Background and Dynamics," *The Jerusalem Quarterly* 4 (Summer 1977), p. 45. See also Handel, *Israel's Political-Military Doctrine,* p. 68, and Eliot Cohen, Michael J. Eisenstadt, and Andrew J. Bacevich, *'Knives, Tanks and Missiles': Israel's Security Revolution* (Washington, DC: The Washington Institute for Near East Policy, 1998), p. 57.

15. See Y. Harkabi, *Arab Attitudes to Israel* (Jerusalem: Keter Publishing House, 1972).

16. Quoted in Yoram Peri, "Afterward," in Yitzhak Rabin, *The Rabin Memoirs* (Berkeley: University of California Press, 1979), p. 399 (emphasis added).

17. Rabin's June 1967 speech at the Hebrew University of Jerusalem, as recalled by Rabin himself in *The Rabin Memoirs*, p. 120 (emphasis added). The actual words of the speech were, "today, the university has conferred this honorary title on us in recognition of our army's superiority of spirit and morals as it was revealed in the heat of war, for we are standing in this place by virtue of battle which though forced upon us was forged into a victory astounding the world." Copy of speech provided to the author courtesy of Colonel (Ret.) Mordechai Bar-On.

18. Luttwak and Horowitz, *The Israeli Army*, pp. 12–14.

19. Past-Deputy Foreign Minister Yossi Beilin acknowledges this dichotomy between the "criticism [the war] aroused among the other Western participants" and the Israeli view, noting that "the Suez war was not a controversial issue in Israel." Beilin, *Israel: A Concise Political History* (New York: St. Martin's Press, 1992), p. 83.

20. Michael I. Handel, *Israel's Political-Military Doctrine* (Cambridge: Center for International Affairs, Harvard University, 1973), pp. 21–23.

21. Ariel Levite, *Offense and Defense in Israeli Military Doctrine* (Boulder: Westview Press, 1989), p. 55.

22. Colonel Mordechai Bar-On, ed., *Israel Defence Forces: The Six Day War* (Israeli Ministry of Defense, 1968), p. 229 (emphasis added).

23. Ibid.

24. Ben-Gurion, *Memoirs*, passage reprinted in David Hardan, ed., *The Moral and Existential Dilemmas of the Israeli Soldier* (Jerusalem: World Zionist Organization, 1985), p. 8.

25. Berl Katznelson, *Collected Writings*, passage reprinted in Hardan, ed., *The Moral and Existential Dilemmas of the Israeli Soldier*, p. 5.

26. Luttwak and Horowitz, *The Israeli Army*, p. 23.

27. Speech by Chief of Staff Yitzhak Rabin to the Hebrew University of Jerusalem on receiving an honorary doctorate, Mount Scopus, Jerusalem (28 June 1967).

28. Amos Elon, *The Israelis: Founders and Sons* (New York: Penguin Books, 1971, 1981), p. 7.

29. In Rafi Mann, *It's Inconceivable* (Or Yehuda: Hed Arzi, 1998), p. 45 (in Hebrew).

30. In Ella Shohat, *Israeli Cinema: East/West and the Politics of Representation* (Austin: University of Texas Press, 1989), p. 79.

31. 1981 article cited in Levite, *Offense and Defense in Israeli Military Doctrine*, p. 167 n.10.

32. Levite, *Offense and Defense in Israeli Military Doctrine*, p. 28.

33. Handel, *Israel's Political-Military Doctrine*, p. 48.

34. Cohen et al., '*Knives, Tanks and Missiles*', p. 26. See also Van Creveld, *The Sword and the Olive*, pp. 277–280.

35. Levite, *Offense and Defense in Israeli Military Doctrine*, pp. 38–39.

36. For a brief discussion of the debate among Israeli military thinkers over the use of territorial gains, see Levite, *Offense and Defense in Israeli Military Doctrine*, pp. 32–33.

37. Graham Evans and Jeffrey Newnham, *The Penguin Dictionary of International Relations*, (London: Penguin Books, 1998), p. 325.

38. Ben-Eliezer, *The Making of Israeli Militarism*, p. 7.

39. Elon, *The Israelis*, p. 9.

40. See Maoz Azaryahu, "The Independence Day Military Parade: A Political History of a Patriotic Ritual," in Edna Lomsky-Feder and Eyal Ben-Ari, eds., *The Military and Militarism in Israeli Society* (Albany: State University of New York Press, 1999); and Dan Horovitz, "Is Israel a Garrison State?" *The Jerusalem Quarterly* 4 (Summer 1977), pp. 58–75, which uses the lack of militarism to reject the idea that Israel might be a "garrison state."

41. It is not uncommon to see a newspaper headline proclaiming the latest activites of "Raful" (Rafael Eytan), "Gandhi" (Rehavam Ze'evi), "Cheech" (Shlomo Lahat), "Fuad" (Binyamin Ben-Eliezer), "Baiga" (Avraham Shohat), and "Bibi" (Binyamin Netanyahu) to name a few Israeli politicians circulating the ranks of politics in recent years, some of them senior ex-military officers.

42. "Brass in the House," *The Jerusalem Report* (4 May 1995).

43. See Tamar Katriel, *Talking Straight: Dugri Speech in Israeli Sabra Culture* (Cambridge: Cambridge University Press, 1986); and Ezrahi, *Rubber Bullets*, pp. 97–98.

44. David Biale, *Power and Powerlessness in Jewish History* (New York: Schocken Books, 1986), pp. 98–99.

45. David Ben-Gurion, *Letters to Paula* (Pittsburgh: University of Pittsburgh Press, 1971), p. 90.

46. Ibid., p. 93.

47. In particular, compare the Chinese legend of Mulan with Isaac Bashevis Singer's Yentl fable.

48. Cohen et al., *'Knives, Tanks, and Missiles,'* p. 31.

49. Summary of meetings between M. Shertok, Count Bernadotte and Assistants (Tel Aviv, 17–18 June 1948), reprinted in Yehoshua Freundlich, ed., *Documents on the Foreign Policy of Israel, vol. 1, 14 May to 30 September 1948* (Jerusalem: Israel State Archives, 1981), p. 183.

50. Myron J. Aronoff, *Israeli Visions and Divisions: Cultural Change and Political Conflict* (New Brunswick: Transaction Publishers, 1989), p. xx.

51. Quoted in Luttwak and Horowitz, *The Israeli Army*, p. 61.

52. Cohen, et al., *'Knives, Tanks, and Missiles,'* p. 52.

53. Ibid., pp. 18–19.

54. Colonel Mordechai M. Bar-On, "Education Processes in the Israel Defense Forces," in Sol Tax, ed., *The Draft: A Handbook of Facts and Alternatives* (Chicago: University of Chicago Press, 1967), pp. 138-166.

55. See Schiff, *A History of the Israeli Army*, pp. 115–123.

56. As related by Major General Yeshayahu Gavish, OC Southern Command during the Six Day War, in author's interview; 19 March 2000, Tel Aviv.

57. Rabin, *The Rabin Memoirs*, p. 81.

58. For a discussion of Israel's security doctrine written by then-Deputy Minister of Defence, see Tal, "Israel's Doctrine of National Security; Background and Dynamics," pp. 44–57.

59. Rabin, *The Rabin Memoirs*, p. 118.

60. Handel, *Israel's Political-Military Doctrine*, p. 5.

61. Tal, "Israel's Doctrine of National Security," p. 51.

62. Author's interview with Major General (Ret.) Gavish, 19 March 2000, Tel Aviv.

63. Horovitz, "Is Israel a Garrison State?" p. 58.

FIVE. ISRAEL AND THE LEBANON WAR

1. In June 1985, the IDF withdrew from most of Lebanon, remaining in a southern strip that was dubbed the "security zone." The IDF withdrew completely in May 2000.

2. Richard A. Gabriel, *Operation Peace for Galilee: The Israeli-PLO War in Lebanon* (New York: Hill and Wang, 1984), p. 224.

3. See, for instance, Daniel Lieberfeld, *Negotiation and Threat Perception in South Africa and Israel/Palestine* (Westport, CT: Praeger, 1999), pp. 58–59, 73, 79. While elsewhere in this chapter I point to a more normative criticism of the war from Yossi Beilin, Beilin has also written that "it seemed that among the Israeli public there was a growing awareness of the limitations of force." Beilin, *Touching Peace: From the Oslo Accord to a Final Agreement* (London: Weidenfeld & Nicolson, 1999), p. 15.

4. Baruch Kimmerling, "The Power-Oriented Settlement: PLO-Israel— The Road to the Oslo Agreement and Back?," in Avraham Sela and Moshe Ma'oz, eds., *The PLO and Israel: From Armed Conflict to Political Solution, 1964-1994* (New York: St. Martin's Press, 1997), p. 259.

5. See Tessler, *A History of the Israeli-Palestinian Conflict,* pp. 528–531.

6. One hundred twenty thousand Palestinians fled from Palestine to Lebanon in 1948, in the course of Israel's War of Independence. By the late 1960s, the population had grown to approximately 250,000. Tessler, *A History of the Israeli-Palestinian Conflict,* pp. 280 and 449.

7. Ze'ev Schiff and Ehud Ya'ari, *Israel's Lebanon War* (New York: Simon and Schuster, 1984), p. 96.

8. In Tessler, *A History of the Israeli-Palestinian Conflict,* p. 573.

9. Tessler, *A History of the Israeli-Palestinian Conflict,* p. 571.

10. Quoted in Tessler, op. cit., p. 572.

11. Yossi Beilin, *Israel: A Concise Political History* (New York: St. Martin's Press, 1992), p. 140.

12. Cited in Ze'ev Schiff, *A History of the Israeli Army: 1874 to the Present* (New York: Macmillan Publishing Company, 1985), p. 245.

13. Schiff, *A History of the Israeli Army,* p. 249.

14. Cited in Moshe Ma'oz, *Syria and Israel: From War to Peacemaking* (Oxford: Oxford University Press, 1995), p. 173.

15. Ma'oz, *Syria and Israel,* p. 175.

16. Robert Slater, *Rabin of Israel: Warrior for Peace* (New York: HarperPaperbacks, 1996), p. 390.

17. Shimon Peres, *Battling for Peace: A Memoir* (New York: Random House, 1995), p. 199.

18. Itim, "Eitan: Begin was Aware of Plans for Lebanon," *The Jerusalem Post* (15 March 1992), p. 10.

19. Yehuda Ben Meir, *Civil-Military Relations in Israel* (New York: Columbia University Press, 1995), p. 156. For a discussion of the war in light of civil-military relations, see pages 148–156.

20. Yehoshafat Harkabi, *Israel's Fateful Hour* (New York: Harper & Row, 1988), pp. 92–104.

21. Author's interview with Hirsh Goodman, 9 November 1999, Jerusalem.

22. In *The Beirut Massacre: The Complete Kahan Commission Report* (Princeton: Karz-Cohl, 1983), p. 14.

23. In ibid., p. 19.

24. In ibid., p. 22.

25. This death toll is the official Israeli estimate, as presented in *The Beirut Massacre*, p. xiii.

26. In ibid., p. 48.

27. The most famous documented blood libel case is that of Mendel Beilis in Russia. See "The Beilis Trial," in Paul R. Mendes-Flohr and Jehuda Reinharz, eds., *The Jew in the Modern World: A Documentary History* (New York: Oxford University Press, 1980), pp. 332–333. For a concise overview of blood libels through the centuries, see Stuart Schoffman, "Tales of Red Matzah," *The Jerusalem Report* (4 April 1991).

28. Speech made by Ariel Sharon to the Knesset on 22 September 1982, reprinted in *The Beirut Massacre*, p. 123.

29. Ibid., speech by Sharon, p. 128.

30. Speech made by Shimon Peres to the Knesset on 22 September 1982, reprinted in *The Beirut Massacre*, p. 130.

31. Beilin, *Israel*, p. 169.

32. Author's interview with Janet Aviad, 11 October 1999, Jerusalem.

33. Cited in Tzaly Reshef, *Peace Now: The Story of the Israeli Peace Movement in the Words of Its Leader* (English translation ms), p. 191.

34. Cited in Reshef, *Peace Now*, p. 192.

35. Kahan Commission Report, in *The Beirut Massacre*, p. 57.

36. In *The Beirut Massacre*, p. xiii (emphasis added).

37. In *The Beirut Massacre*, p. xiv (emphasis added).

38. These were G.O.C. Northern Command Major General Amir Drori; the director of military intelligence, Major General Yehoshua Saguy; and a division commander, Brigadier General Amos Yaron. Kahan Commission Report, in *The Beirut Massacre*, pp. 104–105.

39. Kahan Commission Report, in *The Beirut Massacre*, p. 104.

40. Quoted in Asher Wallfish, "Begin Lieutenant: Protests, Mounting War Casualties, Spurred Resignation," *The Jerusalem Post* (10 March 1992), p. 3.

41. Moshe Zak, "Master Negotiator Menachem Begin," *The Jerusalem Post* (13 March 1992), p. 6.

42. The speech was printed in *Ma'ariv* (20 August 1982); cited in Bar-On, *In Pursuit of Peace*, p. 150.

43. Inbar, "The 'No Choice War' Debate in Israel," p. 25.

44. Author's interview with General (Ret.) Yeshayahu Gavish, 19 March 2000, Tel Aviv.

45. Jacobo Timerman, *The Longest War: Israel in Lebanon* (New York: Vintage Books, 1982), p. 38.

46. Shlomo Aronson and Nathan Yanai, "Critical Aspects of the Elections and their Implications," in Dan Caspi, Abraham Diskin, and Emanuel Gutmann, eds., *The Roots of Begin's Success: The 1981 Elections* (New York: Croom Helm, 1984), pp. 28–29.

47. S. N. Eisenstadt, *The Internal Repercussions of the Lebanon War* (Policy Studies 17, The Leonard Davis Institute for International Relations, The Hebrew University of Jerusalem, August 1986), pp. 10–13.

48. For a discussion of Israeli "operational codes" during the 1992 elections, see Gerald M. Steinberg, "A Nation that Dwells Alone? Foreign Policy in the 1992 Elections," in Daniel J. Elazar and Shmuel Sandler, eds., *Israel at the Polls, 1992* (Lanham, MD: Rowman & Littlefield, 1995), pp. 175–200. For a general formulation, see Alexander George, "The Operational Code: A Neglected Approach to the Study of Political Leaders and Decision Making," *International Studies Quarterly* 13, 2 (June 1969).

49. See Stuart A. Cohen, "Israel and Its Army: The Image of the IDF as an Issue in the 1992 Election Campaign," in Elazar and Sandler, eds., *Israel at the Polls, 1992*, pp. 157–174.

50. Tessler, *A History of the Israeli-Palestinian Conflict*, p. 577.

51. Martin Van Creveld, *The Sword and the Olive: A Critical History of the Israeli Defense Force* (New York: PublicAffairs, 1998), p. 299.

52. Cited in Schiff and Ya'ari, *Israel's Lebanon War*, p. 31 (emphasis added).

53. Yael Yishai, "The Israeli Labor Party and the Lebanon War," *Armed Forces & Society* 11, 3 (Spring 1985), p. 387.

54. Author's interview with Yossi Beilin, 28 November 1999, Jerusalem.

55. Author's interview with Shimon Peres, 15 November 1999, Jerusalem.

56. Ibid.

57. Shimon Peres, *Battling for Peace*, p. 197.

58. Jacob Wirtschafter, "'Peace for Galilee' Helped Bring About Peace Talks—Sharon," *The Jerusalem Post* (4 June 1992), p. 2.

59. Ibid.

60. Yitzhak Rabin, "In the Aftermath of the War in Lebanon: Israel's Objectives," in Joseph Alpher, ed., *Israel's Lebanon Policy: Where To?* (Tel Aviv: Jaffee Center for Strategic Studies, Tel Aviv University, Memorandum No. 12, August 1984), p. 41.

61. Reshef, *Peace Now*, p. 170.

62. Reuven Kaminer, *The Politics of Protest: The Israeli Peace Movement and the Palestinian Intifada* (Brighton, UK: Sussex Academic Press, 1996), p. 35.

63. Ibid., p. 36.

64. Reshef, *Peace Now*, p. 168.

65. Author's interview with Peace Now activist Janet Aviad, 11 October 1999, Jerusalem.

66. Author's interview with Colonel (Ret.) Mordechai Bar-On, 24 November 1999, Jerusalem.

67. Author's interview with MK Naomi Chazan, 6 December 1999, Jerusalem.

68. Author's interview with Colonel (Ret.) Yeshayahu Tadmor, 10 December 1999, Haifa.

69. Mordechai Bar-On, *In Pursuit of Peace: A History of the Israeli Peace Movement* (Washington, DC: United States Institute of Peace Press, 1996), p. 151.

70. In Yael Zerubavel, *Recovered Roots: Collective Memory and the Making of Israeli National Tradition* (Chicago: University of Chicago Press, 1995), p. 175.

71. The original song goes "When we'll die / They will bury us / In the winery of / Rishon Le-Tsiyon. / There are pretty gals there / Who serve glasses / Full of wine [which is] / Reddish red." Zerubavel, p. 175.

72. Lyrics available at: http://the-tech.mit.edu/~orli/silverplatter.html

73. Author's interview with Major General (Ret.) Yeshayahu Gavish, 19 March 2000, Tel Aviv.

74. Author's interview with General (Ret.) Amnon Lipkin-Shahak, 16 March 2000, Jerusalem.

75. Chief of Staff Dan Shomron quoted in Asher Wallfish, "Shomron Rapped for Moves on Rock-Throwers," *The Jerusalem Post* (12 December 1990), p. 1.

76. Carl Schrag, "Fighting Spirit, "*The Jerusalem Post* (4 December 1992), p. 10. The officer in question was cited anonymously.

77. Quoted in Bar-On, *In Pursuit of Peace*, p. 152.

78. Quoted in Yishai, "The Israeli Labor Party and the Lebanon War," p. 391. 79. Baruch Kimmerling, "The Power-Oriented Settlement," p. 228.

80. Bradley Burston, "Lebanon War Tombstone Texts may be Reworded," *The Jerusalem Post* (10 June 1991, p. 2.

81. As Bar-On notes, "The few cases that did occur [during Israel's first three decades] generally involved philosophical pacifists who objected to war in itself, and did not necessarily pass judgment on the specific political circumstances or merits of a particular war." Bar-On, *In Pursuit of Peace*, p. 146. Israel possesses a separate cadre of objectors on very different conscientious grounds: these are members of the ultraorthodox, often non-Zionist segment of society who have entered into an arrangement with the state exempting them from military service in order to dedicate their lives to Torah study.

82. Ruth Linn, "Conscientious Objection in Israel During the War in Lebanon," *Armed Forces & Society* 12, 4 (Summer 1986): 489–511, p. 505 (emphasis in original).

83. Peace Now spokesman cited in Bar-On, *In Pursuit of Peace,* p. 149.

84. In Kaminer, *The Politics of Protest*, p. 37.

85. Linn, "Conscientious Objection," p. 490.

86. Van Creveld, *The Sword and the Olive*, p. 299.

87. Kaminer, *The Politics of Protest*, pp. 38–39.

88. Reuven Gal, "Commitment and Obedience in the Military: An Israeli Case Study," *Armed Forces & Society* 11, 4 (Summer 1985): 553–564, p. 559. Tamar Katriel argues that Geva's protest was made possible by Israeli *dugri* ("straight talk") culture. See Katriel, *Talking Straight: Dugri Speech in Israeli Sabra Culture* (Cambridge: Cambridge University Press, 1986), pp. 89–98.

89. Gal, "Commitment and Obedience in the Military," p. 564 n.9.

90. Interview in *Ma'ariv* with Y. Erez, 26 September 1982, quoted in Gal, "Commitment and Obedience in the Military," p. 559.

91. Author's interview with Hirsh Goodman, 9 November 1999, Jerusalem.

92. Timerman, *The Longest War*, p. 22 (emphasis added).

93. Ibid., p. 16.

94. Daniel J. Elazar, "U.S. Jewry in the 1990s," *The Jerusalem Post* (29 January 1991), p. 8.

95. Quoted in Timerman, *The Longest War*, p. 37.

96. In Calev Ben-David, "Apocalypse Then: Two New Films Recall the Tragic Absurdity of the Lebanon War," *The Jerusalem Report* (20 June 1991).

97. Nurith Gertz, "The Medium That Mistook Itself for War: *Cherry Season* in Comparison with *Ricochets* and *Cup Final*," *Israel Studies* 4, 1 (Spring 1999), p. 170.

98. Ella Shohat, *Israeli Cinema: East/West and the Politics of Representation* (Austin: University of Texas Press, 1989), pp. 103–114.

99. Laurence J. Silberstein, *The Postzionism Debates: Knowledge and Power in Israeli Culture* (New York: Routledge, 1999), pp. 97 and 101.

100. Prominent examples of Israeli "revisionist" scholarship include, inter alia, Benny Morris, *The Birth of the Palestinian Refugee Problem* (Cambridge: Cambridge University Press, 1987); and Tom Segev, *The Seventh Million: The Israelis and the Holocaust* (New York: Hill and Wang, 1993).

SIX. ISRAEL AND THE INTIFADA

1. Cited in Efraim Inbar, "Israel's Small War: The Military Response to the Intifada." *Armed Forces & Society* 18, 1 (1991), p. 37.

2. Tel Aviv University Economist Assaf Razin, cited in Neal Sandler, "The Missing Link," *The Jerusalem Report* (13 December 1990).

3. Mark Tessler, *A History of the Israeli-Palestinian Conflict* (Bloomington: Indiana University Press, 1994), p. 707.

4. Quoted in ibid., p. 708.

5. See Yossi Beilin, *Israel: A Concise Political History* (New York: St. Martin's Press, 1992), p. 47.

6. Avner Shalev, *The Intifada: Causes and Effects* (Boulder: Westview Press, 1991), pp. 149–150.

7. Author's interview with Uri Savir, 17 November 1999, Jerusalem.

8. Author's interview with Avi Gil, 7 December 1999, Tel Aviv.

9. Statement made to the United Nations in Geneva on 14 December 1988. Cited in "An Intifada Chronology," *The Jerusalem Report* (13 December 1990).

10. Author's interview with Uri Savir, 17 November 1999, Jerusalem.

11. Author's interview with Yossi Beilin, 28 November 1999, Jerusalem.

12. Author's interview with Shimon Sheves, 25 November 1999, Tel Aviv.

13. Author's interview with Naomi Chazan, 6 December 1999, Jerusalem.

14. Ze'ev Schiff and Ehud Ya'ari, *Intifada: The Palestinian Uprising—Israel's Third Front* (New York: Simon and Schuster, 1989), pp. 115–116.

15. Tessler, *A History of the Israeli-Palestinian Conflict*, p. 525.

16. Ibid., pp. 525–527.

17. However, during the 1980s, the Israeli right-wing had called for the "Jordanian option," meaning the handover of the West Bank to Jordan, under the assumption that a "Palestinian state" already existed in Jordan—given that a large percentage of Jordanian citizens are of Palestinian origin. (Estimates range from 40 to 60 percent. Lack of public census data makes the number difficult to ascertain with certainty.)

18. Schiff and Ya'ari, *Intifada*.

19. Avner Shalev, *The Intifada: Causes and Effects* (Boulder: Westview Press, 1991), pp. 149–150.

20. Author's interview with IDF Colonel (Ret.) Yeshayahu Tadmor, 10 December 1999, Haifa.

21. Author's interview with Shimon Peres, 15 November 1999, Jerusalem.

22. Mark Tessler, *A History of the Israeli-Palestinian Conflict*, p. 697.

23. Colonel (Ret.) Mordechai Bar-On, "Israeli Reactions to the Palestinian Uprising," *Journal of Palestine Studies* 17, 4 (Summer 1988), p. 48.

24. Schiff and Ya'ari, *Intifada*, p. 117.

25. Author's interview with General (Res.) Nechemia Dagan, 3 January 2000, Jerusalem.

26. Reuven Gal, *A Portrait of the Israeli Soldier* (New York: Greenwood Press, 1986), p. 38.

27. Inbar, "Israel's Small War."

28. See Robert Slater, *Rabin of Israel: Warrior for Peace* (New York: HarperPaperbacks, 1996), pp. 412–414; and Martin Van Creveld, *The Sword and the Olive: A Critical History of the Israeli Defense Force* (New York: PublicAffairs, 1998), p. 167.

29. Author's interview with Naomi Chazan, 6 December 1999, Jerusalem.

30. Shomron made this statement on 23 February 1988. Cited in "An Intifada Chronology," *The Jerusalem Report* (13 December 1990).

31. Quoted in Inbar, "Israel's Small War," p. 34.

32. Ehud Ya'ari, "A War That Musn't Be Won," *Jerusalem Report* (2 April 1992).

33. See Tessler, "The Intifada and Political Discourse in Israel," *Journal of Palestine Studies* 19, 2 (1990).

34. At the time of this writing (2004), there are approximately 230,000 settlers in the West Bank and Gaza living among three million Palestinians. (The vast majority of settlers live in the West Bank, with only 7,000 residing in Gaza.)

35. Author's interview with David Makovsky, 19 October 1999, Jerusalem.

36. Gershom Gorenberg, "The Sinai Convention," *The Jerusalem Report* (3 January 1991).

37. Asher Arian, *Security Threatened: Surveying Israeli Opinion on Peace and War* (New York: Cambridge University Press, 1995), p. 279. By 1993, the mean had increased slightly, to 3.6.

38. Ibid., p. 79.

39. Ibid., p. 80.

40. Cited in Hanna Levinsohn and Elihu Katz, "The *Intifada* Is Not A War: Jewish Public Opinion on the Israel-Arab Conflict," in Akiba A. Cohen and Gadi Wolfsfeld, eds., *Framing the Intifada: People and Media* (Norwood, NJ: Ablex Publishing Corporation, 1993), pp. 58–59.

41. Ibid., p. 60. Neither can this leftward shift be explained simply by generational change: that is, the expectation that as society is distanced from the tumultuous events of the Holocaust and Israeli independence, we can expect a softening of attitudes. An equally strong case could be made against this argument based on what economists and cognitive psychologists working in the tradition of "prospect theory" have identified as the "endowment effect." Individuals tend to value what they have in disproportion to what they stand to gain in a given risky situation. In this case, successive generations of Israelis could have normalized to the occupied territories as a possession, and thus would be less willing to relinquish them. See Janice Gross Stein, "International Co-operation and Loss Avoidance: Framing the Problem," in Janice Gross Stein and Louis W. Pauly, eds., *Choosing to Cooperate: How States Avoid Loss* (Baltimore: Johns Hopkins University Press, 1993).

42. Arian, *Security Threatened*, p. 154.

43. Tessler, *A History of the Israeli-Palestinian Conflict*, p. 706.

44. Eric Silver, "A Marked Shift to the Right," *The Jerusalem Report* (13 December 1990).

45. Lyrics available at: http://www.radiohazak.com/Rl-nga1.html

46. *The Jerusalem Report* (13 Dec 1990).

47. From Calev Ben-David, "The Rocky Horror Intifada Show," *The Jerusalem Report* (27 August 1992).

48. Tessler, *A History of the Israeli-Palestinian Conflict*, pp. 705–706.

49. See Peter Hirschberg, "Bar-Kochba's Revolt," *The Jerusalem Report* (17 January 1991).

50. This sentiment was expressed by one soldier-interviewee in Simcha Jacobovici's 1991 documentary *Deadly Currents*.

51. Eyal Ben-Ari, "Masks and Soldiering: the Israeli Army and the Palestinian Uprising," in Edna Lomsky-Feder and Eyal Ben-Ari, eds., *The Military and Militarism in Israeli Society* (Albany: State University of New York Press, 1999), pp. 173–174.

52. Quoted in Tessler, *A History of the Israeli-Palestinian Conflict*, p. 700.

53. Quoted in Yoram Peri, "Afterword," in Yitzhak Rabin, *The Rabin Memoirs* (Berkeley: University of California Press, 1979, 1996), p. 355.

54. Yoram Peri, "The IDF's Identity Crisis," *The Jerusalem Post* (9 December 1992), p. 6.

55. Cited in Martin Van Creveld, *The Sword and the Olive: A Critical History of the Israeli Defense Force* (New York: PublicAffairs, 1998), p. 349.

56. Cited in Tamar Liebes and Shoshana Blum-Kulka, "Managing a Moral Dilemma: Israeli Soldiers in the Intifada," *Armed Forces & Society* 21, 1 (Fall 1994), p. 50.

57. Author's interview with General (Res.) Nechemia Dagan, 3 January 2000, Jerusalem.

58. Carl von Clausewitz, *On War*, edited and translated by Michael Howard and Peter Paret (Princeton: Princeton University Press, 1976), p. 187.

59. Until September 1993. Ruth Linn, *Conscience at War: The Israeli Soldier as a Moral Critic* (Albany: State University of New York Press, 1996), p. 11.

60. Van Creveld, *The Sword and the Olive*, p. 350.

61. Schiff and Ya'ari, *Intifada*, p. 156.

62. Author's interview with General (Res.) Nechemia Dagan, 3 January 2000, Jerusalem.

63. Stephen Langfur, *Confession from a Jericho Jail* (New York: Grove Weidenfeld, 1992), p. 167.

64. Ben-Ari, "Masks and Soldiering," p. 177.

65. Quoted in Schiff and Ya'ari, *Intifada*, p. 157.

66. Ze'ev Schiff, "War of Attrition," *The Jerusalem Report* (20 December 1990).

67. Linn, *Conscience at War*, p. 70 n. 3. See also Ruth Linn, *Not Shooting and Not Crying: Psychological Inquiry into Moral Disobedience* (New York: Greenwood Press, 1989).

68. Quoted in David Horovitz, "A Soldier's Story," *The Jerusalem Report* (13 December 1990).

69. Van Creveld, *The Sword and the Olive*, p. 345.

70. Yaron Ezrahi, *Rubber Bullets: Power and Conscience in Modern Israel* (New York: Farrar, Straus and Giroux, 1997), pp. 204–205.

71. Quoted in Bar-On, "Israeli Reactions to the Palestinian Uprising," p. 52.

72. Comments by the Chairman of the Council of Jewish Settlements in Judea, Samaria, and Gaza, Yisrael Harel, in "How the Army Lost the Intifada," *The Jerusalem Report* (14 January 1993).

73. Schiff and Ya'ari, *Intifada*, pp. 136–137 and 144–145.

74. Quoted in ibid., p. 135.

75. "[Justice] Schiff Clears Mordechai of Brutality Charges," *The Jerusalem Post* (5 December 1994), p. 2.

76. Cited in Van Creveld, *The Sword and the Olive*, p. 347.

77. Yehuda Ben Meir, *Civil-Military Relations in Israel* (New York: Columbia University Press, 1995), p. 114.

78. Quoted in Schiff and Ya'ari, *Intifada*, p. 153.

79. See, for instance, Benyamin Netanyahu's political treatise written prior to his tenure as prime minister. Netanyahu, *A Place among the Nations: Israel and the World* (New York: Bantam Books, 1993).

80. Author's interview with General (Res.) Nechemia Dagan, 3 January 2000, Jerusalem.

81. Cited in Tessler, *A History of the Israeli-Palestinian Conflict*, p. 700.

82. Lee Hockstader, "Israel Explores Dark Pages of Its Past," *Washington Post* (31 October 1999), p. A1.

83. Gadi Wolfsfeld, "Introduction: Framing Political Conflict," in Cohen and Wolfsfeld, eds., *Framing the Intifada*, p. xix.

84. Quoted in David Rudge, "What It Takes to Head GPO," *The Jerusalem Post* (7 August 1992), p. 10.

85. Interview with Defense Minister Rabin on Israel Television (Arabic Service), 16 February 1989, transcribed in Meron Medzini, ed., *Israel's Foreign Relations: Selected Documents 1988–1992, Vol. 11* (Jerusalem: Ministry of Foreign Affairs, 1993), p. 40.

86. Raphael Nir and Itzhak Roeh, "Intifada Coverage in the Israeli Press: Popular and Quality Papers Assume a Rhetoric of Conformity," *Discourse and Society* 3, 1 (1992): 47–60.

87. Ibid., p. 57.

88. Author's interview with past-editor and former military correspondent of *The Jerusalem Post*, Hirsh Goodman, 9 November 1999, Jerusalem.

89. Yehuda Levy, "On Ethics, Lies and Journalism," *The Jerusalem Post* (2 May 1997), p. 10.

90. Author's interview with Avi Gil, 7 December 1999, Tel Aviv.

91. Orli Lubin of Tel Aviv University, quoted in Rochelle Furstenberg, "Don't Look in the Mirror," *The Jerusalem Report* (13 December 1990).

92. Author's interview with Peace Now activist Janet Aviad, 11 October 1999, Jerusalem.

93. Ibid.

94. Bar-On, "Israeli Reactions to the Palestinian Uprising," p. 55.

95. See Reuven Kaminer, *The Politics of Protest: The Israeli Peace Movement and the Palestinian Intifada* (Brighton, UK: Sussex Academic press, 1996).

96. Tzaly Reshef discusses the rise of these peace organizations in *Peace Now: The Story of the Israeli Peace Movement in the Words of Its Leader* (English trans. ms., undated), pp. 278–279.

97. Author's interview with B'Tselem co-founder Edy Kaufman, 5 December 1999, Jerusalem.

98. See Bar-On, "Israeli Reactions to the Palestinian Uprising," pp. 56–58; and Bar-On, *In Pursuit of Peace.*

99. Reshef, *Peace Now*, p. 273.

100. Yossi Beilin, *Israel: A Concise Political History* (New York: St. Martin's Press, 1992), p. 49.

101. Author's interview with Janet Aviad, 11 October 1999, Jerusalem.

102. Bar-On, *In Pursuit of Peace*, p. 232.

103. Author's interview with Uri Savir, 17 November 1999, Jerusalem.

104. Author's interview with Shimon Peres, 15 November 1999, Jerusalem.

105. Author's interview with Yossi Beilin, 28 November 1999, Jerusalem.

106. Author's interview with Avi Gil, 7 December 1999, Tel Aviv.

107. Author's interview with Eitan Haber, 16 November 1999, Tel Aviv.

108 "Intifada Death Toll," *The Jerusalem Report* (13 December 1990).

109. Asher Arian, *Security Threatened*, p. 78.

110. Author's interview with Uri Savir, 17 November 1999, Jerusalem.

111. Author's interview with Colonel (Ret.) Yeshayahu Tadmor, 10 December 1999, Haifa.

112. Uri Savir, *The Process: 1,100 Days That Changed the Middle East* (New York: Vintage Books, 1998), p. 20.

113. Cited in Bar-On, "Israeli Reactions to the Palestinian Uprising," p. 64 n 9.

114. Address by Defense Minister Rabin to the Conference on Jewish Solidarity with Israel, 21 March 1989, transcribed in Medzini, ed., *Israel's Foreign Relations*, p. 74.

115. Yaron Ezrahi discusses the shift in battle narratives, especially among Israeli poets, that took place after the 1967 war: while the early years were characterized by an aesthetic of war glory, after 1967 the narratives began to capture the terrible, unsavory aspects of combat. See Ezrahi, *Rubber Bullets*, pp. 186–187.

SEVEN. FROM DISSONANCE TO RIGHTSIZING

1. Author's interview with Amnon Lipkin-Shahak, 16 March 2000, Jerusalem.

2. *Yediot Ahronot* (in Hebrew), 19 June 1992 (FBIS-NES-92-120; 22 June 1992).

3. Leslie Susser, "Corridors of Power: Negotiators Draw Closer Together on the Couch," *The Jerusalem Report* (26 December 1991).

4. Author's interview with Avi Gil, 7 December 1999, Tel Aviv.

5. Isabel Kershner, "No! No! No!" *The Jerusalem Report* (3 December 1992).

6. Author's interview with Hirsh Goodman, 9 November 1999, Jerusalem.

7. The Jerusalem Report Staff (ed. David Horovitz), *Shalom Friend: The Life and Legacy of Yitzhak Rabin* (New York: Newmarket Press, 1996), p. 125.

8. Author's interview with Shimon Sheves, director-general of Rabin's Prime Minister's Office, 25 November 1999, Tel Aviv.

9. Yossi Beilin, *Touching Peace: From the Oslo Accord to a Final Agreement* (London: Weidenfeld & Nicolson, 1999), p. 45.

10. See Helena Cobban, "Israel and the Palestinians: From Madrid to Oslo and Beyond," in Robert O. Freedman, ed., *Israel Under Rabin* (Boulder: Westview Press, 1995), pp. 92–93.

11. However, this law had often been circumvented by a clause allowing contact under the auspices of academic conferences; this clause was loosely interpreted by various Israeli peace advocates who sought to test PLO intentions. Interview with peace activist Uri Avnery, 23 December 1999, Tel Aviv.

12. For a description of events surrounding the scandal, see The Jerusalem Report Staff (ed. David Horovitz), *Shalom Friend*, pp. 124–129.

13. See Gerald M. Steinberg, "A Nation that Dwells Alone? Foreign Policy in the 1992 Elections," in Daniel J. Elazar and Shmuel Sandler, eds., *Israel at the Polls, 1992* (Lanham, MD: Rowman & Littlefield Publishers, 1995).

14. *Yediot Ahronot* (in Hebrew), 22 June 1992, p. 2. (FBIS-NES-92-121; 23 June 1992).

15. Author's interview with Yossi Beilin, 28 November 1999, Jerusalem.

16. *Yediot Ahronot* (*L'Shabat* supplement) (in Hebrew), 19 June 1992 (FBIS-NES-92-120; 22 June 1992).

17. Author's interview with Shimon Sheves, director-general of the prime minister's office under Rabin , 25 November 1999, Tel Aviv.

18. Stuart Cohen, "Israel and Its Army: The Image of the IDF as an Issue in the 1992 Election Campaign," in Elazar and Sandler, eds., *Israel at the Polls*, p. 165.

19. *IDF Radio* (in Hebrew), 21 May 1992 (FBIS-NES-92-101; 26 May 1992).

20. *Kol Yisrael* (in Hebrew), 22 May 1992 (FBIS-NES-92-102; 27 May 1992).

21. *Kol Yisrael* (in Hebrew), 17 June 1992 (FBIS-NES-92-118; 18 June 1992).

22. *Ha'aretz* (in Hebrew), report by Ilan Shehori, 31 May 1992, pp. A1, 10 (FBIS-NES-92-105; 1 June 1992).

23. "Quote, Unquote," *The Jerusalem Report* (24 September 1992).

24. *Israel Television Network* (in Hebrew), 16 June 1992; FBIS-NES-92-117 (17 June 1992).

25. Ibid.

26. *Al Hamishmar* (in Hebrew) 22 April 1992, p. 3; FBIS-NES92-079 (23 April 1992).

27. Gid'on Levi, "Death Without Trial," in *Ha'aretz* (in Hebrew), 26 April 1992, p. B1; FBIS-NES-92-081 (27 April 1992).

28. *Israel Television Network* (in Hebrew), 30 April 1992; FBIS-NES-92-085 (1 May 1992).

29. *Kol Yisrael* (in Hebrew), 2 May 1992; FBIS-NES-92-086 (4 May 1992).

30. *Kol Yisrael* (in English), 4 May 1992; FBIS-NES-92-087 (5 May 1992).

31. *Kol Yisrael* (in English), 4 June 1992; FBIS-NES-92-108 (4 June 1992).

32. Israel Television Network (in Hebrew), 3 June 1992; FBIS-NES-92-108 (4 June 1992).

33. *Kol Yisrael* (in English), 21 May 1992; FBIS-NES-92-100 (22 May 1992).

34. Ibid.

35. *Kol Yisrael* (in English) 24 May 1992; FBIS-NES-92-101 (26 May 1992).

36. *Israel Television Network* (in Hebrew) 26 May 1992; FBIS-NES-92-102 (27 May 1992).

37. Beilin, *Touching Peace*, p. 63.

38. In Leslie Susser, "Expulsion: The Doves' Counterattack," *The Jerusalem Report* (14 January 1993).

39. Ibid.

40. David Makovsky, *Making Peace with the PLO: The Rabin Government's Road to the Oslo Accord* (Boulder: Westview Press, 1996), pp. 89–90.

41. In *Ha'aretz* (in Hebrew), 4 May 1992, pp. A1, A8; FBIS-NES-92-086 (4 May 1992).

42. *Kol Yisra'el* (in Hebrew) 4 May 1992; FBIS-NES-92-087 (5 May 1992).

43. *Kol Yisrael* (in Hebrew) 27 May 1992; FBIS-NES-92-104 (29 May 1992).

44. *Ha'aretz* (in Hebrew) 31 May 1992, pp. A1, 10; FBIS-NES-92-105 (1 June 1992).

45. *Kol Yisrael* (in Hebrew) 24 May 1992; FBIS-NES-92-101 (26 May 1992).

46. Speech given by Rabin on 13 July 1992; reprinted in *Pursuing Peace: The Peace Speeches of Prime Minister Yitzhak Rabin* (Tel Aviv: Zmura Beitan, 1995) p. 16 (in Hebrew).

47. Knesset speech by Rabin on 13 July 1992, reprinted in *Pursuing Peace* (in Hebrew), p. 66.

48. Author's interview with Shimon Peres, 15 November 1999, Jerusalem.

49. Poll figures cited in Mark Tessler, *A History of the Israeli-Palestinian Conflict* (Bloomington: Indiana University Press, 1994), p. 754.

50. "Israel Holding Talks with PLO since March," *The Jerusalem Report* (29 July 1993).

51. Beilin's written account of the Oslo process indicates that he informed Peres in the wake of the February Round. Beilin, *Touching Peace*, pp. 72–74. According to journalist and author David Makovsky, however, Peres informed Rabin of the talks during the first week of February. Makovsky, *Making Peace with the PLO*, p. 23.

52. Author's interview with Rabin pollster, 16 November 1999, Ramat Gan, Israel.

53. Citations from the DOP are taken from the reprint of the document in Makovsky, *Making Peace with the PLO*, pp. 205–210.

54. The *Jerusalem Report* Staff (Horovitz, ed.), *Shalom Friend*, p. 153.

55. Reprinted in Makovsky, *Making Peace with the PLO*, p. 223.

56. In Hirsh Goodman, "Good Morning Palestine," *The Jerusalem Report* (28 July 1994).

57. Author's interview with Naomi Chazan, 6 December 1999, Jerusalem.

EIGHT. CONCLUSION

1. David Makovsky, "The Right Fence for Israel," *Foreign Affairs* (March/April 2004), p. 55.

2. Jerusalem Media & Communications Centre (JMCC): Public Opinion Polls, vol. 3, no. 11 (December 2002). Available at: http://www.jmcc.org/publicpoll/pop/02/dec/pop11.htm#one

3. JMCC Public Opinion Poll No. 39—Part Two: Four Months after the Beginning of the Palestinian Intifada: Attitudes of the Israeli and Palestinian Publics towards the Peace Process. Available at: http://www.jmcc.org/publicpoll/results/2000/no39b.htm

4. Stated a leader of Yesh Gvul: the reservists "are not willing to pay the price and risk their lives for something they don't believe in....The army needs to understand that fewer and fewer people are willing to do their dirty work in the territories." See Inigo Gilmore, "Israel Jails 600 Reserve Soldiers in Crackdown on Draft Dodging," *Telegraph* (on-line edition; 1 April 2001).

5. Amos Oz, "Doves over a Barrel," *The Globe and Mail* (6 February 2002), p. A15.

6. Ze'ev Schiff, "What Makes the IDF Unique," *Ha'aretz* (on-line edition), 5 March 2004.

7. Ephraim Yaar and Tamar Hermann, "Peace Index / Most Israelis Support the Attack on Iraq," *Ha'aretz* (on-line edition), 6 March 2003.

8. Ephraim Yaar and Tamar Hermann, "Peace Index: January 2004" (The Tami Steinmetz Center for Peace Research, Tel Aviv University). Available at http://spirit.tau.ac.il/socant/peace/peaceindex/2004/files/Jan2004e.pdf.

9. Akiva Eldar, "The Occupation Corrupts from Above," *Ha'aretz* (on-line edition; 24 November 2003).

10. Chris McGreal, "We're Air Force Pilots, Not Mafia. We Don't Take Revenge," *The Guardian* (on-line edition; 2 December 2003).

11. "Ex-Security Chiefs Chide Israel," *BBC News World Edition* (on-line edition; 14 November 2003).

12. Reuters, "U.S. Envoys, Sharon Discuss Disengagement Plan," *The New York Times* (on-line edition; 11 March 2004).

13. As the Israeli-Palestinian joint statement of 27 January 2001 stated, "We leave Taba in a spirit of hope and mutual achievement, acknowledging that the foundations have been laid both in reestablishing mutual confidence and in having progressed in a substantive engagement on all core issues." *The Jerusalem Post* (28 January 2001), p. 2. For a detailed recounting of the issues discussed at the talks, see Akiva Eldar, "Text: 'Moratinos Document'—The Peace that Nearly Was at Taba," *Ha'aretz* (14 February 2002). Document available at http//www. arts. mcgill. ca/MEPP/PRRN/papers/ moratinos.html.

14. The full text of the Geneva Initiative is available at http://www.heskem. org.il/Heskem_en.asp.

15. The text of the road map is available at http://www.state.gov/r/pa/prs/ ps/2003/20062.htm.

16. Mark Tessler, ed., *Area Studies and Social Science: Strategies for Understanding Middle East Politics* (Bloomington: Indiana University Press, 1999).

17. For the classic articulation of the perceived "Orientalism" traditionally permeating area-studies scholarship—an accusation stating that Western scholars objectify their subjects based on pernicious self-other constructs of observer-observed and East-West dichotomies—see Edward W. Said, *Orientalism: Western Conceptions of the Orient* (London: Penguin Books, 1978).

Bibliography

Ahad Ha'am. 1909. "The Negation of the Diaspora." Reprinted in Arthur Hertzberg, *The Zionist Idea: A Historical Analysis and Reader*. New York: Atheneum.

Alford, C. Fred. 1989. *Melanie Klein and Critical Social Theory*. New Haven: Yale University Press.

Almond, Gabriel A., and Sidney Verba. 1965. *The Civic Culture*. Boston: Little, Brown.

Anderson, Benedict. 1983, 1991. *Imagined Communities*. London: Verso.

Anderson, David, ed. 1998. *Facing My Lai: Moving Beyond the Massacre*. Lawrence: University Press of Kansas.

Arendt, Hannah. 1963. *Eichmann in Jerusalem: A Report on the Banality of Evil*. New York: Viking Press.

Arian, Asher. 1995. *Security Threatened: Surveying Israeli Opinion on Peace and War*. New York: Cambridge University Press.

Arian, Asher. 1989. *Politics in Israel: The Second Generation*, rev. ed. Chatham, NJ: Chatham House Publishers.

Arian, Asher, and Michal Shamir, eds. 1995. *The Elections in Israel 1992*. Albany: State University of New York Press.

Aronoff, Myron J. 1989. *Israeli Visions and Divisions: Cultural Change and Political Conflict*. New Brunswick: Transaction Publishers.

Aronson, Elliot. 1968. "Dissonance Theory: Progress and Problems." In *Theories of Cognitive Consistency: A Sourcebook*, edited by Robert P. Abelson et al. Chicago: Rand McNally and Company.

Aronson, Shlomo, and Nathan Yanai. 1984. "Critical Aspects of the Elections and their Implications." In Dan Caspi, Abraham Diskin and Emanuel Gutmann, eds., *The Roots of Begin's Success: The 1981 Elections*. New York: Croom Helm.

Atlan, Henri. 1987. "Chosen People." In Arthur A. Cohen and Paul Mendes-Flohr, eds., *Contemporary Jewish Religious Thought: Original Essays on Critical Concepts, Movements, and Beliefs*. New York: Charles Scribner's Sons.

Avineri, Shlomo. 1981. *The Making of Modern Zionism: The Intellectual Origins of the Jewish State*. New York: Basic Books.

Azaryahu, Maoz. 1999. "The Independence Day Military Parade: A Political History of a Patriotic Ritual." In Edna Lomsky-Feder and Eyal Ben-Ari, eds., *The Military and Militarism in Israeli Society*. Albany: State University of New York Press.

Bar-On, Mordechai. 1998. "The Historians' Debate in Israel and the Middle East Peace Process." In Ilan Peleg, ed., *The Middle East Peace Process: Interdisciplinary Perspectives*. Albany: State University of New York Press.

Bar-On, Mordechai. 1996. *In Pursuit of Peace: A History of the Israeli Peace Movement*. Washington, DC: United States Institute of Peace Press.

Bar-On, Mordechai. 1988. "Israeli Reactions to the Palestinian Uprising." *Journal of Palestine Studies* 17, 4.

Bar-On, Mordechai (Col.) ed. 1968. *Israel Defence Forces: The Six Day War*. Israeli Ministry of Defense.

Bar-On, Mordechai M. 1967. "Education Processes in the Israel Defense Forces." In Sol Tax, ed., *The Draft: A Handbook of Facts and Alternatives*. Chicago: University of Chicago Press.

Bar-Tal, Daniel. 1983. *The Masada Syndrome: A Case of Central Belief*, Discussion Paper 3. Tel Aviv: International Center for Peace in the Middle East.

Barnett, Michael N. 1999. "Culture, Strategy, and Foreign Policy Change: Israel's Road to Oslo." *European Journal of International Relations* 5, 1.

Barnett, Michael N. 1998. *Dialogues in Arab Politics: Negotiations in Regional Order*. New York: Columbia University Press.

Barnett, Michael N. 1996a. "Identity and Alliances in the Middle East." In Peter J. Katzenstein, ed., *The Culture of National Security: Norms and Identity in World Politics*. New York: Columbia University Press.

Barnett, Michael N., ed. 1996b. *Israel in Comparative Perspective: Challenging the Conventional Wisdom*. Albany: State University of New York Press.

Bates, Robert H. 1997. "Area Studies and the Discipline: A Useful Controversy." *PS: Political Science and Politics* 30, 2.

Beilin, Yossi. 1999. *Touching Peace: From the Oslo Accord to a Final Agreement*. London: Weidenfeld & Nicolson.

Beilin, Yossi. 1992. *Israel: A Concise Political History*. New York: St. Martin's Press.

Ben-Ari, Eyal. 1999. "Masks and Soldiering: the Israeli Army and the Palestinian Uprising." In Edna Lomsky-Feder and Eyal Ben-Ari, eds., *The Military and Militarism in Israeli Society*. Albany: State University of New York Press.

Ben-Eliezer, Uri. 1998. *The Making of Israeli Militarism*. Bloomington: Indiana University Press.

Ben-Gurion, David. 1971. *Letters to Paula*. Pittsburgh: University of Pittsburgh Press.

Ben Meir, Yehuda. 1995. *Civil-Military Relations in Israel*. New York: Columbia University Press.

Ben-Yehuda, Nachman. 1999. "The Masada Mythical Narrative and the Israeli Army." In Edna Lomsky-Feder and Eyal Ben-Ari, eds., *The Military and Militarism in Israeli Society*. Albany: State University of New York Press.

Ben-Yehuda, Nachman. 1995. *The Myth of Masada: Collective Memory and Mythmaking in Israel*. Madison: University of Wisconsin Press.

Bennett, Andrew. 1999. *Condemned to Repetition? The Rise, Fall, and Reprise of Soviet-Russian Military Interventionism, 1973–1996*. Cambridge, MA: MIT Press.

Berger, Peter L., and Thomas Luckmann.1966. *The Social Construction of Reality: A Treatise in the Sociology of Knowledge*. New York: Anchor Books.

Bernstein, Jerome S. 1989. *Power and Politics: The Psychology of Soviet-American Partnership*. Boston: Shambhala Publications, Inc.

Biale, David. 1992. "Zionism as an Erotic Revolution." In Howard Eilberg-Schwartz, ed., *People of the Body: Jews and Judaism from an Embodied Perspective*. Albany: State University of New York Press.

Biale, David. 1986. *Power and Powerlessness in Jewish History*. New York: Schocken Books. Blumer, Herbert. 1986. "The Methodological Position of Symbolic Interactionism." In Blumer, *Symbolic Interactionism: Perspective and Method*. Berkeley: University of California Press.

Blumstein, Philip. 1991. "The Production of Selves in Personal Relationships." In Judith A. Howard and Peter L. Callero, eds., *The Self-Society Dynamic*. Cambridge: Cambridge University Press.

Bornstein, Robert F. 1993. "Implicit Perception, Implicit Memory, and the Recovery of Unconscious Material in Psychotherapy." *The Journal of Nervous and Mental Disease* 181, 6.

Brass, Paul R. 1991. *Ethnicity and Nationalism: Theory and Comparison.* Newbury Park, CA: Sage Publications.

Brecher, Michael. 1975. *Decisions in Israel's Foreign Policy.* New Haven: Yale University Press.

Brown, Michael E. 1993. "Causes and Implications of Ethnic Conflict." In Brown, ed., *Ethnic Conflict and International Security.* Princeton: Princeton University Press.

Bukovansky, Mlada. 2002. *Legitimacy and Power Politics: The American and French Revolutions in International Political Culture.* Princeton: Princeton University Press.

Burke, Peter J. 1991a. "Attitudes, Behavior and the Self." In Judith Howard and Peter Callero, eds., *The Self-Society Dynamic.* Cambridge: Cambridge University Press.

Burke, Peter J. 1991b. "Identity Process and Social Stress." *American Sociological Review* 56.

Burns, Tom R., and Erik Engdahl. 1998. "The Social Construction of Consciousness, Part 2: Individual Selves, Self-Awareness, and Reflectivity." *Journal of Consciousness Studies* 5, 2.

Callero, Peter L. 1991. "Toward a Sociology of Cognition." In Judith A. Howard and Peter L. Callero, eds., *The Self-Society Dynamic.* Cambridge: Cambridge University Press.

Carveth, Donald. 1982. "Sociology and Psychoanalysis: The Hobbesian Problem Revisited." *Canadian Journal of Sociology* 7, 2.

Charon, Joel M. 1992. *Symbolic Interactionism: An Introduction, an Interpretation, an Integration.* Englewood Cliffs, NJ: Prentice-Hall.

Chazan, Naomi. 1997. "The Role of Women and Female Leadership in the Intifada and the Peace Process." In Avraham Sela and Moshe Ma'oz, eds., *The PLO and Israel: From Armed Conflict to Political Solution, 1964–1994.* New York: St. Martin's Press.

Cheesman, Jim, and Philip M. Merikle. 1997. "Subliminal Exposure to Death-Related Stimuli Increases Defense of the Cultural Worldview." *Psychological Science* 8, 5.

Cheesman, Jim, and Philip M. Merikle. 1986. "Distinguishing Conscious from Unconscious Perceptual Processes." *Canadian Journal of Psychology* 40, 4.

Cobban, Helena. 1995. "Israel and the Palestinians: From Madrid to Oslo and Beyond." In Robert O. Freedman, ed., *Israel Under Rabin.* Boulder: Westview Press.

Cohen, Eliot, Michael J. Eisenstadt, and Andrew J. Bacevich. 1998. *'Knives, Tanks and Missiles': Israel's Security Revolution.*

Washington, DC: The Washington Institute for Near East Policy.

Cohen, Stuart A. 1995. "Israel and Its Army: The Image of the IDF as an Issue in the 1992 Election Campaign." In Daniel J. Elazar and Shmuel Sandler, eds., *Israel at the Polls, 1992*. Lanham, MD: Rowman & Littlefield.

Cohen, Stuart A. 1994. "How Did the *Intifada* Affect the IDF?" *Conflict Quarterly* 14, 3.

Collier, David. 1993. "The Comparative Method." In Ada W. Finifter, ed., *Political Science: The State of the Discipline*. 2nd ed. Washington, DC: American Political Science Association.

Connerton, Paul. 1989. *How Societies Remember*. Cambridge: Cambridge University Press.

Crawford, Neta C. 2000. "The Passion of World Politics: Propositions on Emotion and Emotional Relationships." *International Security* 24, 4.

Crayton, John W. 1983. "Terrorism and the Psychology of the Self," in Lawrence Zelic Freedman and Yonah Alexander, *Perspectives on Terrorism*. Wilmington: Scholarly Resources Inc.

Dankner, Amnon, and David Tartakover. 1996. *Where We Were and What We Did: An Israeli Lexicon of the Fifties and the Sixties*. Jerusalem: Keter Publishing House, Ltd. (in Hebrew).

Dittmer, Lowell, and Samuel S. Kim. 1993. "In Search of a Theory of National Identity." In Dittmer and Kim, eds., *China's Quest for National Identity*. Ithaca: Cornell University Press.

Douglas, Mary. 1986. *How Institutions Think*. Syracuse: Syracuse University Press.

Dowty, Alan. 1998. "Israeli Foreign Policy and the Jewish Question." *Middle East Review of International Affairs* 3, 1., internet edition.

Eisenstadt, S.N. 1986. *The Internal Repercussions of the Lebanon War*. Policy Studies 17, The Leonard Davis Institute for International Relations, The Hebrew University of Jerusalem.

Elon, Amos. 1971, 1981. *The Israelis: Founders and Sons*. New York: Penguin Books.

Elster, John. 1983. *Sour Grapes: Studies in the Subversion of Rationality*. Cambridge: Cambridge University Press.

Epstein, Helen. 1979. *Children of the Holocaust: Conversations with Sons and Daughters of Survivors*. New York: Bantam Books.

Evangelista, Matthew. 1991. "Sources of Moderation in Soviet Security Policy." In Philip E. Tetlock, Jo L. Husbands, Robert Jervis,

Paul C. Stern, and Charles Tilly, eds., *Behavior, Society and Nuclear War*, vol. 2. New York: Oxford University Press.

Ezrahi, Yaron. 1997. *Rubber Bullets: Power and Conscience in Modern Israel*. New York: Farrar, Straus and Giroux.

Farrell, Theo. 2002. "Constructivist Security Studies: Portrait of a Research Program." *International Studies Review* 4, 1.

Fearon, James. 1997. "What Is Identity (as We Now Use the Word)?" Unpublished manuscript. University of Chicago.

Fentress, James, and Chris Wickham. 1992. *Social Memory*. Oxford: Blackwell.

Festinger, Leon. 1957, 1968. *A Theory of Cognitive Dissonance*. Stanford: Stanford University Press.

Finnemore, Martha. 1996. *National Interests in International Society*. Ithaca: Cornell University Press.

Freud, Sigmund. 1955. "Group Psychology and the Analysis of the Ego." In vol. 18 of *The Standard Edition of the Complete Psychological Works of Sigmund Freud*. London: Hogarth Press.

Freud, Sigmund. 1933. "New Introductory Lectures on Psychoanalysis." In vol. 22 of *The Standard Edition of the Complete Psychology Works of Sigmund Freud*. London: Hogarth.

Freundlich, Yehoshua, ed. 1981. *Documents on the Foreign Policy of Israel. Vol. 1, 14 May to 30 September, 1948*. Jerusalem: Israel State Archives.

Gabriel, Richard A. 1984. *Operation Peace for Galilee: The Israeli-PLO War in Lebanon*. New York: Hill and Wang.

Gal, Reuven. 1986. *A Portrait of the Israeli Soldier*. New York: Greenwood Press.

Gal, Reuven. 1985. "Commitment and Obedience in the Military: An Israeli Case Study." *Armed Forces & Society* 11, 4.

Geertz, Clifford. 1973. *The Interpretation of Cultures*. New York: Basic Books, Inc.

Gertz, Nurith. 2000. *Myths in Israeli Culture: Captives of a Dream*. London: Vallentine Mitchell.

Gertz, Nurith. 1999a. "From Jew to Hebrew: The 'Zionist Narrative' in the Israeli Cinema of the 1940's and 1950's." In Dan Urian and Efraim Karsh, eds., *In Search of Identity: Jewish Aspects in Israeli Culture*. London: Frank Cass.

Gertz, Nurith. 1999b. "The Medium That Mistook Itself for War: *Cherry Season* in Comparison with *Ricochets* and *Cup Final*." *Israel Studies* 4, 1.

George, Alexander. 1969. "The Operational Code: A Neglected Approach to the Study of Political Leaders and Decision Making." *International Studies Quarterly* 13, 2.

George, Alexander and Juliet George. 1964. *Wilson and Colonel House: A Personality Study.* New York. Dover Publications.

George, Alexander L., and Timothy J. McKeown. 1985. "Case Studies and Theories of Organizational Decision Making." In *Advances in Information Processing in Organizations.* Greenwich: JAI Press.

Gilbert, Margaret. 1989. *On Social Facts.* Princeton: Princeton University Press.

Gilbert, Margaret. 1987. "Modelling Collective Belief." *Synthese* 73.

Goemans, H.E. 2000. *War and Punishment: The Causes of War Termination and the First World War.* Princeton: Princeton University Press.

Goldberg, David J. 1996. *To the Promised Land: A History of Zionist Thought from Its Origins to the Modern State of Israel.* London: Penguin Books.

Goldgeier, James M. 1997. "Psychology and Security." *Security Studies* 6, 4.

Gollwitzer, Peter M., and Robert A. Wicklund. 1985. "The Pursuit of Self-Defining Goals." In Julius Kuhl and Jurgen Beckmann, eds., *Action Control: From Cognition to Behavior.* Berlin: Springer-Verlag.

Hall, Rodney Bruce. 1999. *National Collective Identity: Social Constructs and International Systems.* New York: Columbia University Press.

Handel, Michael I. 1973. *Israel's Political-Military Doctrine.* Cambridge: Center for International Affairs, Harvard University.

Hardan, David, ed. 1985. *The Moral and Existential Dilemmas of the Israeli Soldier.* Jerusalem: World Zionist Organization.

Harkabi, Yehoshafat. 1988. *Israel's Fateful Hour.* New York: Harper & Row.

Harkabi, Y. 1972. *Arab Attitudes to Israel.* Jerusalem: Keter Publishing House.

Harmon-Jones, Eddie, and Judson Mills. 1999. "An Introduction to Cognitive Dissonance Theory and an Overview of Current Perspectives on the Theory." In *Cognitive Dissonance: Progress on a Pivotal Theory in Social Psychology*, edited by E. Harmon-Jones and J. Mills. Washington, DC: American Psychological Association.

Herman, Edward S., and Noam Chomsky. 1988. *Manufacturing Consent: The Political Economy of the Mass Media.* New York: Pantheon Books.

Hogg, Michael A., Deborah J. Terry, and Katherine M. White. 1995. "A Tale of Two Theories: A Critical Comparison of Identity Theory with Social Identity Theory." *Social Psychology Quarterly* 58, 4.

Hollis, Martin, and Steve Smith. 1990. *Explaining and Understanding International Relations.* Oxford: Clarendon Press.

Holsti, K.J. 1970. "National Role Conceptions in the Study of Foreign Policy." *International Studies Quarterly* 14, 3.

Horovitz, Dan. 1977. "Is Israel a Garrison State?" *The Jerusalem Quarterly* 4.

Horovitz, David, ed. (The Jerusalem Report Staff). 1996. *Shalom Friend: The Life and Legacy of Yitzhak Rabin.* New York: Newmarket Press.

Inbar, Efraim. 1991. "Israel's Small War: The Military Response to the Intifada." *Armed Forces & Society* 18, 1.

Inbar, Efraim. 1989. "The 'No Choice War' Debate in Israel." *Journal of Strategic Studies* 21, 1.

Inbar, Efraim. 1987. "War in Jewish Tradition," *The Jerusalem Journal of International Relations* 9, 2.

(The State of) Israel (*Va`adah la-hakirat ha-eru`im be-mahanot ha-pelitim be-Beirut*). 1983. *The Beirut Massacre: The Complete Kahan Commission Report.* Princeton: Karz-Cohl.

Jentleson, Bruce. 1992. "The Pretty Prudent Public: Post Post-Vietnam American Opinion on the Use of Military Force." *International Studies Quarterly* 36, 1.

Jervis, Robert. 1985. "Perceiving and Coping with Threat." In Robert Jervis, Richard Ned Lebow, and Janice Gross Stein, *Psychology and Deterrence.* Baltimore: The Johns Hopkins University Press.

Jervis, Robert. 1978. "Cooperation Under the Security Dilemma." *World Politics* 30, 2.

Jervis, Robert. 1976. *Perception and Misperception in International Politics.* Princeton: Princeton University Press.

Johnston, Alastair Ian. 1995. "Thinking about Strategic Culture." *International Security* 19, 4.

Jung, C. F. 1959. *The Archetypes and the Collective Unconscious.* Trans. R. F. C. Hull. New York: Pantheon Books.

Kaminer, Reuven. 1996. *The Politics of Protest: The Israeli Peace Movement and the Palestinian Intifada.* Brighton, UK: Sussex Academic Press.

Kaplan, Morton A. 1957, 1975. *System and Process in International Politics.* Huntington: Robert E. Krieger.

Katriel, Tamar. 1986. *Talking Straight: Dugri Speech in Israeli Sabra Culture.* Cambridge: Cambridge University Press.

Katzenstein, Peter J., ed. 1996. *The Culture of National Security: Norms and Identity in World Politics.* New York: Columbia University Press.

Kelman, Herbert C. 1995. "Contributions of an Unofficial Conflict Resolution Effort to the Israeli-Palestinian Breakthrough." *Negotiation Journal* 11.

Kier, Elizabeth. 1997. *Imagining War: French and British Military Doctrine between the Wars.* Princeton: Princeton University Press.

Kimmerling, Baruch. 1999. "Between Hegemony and Dormant *Kultur-kampf* in Israel," In Dan Urian and Efraim Karsh, eds., *In Search of Identity: Jewish Aspects in Israeli Culture.* London: Frank Cass.

Kimmerling, Baruch. 1997. "The Power-Oriented Settlement: PLO-Israel—The Road to the Oslo Agreement and Back?" In Avraham Sela and Moshe Ma'oz, eds., *The PLO and Israel: From Armed Conflict to Political Solution, 1964–1994.* New York: St. Martin's Press.

Klotz, Audie. 1995. *Norms in International Relations: The Struggle Against Apartheid.* Ithaca: Cornell University Press.

Kohut, Heinz. 1972. "Thoughts on Narcissism and Narcissistic Rage." *The Psychoanalytic Study of the Child* 27.

Krasner, Stephen D. 1978. *Defending the National Interest: Raw Materials Investments and U.S. Foreign Policy.* Princeton: Princeton University Press.

Kupchan, Charles. A. 1998. "After Pax Americana: Benign Power, Regional Integration, and the Sources of a Stable Multipolarity." *International Security* 23, 2.

Kupchan, Charles A. 1991. *The Vulnerability of Empire.* Ithaca: Cornell University Press.

Langfur, Stephen. 1992. *Confession from a Jericho Jail.* New York: Grove Weidenfeld.

Laqueur, Walter, and Barry Rubin, eds. 1984. *The Israel-Arab Reader: A Documentary History of the Middle East Conflict.* New York: Penguin Books.

Lepgold, Joseph, and Timothy McKeown. 1995. "Is American Foreign Policy Exceptional? An Empirical Analysis." *Political Science Quarterly* 110, 3.

Levinsohn, Hanna, and Elihu Katz. 1993. "The *Intifada* Is Not a War: Jewish Public Opinion on the Israel-Arab Conflict." In Akiba A. Cohen and Gadi Wolfsfeld, eds., *Framing the Intifada: People and Media*. Norwood, NJ: Ablex Publishing Corporation.

Levite, Ariel. 1989. *Offense and Defense in Israeli Military Doctrine*. Boulder: Westview Press.

Levy, Jack S. 1994. "Learning and Foreign Policy: Sweeping a Conceptual Minefield." *International Organization* 48, 2.

Liberman, Peter. "The Spoils of Conquest." *International Security* 18, 2 (Fall 1993).

Lieber, Robert J. 2000. "U.S.-Israel Relations since 1948." In Robert O. Freedman, ed., *Israel at Fifty*. Gainesville: University of Florida Press.

Lieberfeld, Daniel. 1999. *Negotiation and Threat Perception in South Africa and Israel/Palestine*. Westport: Praeger.

Liebes, Tamar, and Shoshana Blum-Kulka. 1994. "Managing a Moral Dilemma: Israeli Soldiers in the Intifada." *Armed Forces & Society* 21, 1.

Linn, Ruth. 1996. *Conscience at War: The Israeli Soldier as a Moral Critic*. Albany: State University of New York Press.

Linn, Ruth. 1989. *Not Shooting and Not Crying: Psychological Inquiry into Moral Disobedience*. New York: Greenwood Press.

Linn, Ruth. 1986. "Conscientious Objection in Israel During the War in Lebanon." *Armed Forces & Society* 12, 4.

Lowi, Miriam R. 1993. *Water and Power: The Politics of a Scarce Resource in the Jordan River Basin*. New York: Cambridge University Press.

Luttwak, Edward N., and Daniel Horowitz. 1983. *The Israeli Army 1948–1973*. Cambridge: Abt Books.

McGuire, William J. 1968. "Resume and Response from the Consistency Theory Viewpoint." In *Theories of Cognitive Consistency: A Sourcebook*, edited by Robert P. Abelson et al. Chicago: Rand McNally and Company.

Makovsky, David. 1996. *Making Peace with the PLO: The Rabin Government's Road to the Oslo Accord*. Boulder: Westview Press.

Mann, Rafi. 1998. *It's Inconceivable*. Or Yehuda: Hed Arzi (in Hebrew).

Ma'oz, Moshe. 1995. *Syria and Israel: From War to Peacemaking*. Oxford: Oxford University Press.

Mead, George H. 1934. *Mind, Self and Society*. Chicago: University of Chicago Press.

Medzini, Meron, ed. 1993. *Israel's Foreign Relations: Selected Documents 1988–1992, Vol. 11.* Jerusalem: Ministry of Foreign Affairs.

Meir, Golda. 1975. *My Life.* New York: Dell.

Mendes-Flohr, Paul R., and Jehuda Reinharz. 1980. *The Jew in the Modern World: A Documentary History.* New York: Oxford University Press.

Mercer, Jonathan. 1999. "Emotion and Identity." Unpublished manuscript. Harvard University, University of Washington.

Mercer, Jonathan. 1995. "Anarchy and Identity." *International Organization* 49, 2.

Merikle, Philip M. 1998. "Psychological Investigations of Unconscious Perception." *Journal of Consciousness Studies* 5, 1.

Merom, Gil. 1999. "Israel's National Security and the Myth of Exceptionalism." *Political Science Quarterly* 114, 3.

Morris, Benny. 1987. *The Birth of the Palestinian Refugee Problem, 1947–1949.* Cambridge: Cambridge University Press.

Netanyahu, Benyamin. 1993. *A Place among the Nations: Israel and the World.* New York: Bantam Books.

Nir, Raphal, and Itzhak Roeh. 1992. "Intifada Coverage in the Israeli Press: Popular and Quality Papers Assume a Rhetoric of Conformity." *Discourse and Society* 3, 1.

Orange, Donna M., George E. Atwood, and Robert D. Stolorow. 1997. *Working Intersubjectively: Contextualism in Psychoanalytic Practice.* Hillsdale, NJ: The Analytic Press.

Peres, Shimon. 1995. *Battling for Peace: A Memoir.* New York: Random House.

Peri, Yoram. 1984. "Coexistence or Hegemony? Shifts in the Israeli Security Concept," in Dan Caspi, Abraham Diskin, and Emanuel Gutmann, eds., *The Roots of Begin's Success: The 1981 Israeli Elections.* New York: St. Martin's Press.

Piven. 1999. *Piven: Works 1990–1999.* Tel Aviv: Am Oved (in Hebrew).

Pogrebin, Letty Cottin. 1991. *Deborah, Golda, and Me: Being Female and Jewish in America.* New York: Crown Publishers.

Polkinghorne, Donald E. 1988. *Narrative Knowing and the Human Sciences.* Albany: State University of New York Press.

Posen, Barry R. 1993. "The Security Dilemma and Ethnic Conflict." In Michael E. Brown, ed., *Ethnic Conflict and International Security.* Princeton: Princeton University Press.

Potok, Chaim. 1967. *The Chosen.* Greenwich: Fawcett Publications, Inc.

Putnam, Robert D. 1988. "Diplomacy and Domestic Politics: The Logic of Two-Level Games." *International Organization,* 42, 3.

Rabin, Yitzhak. 1979, 1996. *The Rabin Memoirs.* Berkeley: University of California Press.

Rabin, Yitzhak. 1995. *Pursuing Peace: The Peace Speeches of Prime Minister Yitzhak Rabin.* Tel Aviv: Zmura Beitan (in Hebrew).

Rabin, Yitzhak. 1984. "In the Aftermath of the War in Lebanon: Israel's Objectives." In Joseph Alpher, ed., *Israel's Lebanon Policy: Where To?* Tel Aviv: Jaffee Center for Strategic Studies, Tel Aviv University, Memorandum No. 12.

Ravitzky, Aviezer. 1987. "Peace." In Arthur A. Cohen and Paul Mendes-Flohr, eds., *Contemporary Jewish Religious Thought: Original Essays on Critical Concepts, Movements, and Beliefs.* New York: Charles Scribner's Sons.

Reshef, Tzaly. Undated. *Peace Now: The Story of the Israeli Peace Movement in the Words of Its Leader.* English translation manuscript.

Rock, Stephen. 1989. *When Peace Breaks Out: Great Power Rapprochement in Historical Perspective.* Chapel Hill: University of North Carolina Press.

Said, Edward W. 1999. *Out of Place: A Memoir.* New York: Alfred A. Knopf.

Said, Edward W. 1978. *Orientalism: Western Conceptions of the Orient.* London: Penguin Books.

Sandelands, Lloyd, and Lynda St. Clair. 1993. "Toward an Empirical Concept of Group." *Journal for the Theory of Social Behaviour* 23, 4.

Sarnoff, Irving. 1968. "Psychoanalytic Theory and Cognitive Dissonance." In *Theories of Cognitive Consistency: A Sourcebook,* edited by Robert P. Abelson et al. Chicago: Rand McNally and Company, 1968.

Savir, Uri. 1998. *The Process: 1,100 Days that Changed the Middle East.* New York: Vintage Books.

Schiff, Ze'ev. 1985. *A History of the Israeli Army: 1874 to the Present.* New York: Macmillan.

Schiff, Ze'ev, and Ehud Ya'ari. 1989. *Intifada: The Palestinian Uprising—Israel's Third Front.* New York: Simon and Schuster.

Schiff, Ze'ev, and Ehud Ya'ari. 1984. *Israel's Lebanon War.* New York: Simon and Schuster.

Schweller, Randall. 1996. "Neorealism's Status-Quo Bias: What Security Dilemma?" *Security Studies* 5, 3.

Segev, Tom. 1993. *The Seventh Million: The Israelis and the Holocaust.* New York: Hill and Wang.

Sewell, Jr., William H. 1992. "Introduction: Narratives and Social Identities." *Social Science History* 16, 3.

Shalev, Avner. 1991. *The Intifada: Causes and Effects.* Boulder: Westview Press.

Shohat, Ella. 1989. *Israeli Cinema: East/West and the Politics of Representation.* Austin: University of Texas Press.

Silberstein, Laurence J. 1999. *The Postzionism Debates: Knowledge and Power in Israeli Culture.* New York: Routledge.

Slater, Robert. 1996. *Rabin of Israel: Warrior for Peace.* New York: HarperPaperbacks.

Snyder, Jack L. 1991. *Myths of Empire: Domestic Politics and International Ambition.* Ithaca: Cornell University Press.

Stein, Janice Gross. 1996. "Image, Identity, and Conflict Resolution." In Chester A. Crocker and Fen Osler Hampson with Pamela Aall, eds., *Managing Global Chaos: Sources of and Responses to International Conflict.* Washington, DC: United States Institute of Peace.

Stein, Janice Gross. 1995. "Political Learning by Doing: Gorbachev as Uncommitted Thinker and Motivated Learner." In Richard Ned Lebow and Thomas Risse-Kappen, eds., *International Relations Theory and the End of the Cold War.* New York: Columbia University Press.

Stein, Janice Gross. 1993. "International Cooperation and Loss Avoidance: Framing the Problem." In Stein and Louis W. Pauly, eds., *Choosing to Cooperate: How States Avoid Loss.* Baltimore: Johns Hopkins University Press.

Steinberg, Gerald M. 1995. "A Nation that Dwells Alone? Foreign Policy in the 1992 Elections." In Daniel J. Elazar and Shmuel Sandler, eds., *Israel at the Polls, 1992.* Lanham, MD: Rowman & Littlefield.

Sternhell, Zeev. 1998. *The Founding Myths of Israel: Nationalism, Socialism and the Making of the Jewish State.* Princeton: Princeton University Press.

Stolorow, Robert, George Atwood, and Bernard Brandchaft, eds., 1994. *The Intersubjective Perspective.* Northvale, NJ: Jason Aronson, Inc.

Stryker, Sheldon, and Anne Statham. 1985. "Symbolic Interaction and Role Theory." In G. Lindzey and E. Aronson, eds., *Handbook of Social Psychology*, vol. I. New York: Random House.

Sucharov, Maxwell S. 1994. "Psychoanalysis, Self Psychology, and Intersubjectivity." In Robert Stolorow, George Atwood, and

Bernard Brandchaft, eds., *The Intersubjective Perspective.* Northvale, NJ: Jason Aronson, Inc.

Sucharov, Mira. 2005. "Security Ethics and the Modern Military: The Case of the Israel Defense Forces." *Armed Forces & Society* 31, 2.

Sucharov, Mira. 1999. "Regional Identity and the Sovereignty Principle: Explaining Israeli-Palestinian Peacemaking." In David Newman, ed., *Boundaries, Territory and Postmodernity.* London: Frank Cass.

Tal, Israel. 1977. "Israel's Doctrine of National Security: Background and Dynamics." *The Jerusalem Quarterly* 4.

Tessler, Mark, ed. 1999. *Area Studies and Social Science: Strategies for Understanding Middle East Politics.* Bloomington: Indiana University Press.

Tessler, Mark. 1994. *A History of the Israeli-Palestinian Conflict.* Bloomington: Indiana University Press.

Tessler, Mark. 1990. "The Intifada and Political Discourse in Israel." *Journal of Palestine Studies* 19, 2.

Tetlock, Philip, and Charles McGuire. 1986. "Cognitive Perspectives on Foreign Policy." In R. White, ed., *Psychology and the Prevention of Nuclear War.* New York: New York University Press.

Timerman, Jacobo. 1982. *The Longest War: Israel in Lebanon.* New York: Vintage Books.

Van Creveld, Martin. 1998. *The Sword and the Olive: A Critical History of the Israeli Defense Force.* New York: PublicAffairs.

Van Evera, Stephen. 1997. *Guide to Methods for Students of Political Science.* Ithaca: Cornell University Press.

Volkan, Vamik D. 1998a. "Psychoanalysis and Diplomacy: Potentials for and Obstacles against Collaboration." Unpublished manuscript. University of Virginia.

Volkan, Vamik D. 1998b. "Psychoanalysis and Diplomacy: Part II—Large-Group Rituals." Unpublished manuscript. University of Virginia.

Vollmer, Fred. 1993. "Intentional Action and Unconscious Reason." *Journal for the Theory of Social Behavior* 23, 3.

von Clausewitz, Carl. 1976. *On War.* Edited and translated by Michael Howard and Peter Paret. Princeton: Princeton University Press.

Walker, Stephen G. 1987. *Role Theory and Foreign Policy Analysis.* Durham, NC: Duke University Press.

Walt, Stephen M. 1987. *The Origins of Alliances.* Ithaca: Cornell University Press.

Waltz, Kenneth. 1979. *Theory of International Politics.* Reading: Addison-Wesley.

Walzer, Michael. 1992. *Just and Unjust Wars: A Moral Argument with Historical Illustrations, 2nd ed.* New York: Basic Books.

Watkins, J. W. N. 1957. "Social Phenomena Result from the Activities of Individual Agents." *British Journal for the Philosophy of Science* 8.

Weinberger, Joel, and Lloyd H. Silverman. 1990. "Testability and Empirical Verification of Psychoanalytic Dynamic Propositions Through Subliminal Psychodynamic Activation." *Psychoanalytic Psychology* 7, 3.

Wendt, Alexander. 1999. *Social Theory of International Politics.* New York: Cambridge University Press.

Wendt, Alexander. 1994. "Collective Identity Formation and the International State." *American Political Science Review* 88.

Wendt, Alexander. 1992. "Anarchy is What States Make of It: The Social Construction of Power Politics." *International Organization* 46.

Wendt, Alexander. 1987. "The Agent-Structure Problem in International Relations Theory." *International Organization* 41, 3.

Wittes, Tamara Cofman. 2000. "Symbols and Security in Ethnic Conflict: Confidence-Building in the Palestinian-Israeli Peace Process, 1993–1995." Ph.D. Dissertation. Georgetown University.

Wolfsfeld, Gadi. 1993. "Introduction: Framing Political Conflict." In Akiba A. Cohen and Gadi Wolfsfeld, eds., *Framing the Intifada: People and Media.* Norwood, NJ: Ablex Publishing Corporation.

Wolfsfeld, Gadi. 1988. *The Politics of Provocation: Participation and Protest in Israel.* Albany: State University of New York Press.

Yaniv, Avner. 1993. "Israel Faces Iraq: The Politics of Confrontation." In Amatzia Baram and Barry Rubin, eds., *Iraq's Road to War.* New York: St. Martin's Press.

Yishai, Yael. 1985. "The Israeli Labor Party and the Lebanon War." *Armed Forces & Society* 11, 3.

Zerubavel, Yael. 1995. *Recovered Roots: Collective Memory and the Making of Israeli National Tradition.* Chicago: University of Chicago Press.

Index